A People's Dictionary to the 'Exceptional Nation'

Ben Schreiner

A People's Dictionary to the 'Exceptional Nation'

Copyright © 2015 Ben Schreiner

Inquiries regarding requests to reprint all or part of *A People's Dictionary to the 'Exceptional Nation'* should be addressed to the author.
For contact visit: www.workingleft.blogspot.com

Published by Ben Schreiner
Salem, Oregon.

ISBN-10: 1508413959

ISBN-13: 978-1508413950

To my incredible mom, dad, and sister — for helping to make this, and so much more, possible.

Contents

A Note on the Text

This is a dictionary of the official hubris, hypocrisy, and outright duplicity of the United States of America. It is a common person's reference guide to the through the looking-glass world of American propaganda; a world in which military aggression abroad is celebrated as "liberation," plutocracy at home branded "democracy."

Focusing largely, although not exclusively, on the post 9/11 "war on terror" era, the dictionary defines some of the major political, cultural, social, and economic buzzwords and newspeak euphemisms common to the vernacular of the self-styled "exceptional nation." Eschewing the humorless formality found in more "respectable circles," the definitions offered within are meant to amuse as much as enlighten. The U.S., after all, is never a land short on irony. And though the definitions are therefore by no means strictly technical or all inclusive in nature, each still seeks to capture a certain important or particularly neglected reality or truth, while in the process also endeavoring to shed some light on the mentality of those who "own the country."

Considering that many of the book's entries and definitions derive directly from the words of officials, or are otherwise terms perhaps foreign to the general reader, ample footnotes have been included throughout the text. All readers are highly encouraged to consult the footnotes. Attention also needs to be drawn at the outset to the use of *italics* within definitions, which are used to connote terms that are themselves defined within the dictionary.

In an effort to ease one's reading, the dictionary is divided into three thematically organized sections containing a total of 12 chapters. The first section, comprised of five chapters, focuses broadly on U.S. "exceptionalism" in the domestic realm, with chapters on domestic U.S. politics; poverty and the accompanying "dependency culture"; the education "reform" movement; the "free press"; the "justice" system; and, lastly, American society. The second section, made up of two chapters, focuses on the economy, with one chapter on the vaunted U.S. "free-enterprise system" and a second on the American way of work. The final four chapters found in the concluding section turn their attention to U.S. foreign policy, with chapters on American "diplomacy"; a view of the world as seen from Washington; the U.S. military (i.e., "the global force for good"); and the "war on terror."

The book's configuration notwithstanding, no true linear progression exists from chapter to chapter, leaving readers free to read the chapters, or even the entries within chapters, out of order. Those looking for any one term in particular should of course take note of the index. With that said, one should know the book's terms and definitions do play on one another to a certain extent and are frequently cross referenced, leaving a complete reading of the dictionary, no matter the means or order, the best way through which to obtain the most complete understanding of each individual term, as well as the larger scope of the Made in USA hubris, hypocrisy, and duplicity the dictionary lays bare.

Part 1:
Indispensable Exceptionalism

I believe America is exceptional – in part because we have shown a willingness through the sacrifice of blood and treasure to stand up not only for our own narrow self-interests, but for the interests of all.

- *President Barack Obama, 2013*[1]

Lying – one of the few growth industries in Washington.

- *William Blum*, Killing Hope[2]

---

[1] Barack Obama. "Remarks by President Obama in Address to the United Nations General Assembly." Whitehouse.gov. (24 Sept 2013).
[2] William Blum. *Killing Hope: U.S. Military and C.I.A. Interventions Since World War II.* (Monroe: Common Courage Press, 2004): 269.

1.   American Politics

Those who succeed in politics, as in most of the culture, are those who create the most convincing fantasies.

- *Chris Hedges,* Empire of Illusion[1]

1%, the

The top 1% of all income earners and owners of 40% of the nation's total wealth. In other words, a highly maligned and persecuted minority akin to, say, Jews in Nazi *Germany.*[2]

99%, the

An eclectic mix of bums, vagabonds, and lazy underachievers who simply haven't worked hard enough to be in *the 1%.*

A City on a Hill

A fully barricaded and garrisoned nation, teeming with an outwardly hostile people forever suspicious of any who seek entry into their fair land.

A New Pearl Harbor

An event so upsetting and catastrophic in nature it has the ability to catapult a disconcertedly *peace*-happy public onto a proper *war* footing.[3] (See *9/11,* Chapter 12.)

---

[1] Chris Hedges. *Empire of Illusion: The End of Literacy and the Triumph of Spectacle.* (New York: Nation Books, 2009): 51

[2] Ken Langone, the billionaire co-founder of Home Depot, and Tom Perkins, a prominent venture capitalist, have both separately compared the so-called plight of the American 1% to that faced by Jews in Nazi Germany. As Langone remarked on the rhetorical attacks on the American rich: "if you go back to 1933, with different words, this is what Hitler was saying in Germany." Ben White and Maggie Haberman. "The rich strike back." *Politico.* (18 March 2014).

[3] In 2000, the infamous neocon talk shop, The Project for a New American Century, run by many of the hawks who would come to form policy within the George W. Bush administration, noted that any plans for increasing military spending would not be possible without something "like a new Pearl Harbor." "Rebuilding America's Defenses: Strategies, Forces, and Resources for a New Century." The Project for a New American Century. (Sept 2000): 51.

Activist

A dangerously divisive individual refusing to accept the fact that *there is no alternative* to how things are now.

Alarmist

One who issues dispiriting warnings based on solid scientific evidence.

All the Above Energy Policy

An energy policy dedicated to producing, distributing, and consuming only those sources of energy which can be drilled or fracked.

America/American

God's chosen land and his chosen people. Alternatively known as the United States of America and the citizens thereof. But only the citizens thereof. Use specific nationalities when describing those living throughout the rest of the American continent (i.e., *America's backyard*).

American Citizen

A *consumer*.

American Dream

The idea that through sheer grit and determination, anyone in *America* – regardless of race, class, or creed – can *work* their way to the top and live a life of their dreams. Of course, only about 1% of *Americans* actually possesses such grit and determination.

American Empire

The only truly benign empire in all of *history*. Indeed, unlike *evil empires*, the American Empire never wantonly sacrifices the blood and treasure of faraway *unpeople* for territory or resources, but because it is simply the right and morally just thing to do.[4]

---

[4] As President Obama remarked on the Iraq war at the close of 2011, "Unlike the old empires, we don't make these sacrifices for territory or for resources. We do it because it's right." Barack Obama. "Remarks by the President and First Lady on the End of the War in Iraq." Whitehouse.gov. (14 Dec 2011).

American Exceptionalism

The belief, nay knowledge, that *America* is the one and only necessary nation. Or as every *American politician* must come to declare, *the world*'s lone indispensable nation.

American History

The time from 1776 to 1991 (i.e., the *end of history*) during which a lot of really great, exceptional *Americans* (think wealthy white men) did a lot of really great, exceptional things (think amassed ever greater personal wealth and *power*). Certainly, mistakes may have been made in there somewhere as well (think slavery, the *ethnic cleansing* of natives, the nuking of civilians, etc.), but one must never fault the great men of American history for being men of their times.

American Humility

See *American Exceptionalism*.

American Individualism

An ethos innate to the *American* psyche, in which it is understood that everything one has in life is due to one's own personal talents and successes. And then conversely, that everything one doesn't have in life is due to one's own personal faults and failings. (See also, *Personal Responsibility*, Chapter 2.)

American-Israel Political Action Committee – AIPAC

The official arbiters of *American foreign policy* in the *Middle East*.

American Medical Association

The vanguard defenders of the *American health care* system from the *tyranny* that is *socialized medicine*.

American People/Public

A mere rhetorical tool employed by *politicians* and *pundits* alike. To be used in the following manner: "What the American people really want [insert whatever you like here]." The American people/public is not to be confused with *public opinion*.

American Petroleum Institute – API

The trade association championing *sound science* in an effort to ensure *alarmists* never come to derail *Washington*'s *all the above energy policy*.

American Values

An unwavering belief in *freedom* and *democracy*, accompanied by the desire to impose such convictions, by force if necessary, on people *the world* over.

American Way of Life

The non-negotiable right, as President George H.W. Bush once declared, of every *American* to consume as many natural resources as one likes, in addition to buying as many disposable gadgets and trinkets as *credit* will allow.[5]

Anarchism

The nihilistic smashing of bank windows by bandana clad youth. Anarchism is nothing more, nothing less.

Anarchist

A window smashing subversive who must be carefully monitored until the day comes when she can be picked up and safely sent to rot in *prison*.[6]

Animal Rights Activist

Terrorist.[7]

---

[5] President Bush declared that "the American way of life is not negotiable" during the 1992 Earth Summit in Rio, Brazil.

[6] In 2012, law enforcement agencies working within a Joint Terrorism Task Force raided homes of suspected anarchists in Portland, Oregon and Seattle, Washington. The raids were conducted as part of an investigation into vandalism associated with the 2011 May Day protests in Seattle. Three activists were ultimately arrested and, after refusing to testify before a grand jury, imprisoned. Two of the activists, Matthew Dyran and Katherine Olejnik, were held for a total of 5 months, most of which was spent in solitary confinement, despite never being charged with any crime. See "Seattle grand jury resisters." Wikipedia. <http://en.wikipedia.org/wiki/Seattle_grand_jury_resisters>

[7] In 2005, John Lewis, an FBI deputy assistant director and top official in charge of domestic terrorism, declared, "The No. 1 domestic terrorism threat is the eco-terrorism, animal-rights movement." Henry Schuster. "Domestic terror: Who's most dangerous?" CNN. (24 Aug 2005).

Animal Rights Movement

An *un-American* movement seeking to *destroy* the *family farm* and kill *jobs*.

Anti-Americanism

Any articulated skepticism of *American exceptionalism*. Such *treason* entails nothing less than an irrational hostility toward *American values*, a hysterical contempt of the *American way of life*, and an uncontainable hatred of *American freedom* in general.[8]

Anticommunism

Once *America*'s true "national religion,"[9] anticommunism preached a dogmatic doctrine profoundly fearful of global *instability* triggered by any attempt to constrain *freedom* in general and the *free market* in particular. Today, anticommunism has given way to *America*'s new, more enlightened national religion: *counterterrorism*.

Anti-Globalization

Anti-*imperialism* deftly rebranded to discredit any anti-imperialist as a flat earther naively unaware that *there is no alternative*.

Anti-Semite

Someone who holds a deep hostility towards Jews. Also, anyone who criticizes the policies of the Israeli *government*.

Antiwar Movement

A dangerously seditious movement comprised of *radicals* of various stripes holding *un-American* beliefs threatening the very lifeblood of the *American*

---

[8] As President Bush famously declared in his speech to a joint session of Congress soon after the 9/11 attacks: "They hate our freedoms: our freedom of religion, our freedom of speech, our freedom to vote and assemble and disagree with each other." George W. Bush. "Address to a Joint Session of Congress and the American People." (Sept 2001).<http://georgewbush-whitehouse.archives.gov/news/releases/2001/09/20010920-8.html>

[9] Edward Herman and Noam Chomsky. *Manufacturing Consent: The Political Economy of the Mass Media.* (New York: Pantheon, 2002): 2.

economy. No expense is therefore to be spared in infiltrating, spying on, and otherwise sabotaging such a traitorous movement.[10]

Antiwar Veteran

A mentally unstable turncoat engaging in disloyal political activities as part of an ill-conceived attempt to reach catharsis.[11]

Appearing Presidential

Carrying oneself in such a manner as to establish one's worthiness of holding the highest elected office in the land. Realized by (1) visiting *Israel* and solemnly pledging loyalty to the *lone democracy in the Middle East*; (2) visiting *Wall Street* and solemnly pledging loyalty to one's *super donors*; and (3) going before the *American public* and solemnly pledging that once one is *president, all* options will always remain *on the table* when dealing with *rogue states.*

Appeasement

Questioning the tactics of the latest *just war* against the *next Hitler.*

Aspirations

The desire of every *American* to live nothing but the *American way of life.*

---

[10] The long, sordid history of government harassment of antiwar groups is well beyond the scope of this book, but suffice to say such illegal practices are hardly confined to history. For instance, as was first reported in 2009, an officer with the Force Protection Service at Fort Lewis Army base in Tacoma, Washington was discovered to have infiltrated both the Students for a Democratic Society and the Port Militarization Resistance in Washington State, and for years spied on the groups' antiwar activities related to the Afghanistan and Iraq wars. Heidi Boghosian. *Spying on Democracy: Government Surveillance, Corporate Power, and Public Resistance.* (San Francisco: City Lights Books, 2013): 107-111.

[11] As Jerry Lembcke briefly remarks on the establishment of antiwar veterans as somehow mentally unstable: "When members of Vietnam Veterans Against the War (VVAW) rallied to Miami Beach, Florida in 1972 to protest the Republican Party's renomination of Richard Nixon as its candidate for President, the [*New York*] *Times* filled its front-page coverage with mental-health terms such as 'psychiatric casualty,' 'emotional illness,' and 'mental breakdown.' Thenceforth, veterans' protest would be understood as a form of catharsis, a kind of acting-out to relieve the stress of their war trauma." Jerry Lembcke. "War Trauma and the New York Times: Reporting or Promoting PTSD?" *CounterPunch.* (17 April 2014).

Authoritarianism

A political system in which there exists a strict deference and obedience to *power* and those that possess *power*. What may appear as authoritarian tendencies within the *American* system – especially from within the *free press* – are, according to *official sources*, not worth getting all that worried about. After all, as officials note, *freedom* reigns in *America*.

Authorities

Those entrusted with making two plus two equal five.

Battleground State

A state subjected to a carpet bombing of *campaign advertising* each election cycle in an attempt to *win the hearts and minds* of the local *swing voter*.

Big Government

The troubling and needless expansion of the *government* into the affairs of its people in regards to protecting the environment, ensuring workplace safety, and providing social services. Military affairs and domestic surveillance, of course, don't constitute Big Government.

Bill of Rights

The document containing the non-*war on terror* inhibiting rights conferred to every *American* citizen.

Billionaire's Primary

A preliminary primary in which *super donors* carefully vet the field of potential *presidential candidates*, ultimately selecting those who will later be put before voters in a formal *primary election*.[12]

---

[12] In the early months of 2014, all the "serious" 2016 Republican presidential hopefuls jetted off to Las Vegas to grovel at the feet of billionaire casino mogul and "super donor" Sheldon Adelson. Indicative of the power of Adelson, New Jersey Governor Chris Christie had to issue a formal apology to the ultra-Zionist Adelson during his stay in Vegas for the faux pas of uttering the phrase "occupied territories" when speaking of the West Bank. Kenneth P. Vogel. "Chris Christie apologies for 'occupied territories' remark." *Politico.* (29 March 2014).

Bipartisanship

The reaching of consensus by both national political parties on every issue of substantial consequence to the average *American*.[13]

Blue State

A state much preferring a cabal of corrupt *Democrats* to oversee to their affairs than a cabal of corrupt *Republicans*.

Border Security

The use of fences, *drones*, armed vigilantes, and trigger-happy *law* enforcement officers in order to keep the Mexicans out. Well, but not all the Mexicans. *Americans* still need their lawns mowed, their crops harvested, and their houses cleaned.[14]

Budget

A bludgeon used to both beat back the uppity poor and reassure the *military-industrial complex* that when it comes to defending the *land of opportunity*, no expense shall be spared.[15]

Bureaucrat

An extravagantly compensated *public sector* employee (i.e., any *public sector* worker earning more than a *poverty* wage).

Campaign Advertising

The prolific use of *fear* in the *marketing* of snake *oil*.

---

[13] The other great unifier of the supposedly feuding parties is the ever present desire for self-enrichment. As Mark Leibovich notes, "Washington becomes a determinedly bipartisan team when there is money to be made." Mark Leibovich. *This Town: Two Parties and a Funeral – plus plenty of valet parking! – in America's Gilded Capital.* (New York: Blue Rider Press, 2013): 142.

[14] In 2012, Republican presidential nominee Mitt Romney ran on an immigration platform of self-deportation. This, of course, being the same Romney who once had his lawn cared for by undocumented immigrants while serving as governor of Massachusetts. See Jonathan Saltzman, Maria Cramer, and Connie Paige. "Illegal immigrants toiled for governor." *Boston Globe.* (1 Dec 2006).

[15] 45% of the 2015 fiscal year federal budget is devoted to military spending. See "Where Your Income Tax Money Really Goes: U.S. Federal Budget Fiscal Year 2015." WarResistersLeague.org.

Campaign Finance Reform

No longer necessary. Campaign financing was all sorted out back in 2010. (See *Citizens United*.)

Centrist

A most serious person, falling in the middle of the official *American* political spectrum. In other words, someone who supports *entitlement reform*, *education reform*, and *war*.

Change You Can Believe In

An award-winning defense of the status quo.[16]

Checks and Balances

The total acquiescence by the legislative and judicial branches of *government* to the executive branch in matters of *war* and *peace*.[17]

Chicken Hawk

A "wounded" never warrior courageously seeking to live vicariously through today's more privileged deprived service members by championing their deployment at every *opportunity*.

Citizens United

A landmark 2010 *Supreme Court* ruling advancing *American freedom* by equating *money* to speech and conferring the rights of free political speech to *corporations*.

---

[16] President Obama's 2008 campaign slogan won *Advertising Age*'s "Marketer of the Year" award.

[17] For example, in March 2011, President Obama, acting under the authority of the War Powers Act (WPA), ordered the bombing of Libya in an effort to establish a "no-fly zone." Once the provisions granting the president power to deploy force abroad found in the WPA had lapsed, however, the U.S. Congress and federal courts stood idly by. Ten renegade lawmakers did ultimately end up suing President Obama in June of 2011 for keeping U.S. forces in Libya beyond the 90 day maximum time period permitted by the WPA, but their lawsuit was dismissed four months later. And in his ruling, U.S. District Court Judge Reggie Walton chastised the lawmakers for having the chutzpa to even bring a suit. As Judge Walton wrote, "the Court finds it frustrating to expend time and effort adjudicating the relitigation of settled questions of law." See Josh Gerstein. "Judge zings lawmakers, dismisses lawsuit over Libya mission." *Politico*. (20 Oct 2011).

Civil Society

All groups and organizations working independently from *government* and *small businesses*. Or, those whose opinions are utterly irrelevant to the forming of official *American* policy.

Class War

The range of divisive tactics employed by certain *un-American* elements and other political opportunists aiming to: raise the average standard of living, preserve the *social safety net*, and create a more equitable and just *society*.

Useful tip: Cry class war to smear, and ultimately derail, any political opponent's domestic agenda.

Clean Coal

A non-existent entity, which still must be touted by every *politician* whenever discussing *climate change*.

Clean Energy

Clean coal, *natural gas*, waste incineration, and nuclear power.

Climate Change

An *alarmist* hoax necessitating no measure of response other than to tout the marvels of *clean coal*.

Climate Skeptic

A person wholly unlearned in climate *science*, who, nevertheless, possesses an unwavering skepticism toward the overwhelming body of scientific research linking human activity to *climate change*.

Collectivism

A tyrannically *unorthodox* concept for a people standing united as atomized individuals.

Commander-in-Chief

The *president*; or, someone who has been proven so quick to assert that all options are always *on the table* he now finds himself commanding the U.S. armed forces – nuclear weapons and all.

Commission on Presidential Debates

The body in charge of ensuring no major party candidate is ever subjected to the humiliation of having to debate a *third party* candidate.[18]

Communism

Once and forever, the single greatest threat to the *free world.*

Communist

Evil incarnate. And historically, someone to be denied *freedom* and *opportunity* within the *land of opportunity*, while simply *offed* abroad. (In the modern context, see *Muslim*, Chapter 12.)

Congress

The nation's most prestigious (as well as most lucrative[19]) internship program for all those seeking a rewarding career as a corporate *consultant* or *lobbyist*.

Conservation

An altogether immature idea posing a threat to *consumption* and, ultimately, the nonnegotiable *American way of life*. Of course, conservation hasn't held much sway amongst serious thinking people in the U.S. since the day President Jimmy – "too many of us worship self-indulgence and consumption" – Carter was sent packing by one *Ronald Reagan*.[20]

---

[18] For a critical history of the Commission for Presidential Debates, see: George Farah. *No Debate: How the Republican and Democratic Parties Secretly Control the Presidential Debates.* (New York: Seven Stories Press, 2004).

[19] While median household net worth dropped 39% from 2007 to 2010, as the *Washington Post* reported in 2012, "The median estimated wealth of members of the current Congress rose 5 percent during the same period." Dan Keating, Scott Higham, Kimberly Kindy and David S. Fallis. "Capitol Assets: Congress's wealthiest mostly shielded from effects of deep recession." *Washington Post.* (6 Oct 2012).

[20] As Morris Berman notes, the 1980 election pitted Carter, who was warning Americans of the perils of conspicuous consumption, against Reagan, who was telling Americans they could have it all. "The American public, it turned out," Berman writes, "was not interested in some sermon or jeremiad about the limits to growth or the joys of solar power. Rather, they wanted to spend their eyeballs out once again, and it is no surprise that Mr. Reagan, who told them they could and should do it, won by a landslide." Morris Berman. *Why America Failed: The Roots of Imperial Decline.* (Hoboken, NJ: John Wiley & Sons, Inc., 2012): 34-41.

Conservative

Someone who champions the *freedom* of *corporations* to control the national political system so that said *corporations* may more easily exhaust the global ecosystem to the point of collapse.

Conspiracy Theory

Any writings, speeches, or cognitive theses articulated by those of *unorthodox* beliefs.

Constituency

See *Super Donor.*

Constitution

An archaic document in no way applicable to the *war on terror.*

Consultant

A *lobbyist* in waiting.[21]

Controversial

Independent thought.

Courage

Giving voice to *American small businesses* and championing their causes by taking on the powerful juggernaut that is the assorted poor and infirm masses.

Sentence example: It takes real political courage to tackle *Medicare reform.*

Crisis of Democracy

A dangerous and troubling increase in political participation by those who ought not to trouble themselves with such matters (i.e., all those not in the *power elite*).[22]

---

[21] Federal law prohibits former House members from lobbying their former colleagues for one year, while former Senators are barred from lobbying their former colleagues for two years. In order to skirt such restrictions, lobbying shops often hire ex-elected officials as "consultants" rather than registered "lobbyists."

[22] As Samuel Huntington was left to observe in a 1973 report for the Trilateral Commission: "Some of the problems of governance in the United States today stem

Cut and Run

A disparaging phrase used to describe a feckless person's call for the withdrawal of *American* troops from a *mistake*. Needless to say, it is always *un-American* to cut and run.

Dangerous Radical

Someone who just may prove effective in countering the status quo.

Dark Money

The off-the-books *super donor* down payments (or "contributions") lining the pockets of the nation's public servants.

Death Tax

A highly burdensome tax levied on the destitute souls who, by the mere misfortune of birth, are forced into an onerous inheritance of millions and millions of *dollars*.[23]

Decider, the

The 43rd *president* of the United States, George W. Bush.

Debt/Deficit

The main catalysts for *entitlement reform*.

Debt Ceiling

A reoccurring hostage *crisis*, wherein the *American* economy is taken and held until further cuts in *wasteful spending* are made.[24]

---

from an excess in democracy...Needed, instead, is a greater degree of moderation of democracy." Samuel Huntington in Michel J. Crozier, Samuel Huntington, and Joji Watanuki. "The Crisis of Democracy: Report on the Governability of Democracies to the Trilateral Commission." (New York: New York University Press, 1973): 113.
[23] In 2014, the estate tax, or "death tax," only applied to inherited wealth in excess of $5,340,000.
[24] "The Republicans, in collusion with the Democrats, have repeatedly used the raising of the debt ceiling to extract future spending cuts. This, despite the fact that the debt ceiling has nothing to do with future spending, as it is strictly limited to already allocated funds. By raising the debt ceiling, then, Congress simply confers its formal authorization to the executive branch to continue with spending commitments it – Congress – has already authorized. Any failure to raise the debt

Deficit Reduction

Rolling back the *undeserving poor*'s life of abundance.

Democracy

The equal participation of the nation's ruling elite in the management of all governmental affairs. To be achieved via the *containment* and manipulation of *public opinion*.

Democrats

See *Republicans*.

Department of Energy

Federal department tasked with picking up the tab for the nation's cache of nuclear weapons so that the *Pentagon*'s *budget* may appear just a bit more reasonable.[25]

Department of Interior

Federal department tasked with sleeping with *oil* and gas company executives[26] when not already engaged in fire sales of public lands to said companies.[27]

---

ceiling would thus not limit future spending in any way, but merely see the country renege on current financial obligations – i.e., default." Ben Schreiner. "The Politics of The Debt Ceiling: Orchestrated Spectacle." *Dissident Voice*. (2 Aug 2011).

[25] In the 2015 fiscal year budget, the Department of Energy allocated $19 billion toward the nation's nuclear weapons stockpile. See War Resisters League. "Where Your Income Tax Money Really Goes."

[26] In 2008, the Interior Department's inspector general delivered three reports to the Senate detailing systemic abuse and corruption within the Minerals Management Service (since renamed the Bureau of Ocean Energy Management, Regulation and Enforcement). The MMS was the agency within the Interior responsible for collecting royalties related to oil and gas permits. Among the investigation's findings was that several of the officials within the MMS "frequently consumed alcohol at industry functions, had used cocaine and marijuana, and had sexual relationships with oil and gas company representatives." Charlie Savage. "Sex, Drug Use and Graft Cited in Interior Department." *New York Times*. (10 Sept 2008).

[27] In 2008, the climate activist Tim DeChristopher attended a fire sale auction for drilling rights in Utah run by the Bureau of Land Management (an agency within the Interior Department). In an attempt to bid up prices, DeChristopher ended up winning the drilling rights to 22,000 acres of land. For his supposed disruption of a public auction, DeChristopher served 21 months in federal prison. This is despite

Deregulation

The curtailment of *Big Government* intrusions into the affairs of *small businesses*.

Direct Action

A *protest* action undertaken by those lacking the patience, wisdom, and foresight to *work* through the only legitimate channel for public redress in *American democracy*: voting for the lesser evil.

Direct Democracy

A most troubling perversion of *democracy*. (See also, *Tyranny*.)

Dithering

A *president* in the intervening period between the outbreak of an international *crisis* and his eventual decision to lob a few *cruise missiles* at the problem.

Don't Tread on Me!

Tread on *others*!

Dove

Someone who, although embracing the overall strategy, still heretically questions the tactics of the clearly *just war*.

Economic Stimulus

$%#@!

Electoral College

A failsafe mechanism in the effective stewardship of *American democracy*. Requiring that a set of appointed electors directly cast the ballots for the *president* of the United States, the Electoral College helps to ensure there will never be a *crisis of democracy* when it comes to sending one to the White House.

---

the fact that not only was the auction ultimately declared illegal, but DeChristopher had actually raised the money for the land. See Amy Goodman and Juan Gonzalez. "Released from Prison, Climate Activist Tim DeChristopher on Civil Disobedience & Building Movements." *Democracy Now!* (17 May 2013).

Electorate

The ever diminishing number of *Americans* turning out to send future *lobbyists* to *Washington* for their necessary training in the U.S. *Congress*.[28]

Emergency Manager

A guardian of *democracy* given carte blanche to impose *fiscal restraint* in localities unwilling to make *hard choices*.[29]

End of History

The idea that *history* is now over, given that *liberal democracy* represents the "final form of human government."[30] And with *history* finished, the task of *Washington* planners from the end of the *Cold War (old)* to the present day has been twofold. First, to ensure that *history* indeed remains at its end in the *West*. And second, that any revisionists still stuck in *history* are made aware – with the help of the *U.S. military*, if necessary – that all world *history* is now to be stopped.

Energy Exploration

Searching for that very last drop of *oil*.

Entitlement Reform

The shuttering of the *Social Security* Ponzi scheme, accompanied by the effort to finally oust *government* from *Medicare*.[31]

---

[28] Voter turnout for those eligible to vote in the U.S. is around 60% for presidential elections and 40% for off year congressional elections.
See: <http://www.fairvote.org/research-and-analysis/voter-turnout/>

[29] Under Michigan state law, the state's governor has the authority to appoint an unelected "emergency manager" to a local government declared to be in a "financial emergency." Emergency managers are then granted sweeping powers to impose draconian budget cuts without the approval of the locality's elected representatives. Emergency managers have been dispatched to the city of Detroit and the Detroit public school district, along with other cities and municipalities across the state.

[30] As the political scientist Francis Fukuyama wrote in 1989: "What we may be witnessing is not just the end of the Cold War, or the passing of a particular period of post-war history, but the end of history as such: that is, the end point of mankind's ideological evolution and the universalization of Western liberal democracy as the final form of human government." Francis Fukuyama. "The End of History?" *The National Interest*. (Summer 1989).

[31] In 2009, at many raucous congressional town hall meetings focused on the ongoing health care debate, numerous attendees were reported as calling for government to

Environmental Protection Agency – EPA

Federal environmental regulatory agency founded in 1971 under the *liberal* tree hugger Richard Nixon. The EPA has since been rendered void, having been unable to adapt to the imperatives of *competitiveness.*

Environmentalist

Terrorist.[32]

Establishment, the

A pejorative used by elite *politicians* seeking to pander to *Middle America.*[33]

Exceptional Nation, the

A nation violently acting out again and again in response to an untreated case of grandiose delusions.

Executive Action

The dropping of any constitutional pretenses by the imperial chief in the White House.

Executive Privilege

The *power* claimed by the *president* and executive branch to halt any attempts at congressional *oversight.*

Expert

A specialist confirming the *orthodox* views held by corporate and *government* leaders.

Extremist

Someone who opposes *just wars*, questions subsidizing *the 1%*, and critiques *consumption.*

---

get out of the federal health care program Medicare. See Joshua Holland. "Town Hall Lunacy Includes Outraged Calls to 'Keep Government Out of Medicare,' When Medicare Is Government." *AlterNet.* (26 Aug 2009).

[32] See above footnote #7.

[33] In announcing his bid for the Republican presidential nomination in 2015, Ted Cruz positioned himself as an insurgent candidate opposed by, as Cruz proudly touted, "the establishment." This, of course, being the same Cruz who graduated from Harvard Law, married a managing director at Goldman Sachs, and now currently serves in the U.S. Senate.

Faith-Based Community

A *community* comprised of "history's actors"; or, those who believe they are capable of making and remaking *reality* as they deem fit.[34]

Fascism

A form of class struggle waged by threatened *capitalists* as a means of crushing powerful *working class* movements. Contemporary *America* can in no way be deemed a fascist *society*, as there simply exists no powerful *working class* movement for *American capitalists* to crush.

Fear

That which must be instilled in every *American* voter. For the candidate able to gin up the most fear – fear of: immigrants, homosexuals, foreigners, political rivals, etc. – is the candidate primed for *victory*.

Federal Communications Commission – FCC

Agency tasked with providing a secure place of employment for both past and future telecommunications industry *lobbyists*.[35]

Federal Elections Commission – FEC

Agency tasked with facilitating the flow of corporate and *super donor money* to *politicians*.

---

[34] "History's actors" being the term Karl Rove used to describe those working within the Bush administration. As Rove purportedly explained to the journalist Ron Suskind: "We're an empire now, we create our own reality. And while you're studying that reality – judiciously as you will – we'll act again, creating other new realities, which you can study, too, all of you, and that's how things will sort out. We're history's actors…and you, all of you will be left to just study what we do."[34] Ron Suskind. "Faith, Certainty and the Presidency of George W. Bush." *New York Times Magazine.* (17 Oct 2004).

[35] As Robert McChesney argues, "The FCC has become the classic 'captured' regulatory agency." "Most FCC members go on to lucrative careers with those they had been ostensibly regulating previously," McChesney continues. "As more than one skeptic has noted, when a commercial firm's executives comes before the FCC, the members do not know whether to regard him as someone to be regulated or as a possible future employer." Case in point, President Obama's appointed chief of the FCC, Tom Wheeler, formerly worked as a lobbyist for the National Cable and Telecommunications Association, along with the Cellular Telecommunications and Internet Association. Robert W. McChesney. *The Problem of the Media: U.S. Communication Politics in the 21st Century.* (New York: Monthly Review Press, 2004): 45.

Federal Emergency Management Agency – FEMA

Agency tasked with doing a heck of a job in responding to natural disasters.[36]

Feminism

Agitating to get more women into corporate boardrooms. And perhaps someday (knock on wood), a sociopathic woman into the Oval Office.[37]

Feminist

Sarah Palin![38]

Filibuster

A *democracy* safeguard meant to defend minority rights in an institution – the U.S. Senate – in which members are elected based on a formula specifically designed to protect minority rights.[39]

Financial Reform

See *Bank Bailout*, Chapter 7.

Fiscal Cliff

A *crisis* manufactured by the U.S. *Congress* in early 2013 as part of the ever expanding effort to scare *Americans* into acquiescing to the draconian social cuts needed to offset further tax breaks to the *deserving rich*. In other words, a fine example that *bipartisanship* is still possible.

---

[36] As President Bush told FEMA director Michael Brown in the wake of Hurricane Katrina, "Brownie, you're doing a heck of a job."

[37] "The feminism that has mattered to the media and made magazine headlines in recent years has been the feminism most useful to heterosexual, high-earning middle- and upper-middle-class white women," Laurie Penny writes. "Public 'career feminists' have been more concerned with getting more women into 'boardrooms', when the problem is that there are altogether too many boardrooms, and none of them are on fire." Laurie Penny. *Unspeakable Things: Sex, Lies, and Revolution.* (New York: Bloomsbury, 2014): 5.

[38] Palin deemed herself to be a feminist during her infamous 2008 interview with Katie Couric. See Katie Couric. "Palin Opens Up On Controversial Issues." *CBS Evening News.* (30 Sept 2008).

[39] In the U.S. Senate, the little over half a million resident of Wyoming are granted the same number of votes (2) as the nearly 40 million residents of California (2).

Fiscal Responsibility

The need to balance public expenses, because *government* is just like a household: it cannot spend more revenue than it receives. And thus *government* must come to make the *hard choices* any household must come to make every day: Should one raise taxes to pay the cable bill? Should one devalue the currency to pay rent? Fiscal responsibility is to be achieved through *entitlement reform*.

Fiscal Restraint

Putting the rabble on a diet.

Flat Tax

A universal rate of taxation proposed as a means of *simplifying the tax code*, because a progressive tax code is just a little too much "from each according to his mean, to each according to his need."

Flip-Flopper

A principled political hack.

Food and Drug Administration – FDA

Federal agency tasked with ensuring burdensome health and safety regulations in no way come to hinder the *profitability* of the corporate entities falling under its regulatory authority (medical device makers,[40] *processed food* manufactures,[41] etc.).

---

[40] According to a December 2014 *Wall Street Journal* investigation, many of the doctors serving on FDA panels reviewing the safety of various medical devices often receive compensation from the very companies whose devices they are tasked with approving. The *Journal* reported: "In panels evaluating devices involved in cardiology and gynecology from 2012 through 2014, a third of 122 members had received compensation – such as money, research grants or travel and food – from medical-device companies...Nearly 10% of the FDA advisers received something of value from the specific company whose products they were evaluating. The FDA disclosed roughly 1% of these corporate connections." Joseph Walker. "Doctors Advise FDA And Companies, Too." *Wall Street Journal*. (9 Dec 2014): A1.

[41] As Michael Moss writes, "when it comes to nutrition, the role the government plays is less a matter of regulation than it is promotion of some of the industry practices deemed most threatening to the health of consumers." Michael Moss. *Salt, Sugar, Fat: How the Food Giants Hooked Us*. (New York: Random House, 2013): 211.

Foreign Policy

The management of the *American Empire*. Accordingly, far too important a matter to be left to anyone but elite *experts*.

Free Speech Zone

An area specifically cordoned off so that *activists* and *protesters* can come to freely express their opinions in a manner guaranteed not to bother important elites, nor distract the *respectable press* from their ongoing consolations with *official sources*.

Freedom

The uninhibited *liberty* granted to every citizen within a *democracy* to sell one's *labor power* to the proprietors of *small businesses*.

Freedom Isn't Free

An ominous warning to the various *unpeople* of *the world* unfortunate enough to ever encounter an *American* GI at *work*.

Fringe

Anyone in principled opposition to either a *just war* or *reform*.

Fundraising

What your elected representative is doing right now.[42]

Future Generations

Those whose future is best served by disbanding the *freedom* impairing *social safety net*.

Gaffe

A *politician*'s expression of his or her true contempt for the *American public*.

---

[42] A 2013 slide breaking down a model daily schedule for incoming freshman Democratic Congress members prepared by the Democratic Congressional Campaign Committee listed 4 hours daily for "call time," 1 hour for "strategic outreach," and 1-2 hours for "constituent visits." As Ezra Klein explained what this actually entails: "'Call time' is not time spent calling your family, or think tank experts, or ordinary constituents. It's time spent calling donors. Strategic outreach is, of course, also time you can spend with donors, and if your constituent visits include constituents who are donors, then all the better!" Ezra Klein. "The most depressing graphic for members of Congress." *Washington Post* Wonkblog. (14 Jan 2013).

Gender Pay Equality

An attack on *free market principles*, asserting it should be required that women receive the same pay for the same *work* as men, as opposed to simply continuing to let *market forces* efficiently allocate greater pay to men.[43]

Genetically Modified Food (aka GMOs)

A means through which to expropriate the role of Creator from the rather inefficient hands of *God* and place said role in the far more profitable hands of *Monsanto* and friends.

Geoengineering (Climate)

The large-scale alteration of the earth's oceans and atmosphere (what could possibly go wrong?) in an attempt to mitigate the effects of global *climate change*. In other words, plan B should *climate change* for some reason turn out to be real and the mere touting of *clean coal* prove an inadequate response.[44]

Gerrymandering

The redrawing of congressional boundaries in a way that protects public servants from the *tyranny* of the ballot box.[45]

---

[43] In 2010, women earned 77% of what men earned, contributing to a loss of $431,000 over a 40-year career for the average woman. Sarah Jane Glynn and Audrey Powers. "The Top 10 Facts About the Wage Gap." Center For American Progress. (16 April 2012).

[44] The danger of geoengineering goes even beyond the unknown effects to the physical environment. By purposely altering the climate, all extreme weather events will inherently come to be seen by some as the malicious intent of those engaged in geoengineering. As Naomi Klein notes, "A drought in India will come to be seen – accurately or not – as a result of a conscious decision by engineers on the other side of the planet. What was once bad luck could come to be seen as a malevolent plot or an imperialist attack." Naomi Klein. "Geoengineering: Testing the Waters." *New York Times*. (27 Oct 2012).

[45] During the 2012 congressional elections, Democratic candidates for the House received over half a million more votes nationally than Republican candidates, yet Republicans were able to retain a 30-plus seat majority in the House due to gerrymandering. In a particularly striking example, Pennsylvanians cast 2,793,538 votes for Democrats seeking House seats, compared to 2,710,070 who voted for Republican candidates. And yet, Democrats only won five congressional seats in the state, while Republicans won a total of 13. Andrew Hacker. "2014: Another Democratic Debacle?" *New York Review of Books* Vol. LXI No. 1 (9 Jan 2014): 32-34.

God Bless the United States of America

The obligatory concluding line to every *politician*'s public remarks, coming in direct recognition of the separation of church and *state*.

Going Off Message

Inadvertently revealing one's intended policy initiatives while still campaigning.

Government

An inherently *inefficient* entity and rather burdensome constraint on the dynamism of government created *free markets*.

Government Shutdown

A shutdown of the U.S. *government* orchestrated by both political parties as a stunt meant to concoct an illusion of two ideologically divergent parties at some sort of loggerheads.

Grassroots

Super donors and their *super PACs*.

Green

Driving new hybrid cars and/or talking about *sustainability*.

Green Jobs

Cleaning *oil* spills and containing nuclear fallout.

Gridlock

The use of Kabuki theater style antics by both major political parties in an effort to cultivate political apathy and starve off a *crisis of democracy*. (See also, *Government Shutdown*.)

Groupthink

A prerequisite for joining *respectable circles*.[46]

---

[46] Answering the question of what it takes to be a corporate executive in America, C. Wright Mills remarked, "the sound judgment, as gauged by the men of sound judgment who select them.   The fit survive, and fitness means, not formal

Growth Agenda

A legislative agenda based on giving *corporations* and *job-creators* everything they would ever want, so they may be properly empowered to go about raising their share prices.

Hard Choices

The difficult decisions made by wealthy lawmakers over just how much funding to cut from social programs serving the poor.[47]

Hawk

Someone in full agreement on both the tactics and strategy of the *just war*.

Heartland

See *Middle America*.

Hope

Despair.

Hydraulic Fracking

A safe drilling technique involving the safe pumping of pressurized water, sand, and safe toxic chemicals into deep underground wells in order to safely fracture rock formations, enabling *oil* and *natural gas* to safely flow back into the well for easy, safe extraction. Did *we* mention fracking is safe?[48]

I Want My Country Back

A common refrain heard from traditionalists seeking to return *America* to a simpler, more prosperous time – a time when blacks knew their place, woman stayed in the kitchen and bedroom, and nobody was gay.

---

competence…but conformity with the criteria of those who have already succeeded." C. Wright Mills. *The Power Elite*. (New York: Oxford University Press, 2000): 141.

[47] As Tony Judt remarked on such "hard" decisions, "The poor vote in much smaller numbers than anyone else. So there is little political risk in penalizing them: just how 'hard' are such choices?" Tony Judt. *Ill Fares the Land*. (New York: Penguin Books, 2011): 36.

[48] "Safe" being the words used by former Secretary of Energy Steven Chu and former Interior Secretary Ken Salazar to describe fracking. Ashe Schow. "Ken Salazar, Steven Chu praise fracking as 'safe.'" *Washington Examiner*. (24 Sept 2014).

Ideological

Those with career-inhibiting principles preventing them from going along to get along with prevailing *orthodoxy*.

Immigration Customs Enforcement – ICE

Federal agency tasked with deporting *criminals* and gangbangers…or at least those who look like they might be *criminals* or gangbangers.[49]

Immigration Reform

Sending more *drones* to the U.S.-*Mexico* border and delivering more ammo to the good folks in the *Border Control*.

Incumbent

Barring a *political scandal*, someone with no need to sweat reelection.[50]

Independent Voter

A voter too dignified to personally succumb to the whole *Democratic-Republican* shell game, yet still willing to help perpetuate the game itself by diligently voting nonetheless.[51]

Internal Revenue Service – IRS

Federal agency tasked with ensuring (1) that the *competitiveness* of *small businesses*

---

[49] Under President Obama, ICE deportations have reached record levels. And despite assurances from Mr. Obama that only "criminals" and "gangbangers" are targeted, a *New York Times* investigation found that, "two-thirds of the nearly two million deportation cases [since Obama came to office] involve people who had committed minor infractions, including traffic violations, or had no criminal record at all." Those deported because of traffic violations alone have "more than quadrupled from 43,000 during the last five years of President George W. Bush's administration to 193,000 during the five years Mr. Obama has been in office." Ginger Thompson and Sarah Cohen. "More Deportations Follow Minor Crimes, Records Show." *New York Times* (6 April 2014).

[50] From 1964 to 2012, the reelection rate for members of the U.S. House of Representatives has never fallen below 80%. Over the same time period, the reelection rate for senators has never dipped below 50%. "Reelection Rates Over The Years." Center for Responsive Politics. <https://www.opensecrets.org/bigpicture/reelect.php>

[51] As Emma Goldman once quipped, if voting made any difference it would be illegal.

is never burdened by the payment of taxes, and (2) that elites sleep at ease knowing their *money* is safely resting in offshore accounts. (See *Tax Haven.*)

Islamofascism

The reason du jour *something must be done.*

Isolationism

The starkly pessimistic belief that the U.S. can't solve every international *crisis* with *boots on the ground.*

Isolationist

A politically impotent and marginalized individual.

Jobs

The purported central political focus in every even numbered calendar year.

Just War

A morally justifiable *war* conducted in a morally justifiable manner – i.e., every *American war.*

K Street

The siren which beckons one into a life of selfless *public service.*

Keeping Americans Safe

Killing nameless foreigners.

Kleptocracy

A political system in which a profoundly corrupted *state* functions chiefly to enhance the personal *power* and fortunes of its officials. The *American* system avoids the trappings of Kleptocracy by handing the levers of *power* over to those of already immense *power* and affluence.[52] Furthermore, as a failsafe of sorts, the promise of further enrichment in the *American* system is postponed until after one officially leaves *government.* (See *Consultant* and *Lobbyist.*)

---

[52] As the Center for Responsive Politics reported in early 2014, for the first time in history, a majority of those serving in Congress are millionaires. "Millionaires' Club: For First Time, Most Lawmakers are Worth $1 Million-Plus." Center for Responsive Politics Open Secrets Blog. (9 Jan 2014).

Land of Opportunity

A land in which *there is no alternative* but to live the *American way of life*.

Left (Political)

A rabid swarm of traitorous *activists*, *dangerous radicals*, and mentally unstable conspiracy theorists.

Lesser Evilism

Voting for evil over and over again, getting evil over and over again, and yet always expecting a different result come the next election season.

Liberal

A person too materially comfortable to even acknowledge, let alone do anything to address, the root causes of the societal injustices she bemoans.

Liberal Democracy

The highest and last stage of political development mankind will ever know, in which a *representative democracy* functions to protect minority rights (i.e., the rights of the beleaguered *1%*).

Liberalism

An ideology left long ago by *liberals* to bleed out in the jungles of Vietnam.[53]

Libertarianism

An ideology for affluent white males desperately seeking to justify their privileged status by denying any societal role in their own personal success.

Liberty

The *freedom* from repressive *government* regulation granted to every *American small business*.

Limited Government

The *conservative* belief that the *free market* functions best when the *government* limits itself to *bank bailouts* and *wars*.

---

[53] On the death of American liberalism, and more specifically the liberal class, see: Chris Hedges. *Death of the Liberal Class*. (New York: Nation Books, 2010).

Lobbying

The charitable rendering of gifts and cash in an effort to educate a public servant on the grave professional perils of crossing moneyed interests.

Lobbyist

A former public official or representative who has effectively monetized his or her *public service*.[54]

Look Forward, Not Backward

The need to grant one's *criminal* predecessor legal immunity, because his *criminal* policies are to be continued.[55]

Low-Life Scum

See *Protesters*.[56]

Loyal Opposition

The minority party's acceptance that *American politics stops at water's edge*.

Man Up

A derogatory phrase levied at a *politician* wavering in his support of either manly *entitlement reform* or manly *war*.[57]

---

[54] Of course, lawmakers also can monetize their public service while still actually remaining in office by simply pimping their family members out to lobbying firms, as 71 Congressional members were doing as of early 2014. See Legistorm. "Family Ties of Members of Congress."
<http://www.legistorm.com/member_family/list/type_id/11.html>

[55] When asked in early 2009 whether his administration would pursue criminal charges against officials in the George W. Bush administration responsible for torture, then President-elect Obama declared that "we need to look forward as opposed to looking backwards." David Johnston and Charlie Savage. "Obama Reluctant to Look Into Bush Programs." *New York Times*. (11 Jan 2009).

[56] As antiwar Code Pink protesters were being escorted out of a Senate Armed Services committee hearing in January 2015, Senator John McCain averred, "Get out of here, you low-life scum." McCain defended his remarks days later by explaining that the protesters were "terrible people." Andrew Desiderio. "McCain: I Don't Regret Calling Protesters 'Low-Life Scum.'" Mediaite. (1 Feb 2015).

[57] In 2012, Senator Lindsey Graham called for Obama to "man up" and support cuts to Medicare. Meanwhile, *New York Times* columnist David Brooks declared on *Meet the Press* in April 2014 that Obama has "a manhood problem in the Middle East. Is

Sentence example: It's time for the *president* to man up and tackle *Medicare reform*.

Manifest Destiny

A 19th century *American* belief, which held that *America* was divinely destined to expand westward, all native inhabitants be damned. A shocking legacy for many *Americans* to comprehend today, given the country's present role as a *democracy* spreading *global force for good*.

Marxism

A peculiar form of social analysis emphasizing the importance of class and class struggle. Marxism has been proven empirically wrong by the very existence of the class devoid *society* that is the United States of America.

Meritocracy

A system in which personal advancement is based on one's own merit or one's own talent. The *American* system, in which those with *money* disproportionally rise to positions of *power*, is still a thriving meritocracy, given that the accumulation of personal wealth in the U.S. is really the only merit worth having.

Messaging

The *marketing* of unpopular policies and *politicians* to the *electorate*. Electoral losses are to be attributed to messaging problems, never because one's policies and candidates were despised by voters.

Middle America

The rural areas in which *America's* *silent majority* resides.

Middle Class

The largely vanquished class occupying the former space between the rich and poor every *politician* still must swear to be fighting for.[58]

---

he tough enough to stand up to somebody like Assad or somebody like Putin?" Igor Volsky. "Lindsey Graham: Debt Ceiling Will Force Obama To Man Up On Medicare Cuts." Think Progress. (10 Dec 2012); Ben Armbruster. "New York Times' David Brooks Says Obama Has 'A Manhood Problem In The Middle East.'" Think Progress. (20 April 2014).

[58] President Obama has defined "middle class" to entail all those making $250,000 a year or less. And with an official poverty rate for a family of four near $20,000 a

Money

Political speech.

Mountaintop Removal

Decapitating redundant and aesthetically displeasing mountains in order to gain access to *clean coal.*

Muscular

The *foreign policy* line of those always insisting that *something must be done*, albeit always done by people other than themselves.

National Rifle Association – NRA

The organization holding the only vote ever worth counting when it comes to any gun control legislation.

Nationalism

A toxic ideology abroad (see *Nationalism* and *Nationalist*, Chapter 9), which has never been too much of an issue within the indispensable nation. USA! USA! USA!

Natural Gas

Everybody's favorite *green* fossil fuel.[59]

---

year, in strictly monetary terms, we can say the American "middle class" is comprised of families with an income falling between $20,000 and $250,000 per year. Of course, this is absurd, for using such a definition we could say that a worker earning minimum wage working two jobs and a tenured college professor are both "middle class." The truth is that middle class is as much a social class as an economic class. And in that sense, the "middle class" still exists in large numbers. But whenever American politicians invoke the term "middle class" they are speaking to those at the high end of the middle class spectrum. In other words, those far more likely to vote.

[59] As Naomi Oreskes notes of natural gas, celebrated by environmental groups like the Environmental Defense Fund as a "green" alternative to coal and oil: "increased availability and decreased price of natural gas are likely to lead to an increase in U.S. greenhouse gas emissions." This is due to the leaking of methane gas, which accompanies natural gas production and actually contributes more proportionally to global warming than CO_2, which is omitted in the burning of both coal and oil. Indeed, as Oreskes notes: "There have been enormous disagreements among scientists and industry representatives over methane leakage rates, but experts calculate that leakage must be kept below 3 percent for gas to represent an

Neo-conservatism

An ideology advancing the notion that the *American Empire* is so strong, no less than *reality* itself can be compelled to bend to the empire's will.

Neo-conservative

Someone finding gainful employment attempting to bend *reality* at the *U.S. Department of State*, the *Pentagon*, a private *think tank*, or a prominent *news* organization.

New Deal

The set of social spending programs (including *Social Security*) implemented under President Franklin Delano Roosevelt during the Great Depression. The shadow cast by the New Deal lingers to this day, as domestic *American politics* largely revolves around how best to unravel the last remaining remnants of the New Deal without having to bear the political costs of having done so.

Occupy

A short-lived national movement comprised of a bunch of jobless losers who had nothing better to do than risk the health and sanitation of city parks.[60]

Oligarchy

A system in which *power* is concentrated amongst a very small number of people. In the *American* system, a very small number of people – the *power elite* – are granted *power* in order to defend against the concentration of *power* one would expect to find in an oligarchy.

---

improvement over coal in electricity generation, and below 1 percent for gas to improve over diesel and gasoline in transportation. The Environmental Protection Agency (EPA) currently estimates average leakage at 1.4 percent, but quite a few experts dispute that figure. One study published in 2013, based on atmospheric measurements over gas fields in Utah, found leakage rates as high as 6.0 percent." Naomi Oreskes. "A Green Bridge to Hell: Why fossil fuels can't solve the problems created by fossil fuels." *Z Magazine* (Sept 2014): 30-31, 33.

[60] Local officials and police across the country justified the forced clearing of Occupy encampments by claiming that they were unsanitary and posed a health risk.

Opportunism

The rejection of one's principles in the pursuit of political advancement. Charges of opportunism are best deflected by holding political advancement as one's lone principle.

Opportunity

The chance afforded every *American* child born into the top 1% to gain a higher *education* and live a life of material abundance (i.e., the *American Dream*).

Orthodoxy

The total and complete acceptance of the infallibility of *capitalism*, an unconditional love of *freedom*, and a firm conviction that exceptional *American* might does indeed make *the world* right.[61]

Oversight

The Congressional whitewashing of *criminal* conduct, whether it be in the *private* or *public sector*.

Pacifism

A childishly *un-American* ideology threatening the very health of the *American* economy.

Pacifist

A *job*-killing economic saboteur.

Paranoid

Someone who denies that the *exceptional nation* is, and has always been, anything but a pure hearted *global force for good*.

Partisan Politics

The painfully strained efforts undertaken by two feuding wings of the same party to manufacture the illusion of two distinct, ideologically diverse parties.

---

[61] "Orthodoxy means not thinking – not needing to think. Orthodoxy is unconsciousness." George Orwell. *1984*. (New York: Signet Classic, 1961): 47.

Patriot

Someone who *supports the troops* – no questions asked – in the next *just war*, all the while maintaining optimum levels of personal *consumption*.

Patriotism

The unconditional love and support of one's country that comes with the knowledge that one's place of birth is superior to *others*.

Pharmaceutical Research and Manufactures of America – PhRMA

Good guy drug pushers.

Plutocracy

A *state* ruled by the wealthy. Although increasing common, the claims that the United States is now a plutocracy are incorrect. After all, with the formal equation of *money* as speech coming with the *Supreme Court*'s landmark *Citizens United* ruling, wealthy *Americans* cannot be said to rule with the *power* of their *money*, but rather with the *power* of their speech.

Polarization

An illusory chasm dividing the *American public* into two opposing camps on every issue of importance. An illusion, it should be noted, which is necessary for sustaining proper degrees of *gridlock*.[62]

Political Action Committee – PAC

A political organization pooling *money* – er, speech – from individuals and *corporations* as part of a down payment on desired *politicians*.

---

[62] The popular "polarization" meme, as Paul Street notes, is "fundamentally incorrect and deceptive." For instance, Street cites a Program for Public Consultation study analyzing public polling occurring between 2008 and 2013. The report's findings reveal "remarkably little difference between the views of people in red (Republican) districts or states, and those who live in blue (Democratic) districts or states." This includes majorities in both blue and red states favoring: background checks for gun purchases, increased spending on Social Security, cuts to military spending, and increased taxes on those making over $500,000 a year, among many other so-called polarizing issues. Paul Street. "Oligarchy: The real polarization behind the gridlock game." *Z Magazine*. (Oct 2014): 13-14.

Political Scandal

The discovered tweeting and/or texting of lewd photos by an elective representative. Reports of other miscellaneous sexual transgressions also apply.

Political Suicide

Publicly criticizing or voting against the interests of the *lone democracy in the Middle East*.

Political Weakness

Capitulation to *public opinion*.

Politician

Aspiring *lobbyist*.

Politics

Voting every four years for the lesser evil candidate. And every two years if one is really political.

Politics Stops at Water's Edge

The fact that no matter the domestic *politics*, *politicians* from both political parties will always join together to support a *president*'s call for *war*.

Polls

When showing support for one's position or candidate, a measure of the people's will. When doing the opposite, a mere pulse of the volatile masses most likely suffering from a biased methodology.

Populism

A political movement championing, or appearing to champion, the interests of "the people" over the interests of "the elite."

Populist

A campaigning *Democrat*.

Pork

Congressional expenditures on social programs.

Postal Service

A dangerous example of the *government* providing a useful, valued public service on a national scale. Needless to say, the Postal Service must be destroyed; so as to *save* it, of course.[63]

Power

The ability to compel and, if needed, physically force *others* to accept in their heart of hearts that *there is no alternative.*

Power Elite

Those who own the country.[64]

President

The sociopath heading the executive branch and serving as *Commander-in-Chief* of the armed forces.

Presidential Candidate

There are two kinds of presidential candidates. The first type announces a run for the presidency merely as a means to further her brand and enhance her future earnings potential as a *pundit* or *talking head.* This is the entrepreneurial candidate. The second type is a genuine sociopath willing to use all sorts of unscrupulous means to attain the *power* of the presidency. This is the serious candidate.

Spoiler alert: The serious candidate always wins.

Presidential Debate

A joint *television* appearance by the *Republican* and *Democratic* presidential nominees, during which all the important *political scandals* of the day are

---

[63] In 2006, Congress passed the Postal Accountability and Enhancement Act, which obligates the Postal Service to fully fund its pension liabilities ten years in advance. It is such arbitrary accounting that has greatly exacerbated the present crisis in Postal Service revenue.

[64] C. Wright Mills defines the power elite to be those in the higher circles of the economic, political, and military establishment. "In so far as national events are decided," Mills writes, "the power elite are those who decide them." Mills. *The Power Elite*, 18.

debated and parsed in a series of engrossing two minute sound bites.[65]

Primary Election

An election in which the survivors of each party's *billionaire's primary* are put before the voters.

Pro-Growth

Pro-*American*.

Pro-Life

Someone who cares deeply about the health and well-being of fetuses, but also generally believes *personal responsibility* ought to begin the moment one leaves the womb.

Prosperity

The perpetual material state of *the 1%*.

Protesters

Unwashed attention seekers who clearly don't understand how a *democracy* works.

Protests

Always a most unproductive and unwelcome inconvenience to those rushing home from *work* to watch their shows.

Public Opinion

The misguided policy judgments of the ill-informed and fickle masses.

Public Relations

Concealing the inherently vile and loathsome personal nature of those seeking office from the *electorate*.

---

[65] As John Nichols and Robert McChesney remark, "The United States does not hold presidential debates in any realistic sense of the word. It holds quadrennial joint appearances by major-party candidates who have been schooled in the art of saying little of consequence in the most absurdly aggressive ways." John Nichols and Robert McChesney. *Dollarocracy: How the Money and Media Election Complex is Destroying America.* (New York: Nation Books, 2014): 203.

Public Service

The mandatory prerequisite for any aspiring *lobbyist*.

Public Space

Spaces free and open to the public...unless one enters said space with an intent on exercising the right to political speech. In such cases, public spaces become long overdue for a good power washing. (See *Occupy*.)

Pursuit of Happiness

The dream of every *American* to let unadulterated *greed power* one to the very top of the corporate ladder and then, once having secured one's place of privilege at the top, turn around and kick the ladder away.

Radical

Someone who seeks an inclusive political system and the preservation of the global ecosystem by advocating a reactionary rollback of corporate *freedom*.

Raising the Minimum Wage

Raising the minimum amount an employer can pay an employee to a wage still below that which, accounting for *inflation*, was required over 40 years ago.[66]

Rand, Ayn

Chief economic advisor to the *Republican* Party.[67]

---

[66] In 2014, President Obama called to raise the federal minimum wage from $7.25/hour to $10.10/hour. Yet if the federal minimum wage from the late 1960s had merely kept pace with inflation, workers would have been earning a minimum of $10.52/hour in 2013. Moreover, if the federal minimum wage had kept pace with gains in productivity, workers would stand to earn $21.72/hour. Caroline Fairchild. "Minimum Wage Would Be $21.72 If It Kept Pace With Increases In Productivity: Study." *Huffington Post*. (13 Feb 2013).

[67] As Thomas Frank has noted of the Ayn Rand cult within the Republican Party: "Paul Ryan suggested in 2009 that 'we are right now living in an Ayn Rand novel, metaphorically speaking.' Among the freshman class in Congress, the fandom burns brightly. Senator Ron Johnson of Wisconsin refers to *Atlas Shrugged* as his 'foundational book.' Representative David Schwikert of Arizona cites *Atlas Shrugged* as his favorite book, Representative Rick Crawford of Arkansas quoted Rand on his Twitter feed, and Senator Rand Paul describes *Atlas Shrugged* as a 'must-read classic

Reaching Across the Aisle

The dropping of a faux *populist* posture by a *Democrat* in order to track rightward toward the more *super donor*-friendly position of the *Republicans*. (See also, *Triangulation*.)

Reagan, Ronald

Patron saint of the *Republican Party*.

Reality-Based Community

A *community* comprised of those left trying to make sense of the *faith-based community*'s assertion that *reality* can be made by those suspended in a world devoid of any discernable *reality*.[68]

Red State

A state much preferring a cabal of corrupt *Republicans* to oversee to their affairs than a cabal of corrupt *Democrats*.

Redistribution

When reallocating wealth from top to bottom, an infringement on *liberty* and *freedom*, not to mention a dangerous slide towards *socialism*. When reallocating wealth from the bottom to the top, *sound economics*. (See also, *Trickle-Down Economics*, Chapter 7.)

Reducing the Size of Government

Cutting *handouts*.

Reform

Any sort of transformation undertaken for the betterment of elite interests.

Regulatory Reform

The elimination of all *government* regulations.

---

in the cause of liberty.'" Thomas Frank. *Pity the Billionaire: The Hard-Times Swindle and the Unlikely Comeback of the Right.* (New York: Metropolitan Books, 2012): 141.

[68] As Ron Suskind relayed a 2004 conversation with Karl Rove: "The aide [Rove] said that guys like me were 'in what we call the reality-based community,' which he defined as people who 'believe that solutions emerge from your judicious study of discernible reality.'" Suskind. "Faith, Certainty and the Presidency of George W. Bush." *New York Times Magazine.*

Renewable Energy

The earth's unlimited supply of *clean coal*, *oil*, and *natural gas*.

Representative Democracy

A *democracy* in which elites purchase and then delegate various officials to oversee to their interests.

Republicans

See *Democrats*.

Resolute

Continuing to *support the troops* in the *just war* even after it becomes clear that it was all a *mistake*.

Respectable Circles

All those safely ensconced in the trappings of unbridled wealth, along with their hired apologists and hangers-on.

Responsible Budget

A *budget* with increases in military spending offset by cuts to social programs.

Revolution

An overthrowing or toppling of the existing *government* by the people governed. As Thomas Jefferson argued, a revolution is necessary every 20 years in order to refresh the tree of liberty "with the blood of patriots and tyrants." Of course, Jefferson was speaking at a time when *history* was still in the process of unfolding. In the modern era, that of the *end of history*, revolution is obviously no longer necessary, nor in any way even fathomable.

Revolving Door

The process through which one enters *public service*, then freely moves on to monetize said service in the *private sector*, only to later freely return to *public service* to further enhance one's *private sector* earning potential down the road.[69]

---

[69] A total of 413 members of the 110th and 111th Congress became lobbyists. <http://www.opensecrets.org/revolving/top.php?display=Z>

Save

Cut and destroy. As in, the only way to save *Social Security* and *Medicare* is to make the *hard choices* to cut and ultimately destroy both programs.

Sequestration

A legislative mechanism used to impose across the board *budget* cuts, ultimately meant to facilitate the shrinking of *government* down to the size where it can be safely *offed*. (See *Austerity*, Chapter 7.)

Shared Prosperity

The wealth and privilege passed down to the children of the *1%*.

Shared Sacrifice

The necessary belt tightening undertaken by *the 99%* during times of *crisis*; needed in order to properly ensure the privileged class status of *the 1%* is never seriously imperiled.

Signing Statement

A shadow veto coming in the form of an adjoining statement *presidents* attach to congressional bills signed into *law* stating their intention to not comply with the very bill they just signed into *law*. A perk of *executive privilege*, in other words.

Silent Majority

The hordes of apolitical *Americans* the political elite can just sense agree with all their policy decisions.

Simplifying the Tax Code

Raising taxes on the poor and lowering them on the rich.

Smart People

Those celebrated for instinctually adhering to *Washington*'s prevailing *groupthink*.

Social Agitators

The disreputable elements responsible for any social unrest in an otherwise completely harmonious *society*.[70]

Social Justice

Enduring *communist propaganda*.

Social Movements

Large groupings comprised of various *terrorists* and assorted *un-American others*, which seek to enact social and political change. Social movements are to be mocked as ineffectually small and marginal…until they aren't anymore. At which point they are to be treated as the dire threat to *national security* that they really are.[71]

Socialism

An economic system broadly based on the public ownership of industry and high social expenditures on the masses. In a word, *tyranny*.

Socialist

A most ungodly savage. Also, a devastating political smear levied at a *politician* too crassly posturing as a *populist*.

Soft on Communism

A *Cold War (old)* era term used to describe one who expressed unease with launching a first strike nuclear attack against the Soviet Union. (In the modern context, see *Soft on Terror*, Chapter 12.)

Something Must Be Done

Bombs must be dropped.

---

[70] The World Economic Forum's 2012 Global Agenda Survey placed social unrest as the 14th ranked global trend, with much of the global unrest due to, as the report stated, "small groups of social agitators." "Global Agenda Survey 2012." World Economic Forum. (2012).
 <http://reports.weforum.org/global-agenda-survey-2012/>
[71] As Gandhi remarked, "First they ignore you, then they laugh at you, then they fight you, then you win."

Sound Science

Any spurious assertions meant to cast doubt on the existence of human caused *climate change*.

Southern Strategy

A *Republican* electoral strategy utilizing dog whistle *politics* to court southern white bigots. Amidst changing national demographics, the strategy has become the party's primary form of "minority outreach."[72]

Special Interest

A group looking to advance its own agenda, regardless of whether it benefits the greater *society*. As such, any group working contrary to the interests of *small businesses* (the engines of economic *growth*) or in opposition to *war* (the linchpin of the *American* economy).

State, The

The entity used to ensure the continued *prosperity* of the ruggedly individualist *American power elite*. The state accomplishes this task by: (1) efficiently redistributing state tax revenue into the coffers of *job-creators*; (2) militarily securing lucrative markets abroad; (3) suppressing any *civil unrest* at home threatening to challenge elite privilege; and (4) bailing out elites and their business ventures in times of *crisis*.[73] Any other use of state *power* is to be condemned for what it is: *Big Government*.

Staying on Message

The obscuring of one's true political aims by keeping to focus group tested *talking points*.

Stump Speech

A candidate's standard speech repeated at each campaign stop, containing all the stock lies and distortions necessary for winning over the *electorate*.

---

[72] Following the 2012 election, the Republican National Committee published a review which argued the Republican Party needed to enhance its "minority outreach" to better bolster its national electoral chances.

[73] "Every state is a 'special repressive force' for the suppression of the oppressed class." V.I. Lenin. *State and Revolution*. (New York: International Publishers, 2006): 18.

Supercommittee

A small group of Senators and congressional representatives convened for the purpose of devising the most politically expedient means of destroying *Medicare* and *Social Security*. Realizing, in other words, the bipartisan dream of *entitlement reform*.

Super Donor

An individual with the requisite financial clout to have political opinions that actually count.

Super PAC

Unlike a lowly *PAC*, Super PACs allow for the unlimited collection of *money* – er, speech – for the purposes of purchasing candidates.

Superpower

A country so sure of its limitless *power* that no number of military defeats can leave it humbled.[74] And as many *American* commentators are apt to note, *America* remains *the world*'s lone superpower.

Swing Voter

A highly coveted voter swinging as an inanimate pendulum between the *Democrats* and *Republicans* each election. *American* elections hinge on who can *win the hearts and minds* of these politically ignorant free agents.[75]

Talking Points

The script containing the PR-approved *spin* read by *pundits* and *politicians*.

---

[74] As Sheldon Wolin notes, "we might be tempted to redefine superpower as an imaginary power that emerges from defeat unchastened, more imperious than ever." Sheldon Wolin. *Democracy Inc.: Managed Democracy and the Specter of Inverted Totalitarianism*. (Princeton: Princeton University Press, 2008): 40.

[75] As Jacob Hacker and Paul Pierson write: "Most of the famous 'swing voters,' whom journalist tend to idealize as standing above the fray, carefully sorting among the strengths and weaknesses of each party's offerings, are actually the *least* engaged, *least* well-informed citizens, reaching a final decision (if at all) on the flimsiest grounds." Jacob S. Hacker and Paul Pierson. *Winner-Take-All Politics: How Washington Made the Rich Richer – And Turned Its Back on the Middle Class*. (New York: Simon & Schuster Paperbacks, 2011): 109.

Tax Haven

A *power elite* bank.[76]

Tax Holiday

Permanent tax cut.

Tax Incentive

A tax break given by governments to blackmailing *small businesses*.[77]

Tax Reform

The lessening of the tax burden on those least able to afford it (i.e., all *small businesses* and upper income earners).

Tea Party

An army of pissed-off old white people sent into battle against Mexicans, blacks, gays, and other assorted *socialists* by a cadre of fearless commanders whose battle cries, coming from their corporate overlords, are strategically disseminated on *talk radio* and *Fox News*.

Technocrat

A political hack so ruthlessly *efficient* at imposing *shared sacrifice* he or she appears to transcend *politics*.

Theocracy

A political system ruled by religious leaders, or those working on their behalf. Although a deeply religious nation, the U.S. fortunately places a strict line of separation between church and *state*; a remarkable achievement for one nation under *God*, indivisible, with *liberty* and *justice* for all.

---

[76] A 2012 study published by the Tax Justice Network found wealthy North Americans and Europeans alone keep upwards of $23 trillion of private financial wealth hidden away in offshore tax havens. James S. Henry. "The Price of Offshore Revisited." Tax Justice Network. (July 2012).

[77] State and local governments give away upwards of $80 billion per year in tax incentives to businesses – often on the threat from companies that a failure to receive such largesse will result in a loss of jobs. Such tax giveaways rise to $170 billion when combining federal and state governments. Louise Story. "As Companies Seek Tax Deals, Governments Pay High Price." *New York Times*. (1 Dec 2012).

Think Tank

A place where the intellectual cases for various *reforms* and *humanitarian interventions* are hatched.

Third Party

Irrelevant. (See *Democrats* or *Republicans*.)

Tort Reform

Protecting quacks and negligent *corporations* from the greedy, disfigured hoards.

Totalitarianism

A highly repressive system of *government* common to those *states* – and only those *states* – not allied with the U.S.

Transparency

The shrouding of the everyday affairs of *government* from the prying eyes of the citizenry.[78]

Triangulation

A successful political strategy, first employed by Bill Clinton, in which *Democrats* adopt *Republican* policies to appeal to *super donors* and *small businesses*, knowing that traditional *Democratic* constituencies, like *organized labor*, have no spine and will always come to support the *Democrats*.

Two-Party System

A system in which two rival factions within a single aggressively pro-business party come to possess a *monopoly* hold on political *power*.

Tyranny

The assertion of rights by workers.

---

[78] As President Obama has proudly proclaimed, his is "the most transparent administration in history." And in 2014, the "most transparent administration in history" set a new record for denying and censoring public records requests (39% of all requests made), according to an Associated Press analysis. See: Jonathan Easley. "Obama says his is 'most transparent administration' ever." *The Hill* Briefing Room Blog. (14 Feb 2013); Ted Bridis. "Administration sets record for withholding government files." AP. (18 March 2015).

Un-American

Those who believe in *freedom*, *liberty*, *opportunity*, and the *pursuit of happiness* in the normative sense.

Uncle Sam

The proverbial drunken uncle.

United States Chamber of Commerce

A *small business* champion exhibiting the profound *courage* to stand up for all the little guys listed on the *Dow Jones Industrial Average*.

Unorthodoxy

An inclination toward independent thought, and perhaps the questioning or doubting of the supremacy of *capitalism*, *freedom*, and even *America*'s indispensability. Unorthodoxy is obviously a most heinous offense, never to be left unpunished.[79]

Voter Fraud

A pervasive imaginary problem plaguing the *American* electoral system.

Voter ID Laws

Laws enacted to help remove built-up excesses of *democracy* by disenfranchising people of color, the poor, and the elderly.[80]

War Fatigue

The tendency of a weak-kneed *American public* to waver in its continued support of a *just war*. (See also, *Vietnam Syndrome*, Chapter 9.)

War Powers Act

A 1973 congressional resolution intended to limit a *president*'s *power* to commence military hostilities without formal authorization from *Congress*.

---

[79] "Independent thought," Chris Hedges writes, "is an instant career killer. Doors shut. No longer are you invited on the television talk shows, given grants, feted in the university, interviewed on CNN, invited to the Council on Foreign Relations, given tenure, or asked to write op-ed pieces in the *New York Times*." Hedges. *Death of the Liberal Class*, 143.

[80] Since 2013, 12 states have passed laws making it harder to vote by requiring some form of ID.

Presidents have since learned to skirt the restrains of the War Powers Act through either the use of *covert action* or a simple redefinition of *war*, á la President Obama's most imaginative declaration that the deployment of U.S. forces to *Libya* in 2011 didn't constitute a *war*, because no *American* forces were killed in action.[81] (See also, *Hostilities*, Chapter 9.)

Washington

An accountability-free zone enriching the nation's very best hustlers, hucksters, spinsters, swindlers, and outright sociopaths.

Wasteful Spending

Spending on social programs.

We

A rhetorical sleight of hand used to apply a veneer of popular legitimacy to elite interests and/or elite institutions.[82]

Sentence Example: We all have a stake in ensuring *entitlement reform* comes to pass.

We the People

They the *corporations*.

Weak Leader

A *president* whose answer to every *foreign policy* problem isn't a *no-fly zone* or *boots on the ground*.

---

[81] As the journalist Glen Ford noted, Obama has "redefined war, for U.S. purposes, as limited to conflicts in which Americans are killed in action. Thus, he told Congress in 2011, the massive bombing of Libya did not constitute a war, or even 'hostilities,' since no Americans were killed." Glen Ford. "Obama's War Against Civilization." *Black Agenda Report*. (26 Feb 2014).

[82] As British media critic David Cromwell remarks on the use of "we" in mainstream media and political discourse: "All too often, viewers, readers and listeners are asked, even impelled, to identify with the 'we' that resides in power, sitting in the Cabinet, the White House or the plush offices of corporate executives…The powerful 'we' that so often dominates the news agenda does not, in fact, represent the best interests of the majority of the population, nor the best interests of a sustainable planet." David Cromwell. *Why Are We The Good Guys? Reclaiming Your Mind From the Delusions of Propaganda*. (Washington: Zero Books, 2012): 27.

Welcoming a Debate

Feverishly working to ensure there won't be any more damn debates to welcome by pursuing the *traitor* responsible for the current debate to the very ends of the earth.[83]

Whatever It Takes

Implementing as many social cuts at home, dropping however many bombs abroad.

Xenophobia

The blood pulsating through the *American* body politic.

Yes, We Can

No, you can't.

---

[83] Reacting to the debate over domestic spying stirred by the leaks of Edward Snowden – i.e., the same Snowden the Justice Department was to charge under the Espionage Act and the State Department was to maroon in Moscow – President Obama quite begrudgingly and cynically declared: "I welcome this debate. And I think it's healthy for our democracy. I think it's a sign of maturity." "Transcript: Obama's Remarks on NSA Controversy." *The Wall Street Journal* Washington Wire. (7 June 2013).

2.   Dependency Culture

As a person who has worked extremely hard for more than 40 years, I don't want my tax dollars going to drunkards and drug addicts.

-   *Bill O'Reilly, 2013*[1]

Cadillac Health Plan

An overly lavish *labor union health care* plan, coming complete with excessive and wholly unnecessary services like preventive care. Look for Cadillac health plans to be heavily taxed and otherwise discouraged, given that working people have no right to anything associated with the luxury and comfort of the Cadillac brand.[2]

Child Poverty

The deserved fate of those recklessly selecting parents lacking in *personal responsibility*.[3]

Corporate Welfare

An offensive term used to describe valuable *government* assistance provided to the lone engines of economic *growth: corporations* and *job-creators*.

Dead Broke

A particularly bleak form of privation, leaving one of meager origins struggling to stay financially viable in the intervening months between

---

[1] Bill O'Reilly. "Welfare Nation." BillOReilly.com. (31 Oct 2013).
[2] The ploy of describing generous health plans to be "Cadillac" is no doubt inspired by the tried and true divide and conquer strategy. "Calling them Cadillac plans or gold-plated plans is a rhetorical trick," Samantha Winslow writes. "The point is to pit non-union workers, who have to pay more in premiums and out-of-pocket costs, against union workers, who have successfully negotiated good health plans over the years." Samantha Winslow. "Attack of the Cadillac Tax." *Labor Notes.* (24 Sept 2013).
[3] As Sasha Abramsky notes, "in May 2012, UNICEF reported that of the world's developed countries, the United States had the second highest rate of child poverty, with more than 23 percent of its kids officially poor. Only Romania, still struggling to shed itself of the awful legacy left by Nicolae Ceaușescu's dictatorship, had worse numbers." Sasha Abramsky. *The American Way of Poverty: How The Other Half Still Lives.* (New York: Nation Books, 2013): 10.

residing in the White House and the arrival of multi-million dollar book advances and six-figure speaking fees.[4]

Death Panels

A fictitious board of *government bureaucrats* tasked with ordering that grandma be taken off life support. Not to be confused with actually existing boards of *health insurance* executives denying grandma access to life-saving care because the costs are just too prohibitive to be made compatible with *profitability*.

Dependency Culture

The debilitating reliance on *government handouts* by the *undeserving poor*.

Deserving Poor

Starving, physically disabled whites.

Deserving Rich

All rich people.

Enabling Poverty

Adequately funding any *government* program providing services to those in *poverty*.

Entitlement Culture

A toxic culture in which individuals come to actually believe they are owed – or entitled – to the benefits of the *social safety net* they, themselves, have helped to fund.[5]

---

[4] As Hilary Clinton remarked to ABC's Diane Sawyer in 2014, "We Came out of the White House not only dead broke, but in debt. We had no money when we got there, and we struggled to, you know, piece together the resources for mortgages[!], for houses[!], for Chelsea's education. You know, it was not easy." Lis Kreutz. "Hillary Clinton Defends High-Dollar Speaking Fees." ABC News. (9 June 2014).

[5] The spurious claims made of an "entitlement culture" amongst those relying on social services aside, there does indeed appear to be an entitlement culture in American society. Only it is those at the top of society that demonstrate behavioral tendencies indicating an actual sense of entitlement. University of California-Berkeley professor Paul Piffa, for instance, has found that "higher social class is associated with increased entitlement and narcissism." In one revealing study conducted by Piffa, participants were left alone to wait in a room after being shown

Food Insecurity

An intolerable scourge, which is just going to have to be tolerated so long as a dime more remains for all the bombs, guns, and missiles providing the true security every food insecure *American* so desperately deserves.[6]

Food Stamps

Easily expendable *government* food aid given to *free riders*.

Food Stamp Fraud

The use of *food stamps*.[7]

Food Stamp President

A black *president*.[8]

Free Rider

Someone who receives certain benefits without having to pay for their full cost. All those not in *the 1%* or working as *job-creators* are free riders in *American society*.

---

a jar of individually wrapped candies, which they were then told were for children in a nearby lab. As the study found, "participants in the upper-class rank condition took more candy that would otherwise go to children than in the lower-rank condition." See: Paul K. Piffa, Daniel M. Stancatoa, Stéphane Côtéb, Rodolfo Mendoza-Dentona, and Dacher Keltnera. "Higher social class predicts increased unethical behavior." *PNAC* Vol. 109 No. 11 (13 March 2012): 4086-4091; Paul K. Piffa. "Wealth and the Inflated Self: Class, Entitlement, and Narcissism." *Personality and Social Psychology Bulletin.* Vol. 40 No. 1 (Jan 2014): 34-43.

[6] As the national food bank network Feeding America reports, "In 2013, 49.1 million Americans lived in food insecure households, including 33.3 million adults and 15.8 million children." "Hunger and Poverty Fact Sheet." Feeding America. <http://www.feedingamerica.org/hunger-in-america/impact-of-hunger/hunger-and-poverty/hunger-and-poverty-fact-sheet.html>

[7] In 2013, the *New York Times* reported total losses to the food stamp program attributable to fraud registered at about 4.07%, far less than the rate of loss found in Medicare and Medicaid. Kim Severson. "Food Stamp Fraud, Rare but Troubling." *New York Times.* (18 Dec 2013).

[8] Throughout his 2012 run for the Republican presidential nomination, former House Speaker Newt Gingrich referred to President Obama as the "food stamp president."

Handouts

All benefits one undeservedly receives from *government* social programs; namely, all benefits one receives from *government* social programs. One's previous contributions into such programs (such as one's lifetime contribution into the *Social Security* Trust Fund) are irrelevant, as every form of assistance provided by the *government* is a handout…unless it is provided to *corporations* or the *power elite*. In that case, such warranted assistance is not a handout, but a *tax incentive*.

Health Care

A fringe benefit provided to the financially successful.

Health Care Reform

Ensuring the continued *profitability* of the private *health insurance* industry. (See *Obamacare*.)

Health Insurance (Private)

A thing one is compelled to purchase despite the inevitable declaring of bankruptcy upon any significant medical emergency.[9]

Health Savings Account

An individual tax-advantaged savings account meant to help users meet their high *health insurance* deductible. Put differently, an innovative approach to *health care*, neither trampling *American individualism* nor discouraging *personal responsibility*, all the while insuring the continued *profitability* of insurance companies by *outsourcing* any cost overruns onto policyholders.

Homelessness

A *criminal* act committed by those unwilling to *work* hard.[10]

---

[9] Health care is the number one cause of personal bankruptcy in the U.S., with one study putting the number of Americans with health insurance that still face financial difficulties in paying off their medical bills to be near 10 million. Dan Mangan. "Medical Bills Are the Biggest Cause of US Bankruptcies: Study." CNBC. (25 June 2013).

[10] According to a 2014 report from the National Law Center on Homelessness and Poverty, since 2001, city-wide bans on camping in public have increased 60%; bans on begging have increased by 25%; bans on loitering, loafing, and vagrancy have increased by 35%; bans on sitting or lying down in particular public places have

Individual Mandate (Health Care)

A pillar of *Obamacare*, requiring every *American* to contribute to the collective national effort to boost the share prices of the major *health insurance* companies.[11]

Inner City

The *crime*-infested abode of lazy (i.e., all) *welfare* recipients. In other words, the home for the nation's *undeserving poor*.[12]

Medicare/Medicaid

Widely popular national *health care* programs for the poor and elderly. *Medicare* and *Medicaid* are thus a necessary target for funding cuts (or *reform*), lest the *American people* begin to get any ideas about expanding such programs to cover all *Americans*.

Medicare Reform

Privatizing *Medicare*.

Near Poor

The new *middle class*.[13]

---

increased by 43%; bans on sleeping in vehicles have increased by 119%. See "No Safe Place: The Criminalization of Homelessness in U.S. Cities." National Law Center on Homelessness and Poverty. (July 2014): 8-9.

[11] Since the Affordable Care Act was signed into law in 2010, as the *New York Times* reported in late 2014, the "share prices for four of the major insurance companies — Aetna, Cigna, Humana and UnitedHealth — have more than doubled, while the Standard & Poor's 500-stock index has increased about 70 percent." Robert Pear. "Health Care Law Recasts Insurers As Obama Allies." *New York Times*. (17 Nov 2014).

[12] In March 2014, Wisconsin Rep. Paul Ryan hinted that the poverty blighting inner cities was due to their lazy residents. As Ryan remarked: "We have got this tailspin of culture, in our inner cities in particular, of men not working and just generations of men not even thinking about working or learning the value and the culture of work, and so there is a real culture problem here that has to be dealt with." See Igor Volsky. "Paul Ryan Blames Poverty On Lazy 'Inner City' Men." Think Progress. (12 March 2014).

[13] According to the writer Paul Buchheit, up to half of Americans are either in poverty or near poor (i.e., those with incomes 1.5 times the official poverty threshold). Paul Buchheit. "Overwhelming Evidence that Half of America is In or Near Poverty." *AlterNet*. (23 March 2014).

Obamacare

An insidious *socialist* plot endeavoring to destroy the *free-enterprise system* by lining the pockets of the private *health insurance* companies.

Personal Responsibility

The idea that one ought to take full responsibility for all of one's personal hardships, especially those stemming from the accumulated weight of intractable socioeconomic forces.

Poverty

The condition in which one deservedly lives without sufficient *money* or means of support due to various personal failings. Poverty is alleviated through an acceptance of *personal responsibility* and a devotion to *positive thinking*.

Predatory Lending

The predatory borrowing of *money* by those lacking in *personal responsibility*.

Premium Support

The focus group approved alternative phrasing for a *Medicare voucher*.[14]

Single-Payer Health System

A wholly *un-American* health system, wherein all health costs are paid for by the *government*. Of course, such a scheme will never work in *America*, because, well, it's just *un-American*.

Social Contract

The implicit agreement entered into by *Americans* not of *the 1%*, in which it is understood that they will come to fend for themselves over the course of their lives without turning to the *state* for *handouts*.

---

[14] Rep. Paul Ryan's fiscal year 2013 budget, "The Path to Prosperity," called for a transformation of Medicare into a voucher program. But due to the public's well-known aversion to the word voucher, Ryan maintained his reforms wouldn't provide a medical voucher, but rather a medical "premium support."

Social Safety Net

A "hammock" lulling "able-bodied people into lives of complacency and dependency."[15]

Social Security

A Ponzi scheme devised by greedy senior citizens seeking to siphon wealth from hardworking *Americans*. Also, a grave threat to *fiscal responsibility*.

Socialized Medicine

A ghastly horror. (See also, *Single-Payer Health System*.)

Undeserving Poor

Able-bodied people of color seeking *handouts*.

Undeserving Rich

There is no such thing.

Unemployment Insurance

The *money* given to those supposedly seeking *work*, but supposedly unable to find any…supposedly. Either way, a clear disincentive for anyone to ever *work* a day in their life. Why suffer the humiliation and shame associated with working when one can experience the pride that comes with accepting a *handout*?[16]

War on Poverty

A grave strategic blunder squandering the scarce resources better suited for far more profitable *wars*: on drugs, *communism*, *terrorism*, etc.

---

[15] In his 2011 Republican response to the president's State of the Union address, Rep. Paul Ryan remarked that the social safety net is in grave danger of transforming into "a hammock, which lulls able-bodied people into lives of complacency and dependency."

[16] "Contrary to a widespread assumption that has crept back into Anglo-American political jargon," Tony Judt noted, "few derive pleasure from handouts: of clothes, shoes, food, rent support or children's school supplies. It is, quite simply, humiliating." Judt. *Ill Fares the Land*, 27.

Welfare

A fundamentally flawed idea. After all, give a man a fish and he'll eat, be happy, and probably genuinely thankful. In fact, receiving a fish might even inspire him to buy a fishing rod and boat for himself once he is able to save up enough *money*. But teach a man to fish, and you won't have to give away any more of your damn fish. Instead, you can eat them all yourself. I mean, you taught him how to fish, so what if he doesn't have a pole or a boat? Not your problem. Whatever happened to *American individualism*? Anyway, the point to remember is, welfare only enables *poverty*.

Welfare Queen

A lazy, greedy, sexually promiscuous, black mother from the *inner city* who is seeking a *handout*.

Welfare Recipient

An *inner city* resident.

Welfare Reform

Ending dependency by cutting *handouts* and raising millions out of *poverty* through simply redefining poor as *middle class*.

Workfare

Forcing recipients of *government* aid to enter the workforce. Celebrated as offering a path out of *poverty*, given the long track record of *low-wage jobs* leading to lifelong material comfort.

Working Poor

Those *having it all* – a precarious job to go along with a precarious existence.

3. Education Reform

Did you know that the education sector now represents nearly 9 percent of the country's gross domestic product? That for-profit education is valued at $1.3 trillion, and is one of the largest U.S. investment markets?

- *Advertisement for a Conference on Private Equity Investing in For-Profit Education Companies, 2013*[1]

Charter Schools' New Cheerleaders: Financiers

- New York Times, *2010*[2]

21st Century Literacy Skills

The ability to read and write at a proficient level without ever engaging in any degree of *critical thinking*.

Adjunct Professor

An overeducated *intern*.[3]

---

[1] Quoted in: Valerie Strauss. "Education Reform as a business." *Washington Post* Answer Sheet. (9 Jan 2013).

[2] Trip Gabriel and Jennifer Medina. "Charter Schools' New Cheerleaders: Financiers." *New York Times*. (9 May 2010).

[3] According to the Adjunct Project, "Two-thirds of the faculty standing in front of college classrooms each day aren't full-time or permanent professors," but adjuncts. In 2011, the *Chronicle of Higher Education* described the lives of three such adjuncts as follows: "one adjunct is about to move into a sister's basement. Another, a Ph.D. in African-American Studies, is living in a homeless shelter in Philadelphia that is supposed to be for recovering drug addicts. She is subject to a curfew and to disciplinary action, as if she, too, was a drug addict. Her only crime was to study for over a decade to earn a Ph.D., and to teach for poverty wages. The third adjunct, whose case is the direst right now, is an artist and educator living in California, who will be homeless as of August 15. Even worse, he now faces the possibility of losing his life's work. Most of his paintings and artwork, 30 years worth of work, is stored in a facility that will not give him access because he is several months behind in rent. They have not discarded or destroyed the artwork yet, but that is becoming a real possibility as the month comes to a close." Isaac Sweeney. "Adjunct Emergency Fund." *Chronicle of Higher Education*. (2 Aug 2011).

Apartheid Schools

The over 6,000 schools in a *post-racial America* whose minority population is 99% or greater.[4]

Arts, The

A subject in no way encouraging conformity, nor one easily evaluated by *standardized tests*. In other words, the arts are quite expendable. Unless, of course, one is at private school catering to the heirs of the ruling elite. In that case, the arts are essential for the well-rounded *education* every child of privilege deserves.[5]

Bad Teacher

A teacher unable to adequately improve the *standardized test* scores of *students* living in *poverty*.

Business School

A school where aspiring titans of business are versed in the utter infallibility of the *American free-enterprise system*. A successful business school *student* will graduate assured that the true purpose of life is personal self-enrichment (i.e., the *pursuit of happiness*).

---

[4] Most such apartheid schools are located in the Midwest and Northeast. A 2013 Rutgers University report, for instance, found that during the 2010 to 2011 school year, "26 percent of all black students and almost 13 percent of Latino students" in the state of New Jersey attended an "apartheid school." But even in the federally integrated school systems of the South, apartheid schools are on the rise. "In 1972," Nikole Hannah-Jones writes, "due to strong federal enforcement, only about 25 percent of black students in the South attended schools in which at least nine out of 10 students were racial minorities. In districts released from desegregation orders between 1990 and 2011, 53 percent of black students now attend such schools." See: Naomi Nix. "Rutgers study: Too many N.J. students are in 'apartheid schools.'" NJ.com. (11 Oct 2013); Nikole Hannah-Jones. "Segregation Now: Investigating America's Racial Divide." ProPublica. (16 April 2014).

[5] Prominent school "reformer" Bill Gates, for one, sends his own children to a private school which neither adheres to the national Common Core standards, which Gates advocates for, nor places much emphasis on standardized tests. As the school's mission statement reads in part: "We believe that in today's global world, our students need to know more than one culture, one history, and language." Diane Ravitch. "KrazyTA Explains What Bill Gates Wants for His Own Children." DianeRavitch.net. (19 March 2014).

Charter School

A privately-run, publicly-funded, *union*-free school working to turn a *profit* by carefully selecting the best and brightest students for admission, so to then achieve the most impressive test results.[6]

Common Core

National *education* standards employing product placement laced *standardized tests* to access whether a *student*, and his or her *teacher*, is a success or a failure.[7]

Critical Thinking

That which is to be safely expunged via a rigorous curriculum of *standardized tests*.

Department of Education

Federal department tasked with ensuring no successful test taker is left behind in the *race to the top*.

---

[6] As a 2013 Reuters investigation into U.S. charter schools found that, "charters aggressively screen student applicants, assessing their academic records, parental support, disciplinary history, motivation, special needs and even their citizenship, sometimes in violation of state and federal law." Stephanie Simon. "Special Report: Class Struggle - How charter schools get students they want." Reuters. (15 Feb 2013).
[7] In 2013 and 2014, New York students taking the state's Common Core standardized test were subjected to test questions containing clearly gratuitous product placement. Brands appearing on the 2014 test included: Barbie, iPod, Mug Root Beer, Nike, and Life Savers. On the 2013 test, students encountered: Melmac, IBM, Lego, FIFA, and Mindstorms. As eighth grade test taker Isaiah Schrader wrote in 2013 of one question involving a story of a busboy cleaning up a soda: "The 'busboy' passage in the eighth grade test I took was fictional, written about a dishwasher at a pizza restaurant. In it, the busboy neglects to notice a large puddle of root beer under a table that he clears. His irate employer notifies him about the mess, and he cleans it up. It seems alright at first glace [*sic*]. However, the root beer was referred to at one point as Mug™ Root Beer. It was followed by a footnote, which informed test-takers that Mug™ was a registered trademark of PepsiCo. The brand of soda, the type of soda, and, come to think of it, the exact beverage was not necessary to the development of the story, nor was it mentioned in any of the confusing and analytical questions following the passage." See Valerie Strauss. "Eighth grader: What bothered me most about new Common Core test." *Washington Post* The Answer Sheet. (8 May 2013).

Education

The reason *Americans* don't have enough *jobs*. For if only *Americans* would take their education just a little more seriously, they could all find *work*.[8] That said, public funding for education still constitutes *wasteful spending*, as education is really more of a *personal responsibility*.

Education Reform

The breaking of anti-child *teacher unions* and firing of *bad teachers*, coupled with the *liberation* of *public schools* from meddlesome public *oversight* through the opening of *charter schools*.[9]

---

[8] "The challenge the nation faces as high unemployment persists is not better education and training for those currently unemployed," Lawrence Mishel of the Economic Policy Institute argues. "The problem is a lack of jobs." Mishel continues: "The huge increase in wage and income inequality experienced over the last 30 years is not a reflection of a shortfall in the skills and education of the workforce. Rather, workers face a wage deficit, not a skills deficit. It is hard to find some ever-increasing need for college graduates that is going unmet: college graduates have not seen their real wage rise in 10 years, and the pay gap with high school graduates has not increased in that time period. Moreover, even before the recession college students and graduates were working as free interns, a phenomenon we would not observe if college graduates were in such demand." Lawrence Mishel. "Education is Not the Cure for High Unemployment or for Income Inequality." Report: Wages Income and Growth EPI. (12 Jan 2011).

[9] As Diane Ravitch remarks on what is left out by those calling for education "reform": "Seldom do they protest budget cuts, no matter how massive they may be. They do not complain when governors and legislatures cut billions from public schools while claiming to be reformers. They do not protest rising rates of child poverty. They do not complain about racial segregation. They see no harm in devoting more time and resources to standardized testing. They are not heard from when districts cut the arts, libraries, and physical education while spending more on testing. They do not complain when federal or state or city officials announce plans to test children in kindergarten or even prekindergarten. They do not complain about increased class size. They do not object to scripted curricula or teachers' loss of professional autonomy. They do not object when experienced teachers are replaced by recruits who have only a few weeks of training. They close their eyes to evidence that charters enroll disproportionately small numbers of children with disabilities, or those from troubled homes, or English-language learners…They do not complain when for-profit corporations run charter schools or when educational services are outsourced to for-profit businesses. Indeed, they welcome entrepreneurs into the reform community as investors and partners." Diane Ravitch. *Reign of Error: The Hoax of the Privatization Movement and the Danger to America's Public Schools.* (New York: Alfred A. Knopf, 2013): 35.

Education School

A school where aspiring *teachers* are trained in the administering of *standardized tests*.

Ethnic Studies

A wholly *un-American* subject fostering "hatred" and "division."[10]

Failing School

A public school run by *bad teachers* producing low student test scores. Failing schools are to be closed and converted into *charter schools*. (See *Turnaround School*.)

Geography

The study of the various *dispensable nations* (minus their location, culture, language, *history*, etc.) that come to enter the *American* lexicon after having been subjected to *American* bombs of *liberation*.

History

An appropriate enough subject, just as long as one sticks to *American history*. Indeed, any deviation from *American history* ought not to be tolerated. (See *Ethnic Studies*.)

Homeschool

A school where *students* are safely protected from any indoctrination in the heretics of secularism generally and *evolution* in particular.

Interim Assessment

A *standardized test* given to *students* as a means to prepare for a *standardized test*.

Law School

A school where aspiring lawyers study and train to tirelessly defend corporate *liberty*.

---

[10] In 2010, Arizona banned ethnic studies courses from public and charter schools in the state, claiming such courses promoted "hatred" and "division." Gregory Rodriguez. "Why Arizona banned ethnic studies." *Los Angeles Times*. (20 Feb 2012).

Math

A *standardized test* compatible subject necessary for one to be a productive *associate* manning the register. Which is to say math is a very important subject.

Music

A little too artsy, so off to the chopping block with music. Unless, again, one is at private school catering to the children of the elite.

No Child Left Behind

The leaving of no child with high test scores behind.

Opportunity Scholarship

A school *voucher*, minus the negative connotations associated with *vouchers*.

Physical Education

An unnecessary distraction from test prep. Perhaps in a country with a childhood obesity epidemic physical education might be important, but even then, probably still cut it.

Public School

An archaic and inefficient testing center failing to turn a *profit*.

Race to the Top

National education initiative serving as a pithy reminder that *education*, like life, is a contest – complete with winners (in this case, those with high test scores) and losers (in this case, those with low test scores).

Reading

A most delicate subject. Although necessary for success on *standardized tests*, moderation also must be applied to the teaching of reading. For reading taken beyond *21ˢᵗ century literacy skills* can lead a *student* down a dangerous path of discovery, which may ultimately culminate in the reading of subversive or *unorthodox* material.

Reformer (Education)

A wealthy pro-*charter school*, anti-*bad teacher*, *Wall Street*-type who sends his or her kids to an elite private school, where they embrace the *arts*, *music*, and *physical education*.[11]

School Choice

Removing the *government monopoly* on *education* by allowing parents and *students* the *opportunity* to attend private schools more aligned with the dictates of *competitiveness*.

School Resource Officer

A *peace officer* dispatched to a *public school* in order to ensure the school to *prison* pipeline continues to function at optimum capacity.[12]

School Segregation

A silly *post-racial America* excuse for low *student* achievement made by *bad teachers* and their apologists.[13]

---

[11] According to a 2010 *New York Times* story, Wall Street financiers are some of the biggest champions of the education "reform" movement because they "are drawn to the businesslike way in which many charter schools are run; their focus on results, primarily measured by test scores; and, not least, their union-free work environments, which give administrators flexibility to require longer days and a longer academic year." Of course, the valued worth of the U.S. public educational system (roughly $600 billion in total) is also well known to such "philanthropists." Gabriel and Medina. "Charter Schools' New Cheerleaders: Financiers."

[12] A 2014 *Wall Street Journal* report notes that, "The number of school police officers rose 55% to about 19,000 in the 10 years to 2007." Meanwhile, "260,000 students were reported, or 'referred' in the official language, to law enforcement by schools in 2012 …92,000 students were subject to school-related arrests." To take two cases: "In Texas, a student got a misdemeanor ticket for wearing too much perfume. In Wisconsin, a teen was charged with theft after sharing the chicken nuggets from a classmate's meal – the classmate was on lunch assistance and sharing it meant the teen violated the law, authorities said." Gary Fields and John R. Emshwiller. "For More Teens, Arrests Replace School Discipline." *Wall Street Journal.* (21 Oct 2014): A1, A12.

[13] As part of a 2014 report on the re-segregation of American schools, "ProPublica examined 24 years of demographic data compiled by the National Center for Education Statistics and found that districts grew steadily more segregated after their desegregation orders ended. A separate 2011 study in the American Economic Journal found that within 10 years of being released, school districts unwound about 60 percent of the integration they had achieved under court order." The significance being that, "The achievement gap for black students grows the longer they spend in segregated schools. When they start 8th grade, black students are already three years

Science

An important subject (because it's testable) that still must not be taken too far. For if it is, science can quickly devolve into politically sensitive topics like *climate change* and *evolution*.

Standardized Test

The means through which *American students* of non-elite lineage are taught what to think, rather than how to think.

Student

A data point whose worth is determined via *standardized tests*.

Student Loans

The means through which it is ensured *American students* come to live a life of peonage to *Wall Street*.[14] (See also, *Debt*, Chapter 7.)

Teach for America

A program proudly offering low-wage, inexperienced, and non-unionized temporary *teachers* as a permanent cure for *bad teachers* and *failing schools*.[15]

Teacher

Test administrator.

Teaching to the Test

The curriculum of good *teachers*.

---

behind their white counterparts in math and reading." Hannah-Jones. "Segregation Now."

[14] According to The Project on Student Debt, 71% of college seniors in 2013 graduated with debt, with the average debt for a recent grad coming to $29,400. <http://projectonstudentdebt.org/>

[15] As Ravitch notes of Teach for America, "Today TFA is at the center of the corporate reform movement, supplying young teachers to staff the growing number of non-union, privately managed charter schools across the nation. These inexperienced young men and women will work incredibly hard, as much as seventy or eighty hours a week, trying to perform a job for which they are ill-prepared, with no expectation of a pension or benefits, then move on. TFA is not just a beneficiary of the privatization movement but one of the central drivers of the movement." Ravitch. *Reign of Error*. 140.

Tenure Reform

The removing of *teacher* tenure, which was solely designed to shield *bad teachers* in *failing schools*.

Turnaround School

A once bureaucratic, unprofitable, *union*-staffed *public school* successfully converted into an efficient, profitable, and *union*-free *charter school*.

Voucher (School)

An *opportunity scholarship* offering the panacea for *failing schools* by allowing their most gifted *students* to pack-up and take their public *money* to a far more *efficient* place of testing.

Workforce Development Systems

Public Schools.

4.   The Free Press

George Bush is the president. He makes the decisions…wherever he wants
me to line up, just tell me where, and he'll make the call.

-   *Dan Rather, 2001*[1]

A Word from Our Sponsors

A word from our editors.

Accomplice

A *criminal* enabler posturing as a journalist in order to insidiously conspire
with a *government whistleblower* to publish stories blatantly flaunting all measures
of proper journalistic decorum.[2]

Advocacy Journalism

A journalism failing to demonstrate a proper degree of deference to those in
positions of *power*. In other words, the *criminal* ravings of *accomplices* and *co-conspirators*.

All the News That's Fit to Print

The motto of the *New York Times*, with the paper of record's final decision
on what *news* is really fit to print each day coming after exhaustive
consultations with *official sources*.[3]

---

[1] Quoted in: Robert Jensen. "Dan Rather and the Problem with Patriotism: Steps
Toward the Redemption of American Journalism and Democracy." Jeffery Klaehn,
Ed. *Filtering the News: Essays on Herman and Chomsky's Propaganda Model*. (New York:
Rose Black Books, 2005): 122.

[2] During a January 2014 congressional hearing, U.S. Director of National Intelligence
James Clapper "called on '[Edward] Snowden and his accomplices' to return the
documents the former National Security Agency contractor took, in order to
minimize what Clapper called the 'profound damage that his disclosures have caused
and continued to cause'." Spencer Ackerman. "James Clapper calls for Snowden and
'accomplices' to return NSA documents." *The Guardian*. (29 Jan 2014).

[3] In 2004, the *Times* spiked a report on NSA domestic spying after consultations with
the George W. Bush White House. The paper did eventually publish the report in
late 2005, after President Bush's reelection and a mere month before *Times* reporter
James Risen's book revealing the NSA program, *State of War*, was to be published.

Alternative Media

Amateurs lacking in *credibility*, as evidenced by their lack of *corporate sponsors*.

Blogger

A pejorative coming in handy whenever needing to demean an adversarial journalist scooping the *respectable press*.[4]

Breaking News

Any development in *the world* of *celebrity* and entertainment.[5]

Brought to You By

Beholden to.

Campaign Coverage

The in-depth analysis of *poll* numbers, *fundraising* totals, *television* commercials, and various personal intrigues. Campaign coverage, limited to presidential elections (local elections are just so boring), runs 24-7-365. After all, election night is but a reminder that it's just a little over three short years till the Iowa Caucuses.[6]

---

[4] In 2013, soon after the Edward Snowden leaks began being published, the *New York Times* ran a profile of author and then-*Guardian* journalist Glenn Greenwald with the dismissive title: "Blogger, With Focus on Surveillance, Is at Center of a Debate." (*NYT*, 6 June 2013).

[5] In early 2014, MSNBC's Andrea Mitchel cut away from an on-air interview over NSA spying with former Rep. Jane Harmon for the "breaking news" regarding the latest legal proceedings of the pop singer Justin Bieber. Seven months later, Luke Russert, filling in for Mitchel on MSNBC, cut away from an interview with a congressional representative to break the "news" that the basketball player Lebron James was to sign a contract with the Cleveland Cavaliers. Josh Feldman. "MSNBC Cuts Away from Some Silly NSA Thing to Breaking Bieber News." Mediaite. (24 Jan 2014); Matt Wilstein. "MSNBC's Luke Russert Cuts Off Dem Rep. to Break LeBron James News." Mediaite. (11 July 2014).

[6] It took less than one day after the 2012 presidential election before the media's attention turned to 2016 speculation. As the *Washington Post*'s Chris Cillizza wrote in his November 2012 handicap of the 2016 field: "the line of demarcation between people who like politics and people who are obsessed with politics is that the former's eyes glaze over when talk of the next election begins soon after the end of the last election while the latter's eye take on a wolfish intensity that might scare some." Of course, we might add, that all depends on how one comes to define "politics." Chris Cillizza. "Handicapping the 2016 presidential field." *Washington Post*. (7 Nov 2012).

Censorship

Not needed for a *free press* voluntarily endeavoring to gauge, and then purge, what *government* officials may deem objectionable.[7]

CNN

24-hour cable *news* channel for those too discerning for *MSNBC* or *Fox News*, but still daft enough to voluntarily subject themselves to unadulterated *spin*.

Co-Conspirator

A journalist failing to report an *insider threat* to the proper *authorities*.[8]

Conflict of Interest

There is simply no such thing for a professional *American* journalist working at a respected *news* outlet. So, want to interview your father? No problem.[9]

---

[7] In a particularly blatant example of self-censorship, a Florida newspaper issued instructions to its staff soon after the commencement of the U.S. war in Afghanistan, reading in part: "DO NOT USE photos on page 1A showing civilian casualties from the war on Afghanistan…DO NOT USE wire stories that lead with civilian casualties…They should be mentioned further down in the story. If a story needs rewriting to play down civilian casualties, DO IT." Cited in: Chalmers Johnson. *Nemesis: The Last Days of the American Republic*. (New York: A Holt Paperback, 2007): 30.

[8] In 2010, Fox News chief Washington correspondent James Rosen had his personal email account read and phone records checked by the Department of Justice as part of an investigation into the leaking of documents related to a story Rosen published on North Korea. The leading FBI agent on the investigation, Reginald Reyes, described Rosen as "an aider, abettor and/or co-conspirator." The federal judge who signed off on a search warrant of Rosen's communications agreed "that there was probable cause that Rosen was a co-conspirator." Rosen's source, Stephen Kim, was charged under the Espionage Act and sentenced to over one year in jail. Ann E. Marimow. "A rare peek into a Justice Department leak probe." *Washington Post*. (19 May 2013).

[9] American journalists being allowed to interview their own parents while working for prominent news outlets is fairly common. Consider the following examples: In April 2014, NBC *Today Show* "special correspondent" Jenna Bush-Hager interviewed her father, former President George W. Bush, in a segment on the former president's newfound painting hobby. A little over a year prior, Bush-Hager was sent by *Today* to interview her grandfather, George H.W. Bush. Meanwhile, Mika Brzezinski, co-host of MSNBC's *Morning Joe*, is regularly allowed to interview her father, Zbigniew Brzezinski. See: Judd Legum. "The Ethics Of NBC Letting George W. Bush Be Interviewed By His Daughter." Think Progress. (6 April 2014).

Your brother? Sure.[10] Or, how about your husband? Because that's certainly fine too.[11]

Corporate Media (aka Mainstream Media)

The most vibrant segment of the *American free press*, *brought to you by…*

Corporate Sponsors

Content filters.

Credible Sources

Those refuting the *alarmist* claims of assorted *activists*.

Discredited Allegations

Documented evidence of official criminality sternly denied by anonymous *official sources*.

Echo Chamber

The process through which suspect claims made by *government* officials and *pundits* enter into a positive feedback loop, ultimately culminating in the transformation of wholly unfounded assertions into accepted facts. For instance, a *government* official may leak a story to a reputable *news* outlet, say the *New York Times*, and then use the ensuing report as a *pretext* to comment on dubious intelligence now granted the shiny veneer of legitimacy.[12]

Embedded Reporter

Pentagon spokesperson.

---

[10] In December 2013, CNN viewers were treated to *New Day* anchor Chris Cuomo interviewing his brother, New York Governor Andrew Cuomo. See PoliticsNow. "Chris Cuomo Interviews Governor Andrew Cuomo on New York Train Derailment." YouTube.com. (2 Dec 2013).

[11] In October 2012, CNN's Christiane Amanpour hosted a roundtable discussion with the writer Robert Kagan and former Assistant Secretary of State, and Amanpour's husband, James Rubin. See "How should candidates view Arab Spring?" CNN. (23 Oct 2012).

[12] In 2002, the *New York Times*, citing anonymous officials, reported that Saddam Hussein was engaged in a worldwide hunt to build an atomic bomb using specially designed aluminum tubes. The same day the *Times* report was published, Vice President Dick Cheney appeared on *Meet The Press* and eagerly parroted the line about the specially designed tubes, noting, of course, that he was merely referencing the *Times* report that just so happened to be in that morning's paper.

Fourth Estate

The title conferred upon the *American* media, due to its pivotal role in helping to head off any *crisis of democracy* through the faithful force-feeding of *infotainment* to the *American public*.

Fox and Friends

Fox News' flagship morning *news* program, where loyal viewers are treated to hard hitting *news* and analysis provided by an in house crack team of simpletons (Steve Doocy, Elisabeth Hasselbeck, and Brian Kilmeade) with aggressively *orthodox* beliefs.

Fox News

Pixelated *fear* and hate masquerading as a 24-hour cable *news* channel.

Free Press

A press reliant on *official sources* and indebted to *corporate sponsors*.

Gotcha Question

A question asked by a member of the *liberal media* in a blatant attempt to mock a political candidate from *Middle America*. Examples include: "What newspapers do you read?" And, "Can you name a *Supreme Court* case you disagree with?"[13]

High-Tech Terrorist

A treasonous publisher of *classified information*.[14]

Huffington Post

An innovative online newspaper working to revitalize the *profitability* of journalism by shrewdly eschewing the antiquated practice of financially compensating one's contributors.

---

[13] These being the questions Katie Couric asked in 2008 to then-Vice Presidential candidate Sarah Palin, both of which Palin later deemed to be "gotcha questions."

[14] In late 2010, Senate Minority Leader Mitch McConnell called WikiLeaks founder Julian Assange a "high tech terrorist," to which Vice President Joe Biden was to later second on an appearance on *Meet the Press*. Nisha Chittal. "Sen. Mitch McConnell: Julian Assange Is A 'High Tech Terrorist.'" Mediaite. (5 Dec 2010); "Biden Makes Case For Assange As A 'High-Tech Terrorist'" *Huffington Post*. (19 Dec 2010).

Identity Thief

An independent journalist thrown the book for being too much of a *troublemaker*.[15]

Infotainment

See *News*.

Insider Threat

A potential unauthorized *leaker* of *government* information. More precisely, anyone working within the federal *government*.[16]

Journalism School

A school training stenographers in *letting the facts speak for themselves*.

Leaker

Authorized: a *public relations* official discreetly working to properly inform members of the *respectable press*. Unauthorized: an *insider threat*.

Letting the Facts Speak for Themselves

Letting the *official sources* speak for themselves.

Liberal Media

The entire U.S. media. Well, maybe excluding: *Fox News, talk radio*, the *Wall Street Journal*, the *Washington Times*, the *Washington Post*, network news…

---

[15] In 2012, the muckraking journalist Barrett Brown was charged with, among other things, "aggregated identity theft" for posting a link online to a file containing data stolen from the CIA-linked private intelligence firm Stratfor. Brown hadn't stolen the file, but merely copied a link to the files from a public chat room and then proceeded to post it to another chat room. In early 2014, the identity theft charges were dropped, but in early 2015, Brown was still sentenced to 63 months in prison.
[16] Launched in 2011, the U.S. government's Insider Threat Program – which stretches beyond agencies directly related to national security, to include everything from the Peace Corps to the Department of Education – seeks to educate employees on the signs of a potential leaker working in their midst. The purported signs of a potential "insider threat," as *McClatchy* reported, include "certain life experiences," including "stress, divorce, financial problems" or "frustrations with co-workers or the organization." Marisa Taylor and Jonathan S. Landay. "Obama's crackdown views leaks as aiding enemies of U.S." *McClatchy*. (20 June 2013).

Mass Media

All *news* outlets and journalists tirelessly working to synchronize the *American public* to all the very latest developments in *celebrity*.

Military Analyst

A *consultant* for a defense contractor moonlighting as an "independent" military analyst on radio and TV.[17]

Morning Joe

A morning *news* show on *MSNBC* – formerly "brewed" by Starbucks Coffee – hosted by Joe Scarborough, a former *Republican* representative, and Mika Brzezinski, the daughter of Zbigniew Brzezinski. The show – which was formerly "brewed" by Starbucks – is the place for serious *Washington power* players to discuss the most important issues of the day. The show, incidentally, is also known for its four year corporate sponsorship deal with Starbucks, which included on-air product placement and an ever-discreet, ever-present Starbucks logo displayed on screen. Despite no longer being "brewed" by Starbucks, *Morning Joe* remains a very serious and important show for very serious and important people.

MSNBC

Shrill *liberal* apologetics masquerading as a 24-hour cable *news* channel.

National Public Radio – NPR

The nation's public radio station, offering the public a rare *opportunity* to be told things by *experts*.[18]

---

[17] A 2008 *New York Times* investigation revealed a Pentagon-led campaign to transform media military analysts "into a kind of media Trojan horse — an instrument intended to shape terrorism coverage from inside the major TV and radio networks." The *Times* reported that military analysts for all the major TV networks were equipped with Pentagon-supplied talking points (which included calling the Iraq war a "war of liberation") in return for special access within the Defense Department, which could then be used by the analysts "as a marketing and networking opportunity or as a window into future business possibilities." David Barstow. "Behind TV Analysts, Pentagon's Hidden Hand." *New York Times*. (20 April 2008).

[18] As a 2004 Fairness and Accuracy in Reporting study found: "NPR's guest list shows the radio service relies on the same elite and influential sources that dominate mainstream commercial news, and falls short of reflecting the diversity of the

Native Advertising

Corporate advertising clandestinely designed in partnership with *news* outlets to appear to the *consumer* as actual *news* content. Or, to put it far more succinctly, *news*.[19]

New York Times

The newspaper of the *power elite* vetted record.

News

Native advertising, the weather, *celebrity* intrigue, and the occasional *political scandal*.

Normal Journalistic Outlet

A *news* organization doing the responsible thing by handing control of its publishing schedule over to *government* officials.[20]

Objective Reporting

Giving equal weight to both sides of a story; that is, the claims made by both *government* officials and corporate spokespeople. And as any objective reporter worth his or her salt knows, there's only two sides to a story.[21]

American public." Moreover, countering the presumption that NPR constitutes a liberal new outlet, the FAIR study found that, "Republicans outnumbered Democrats [on air] by more than 3 to 2 (61 percent to 38 percent)." Steve Rendall and Daniel Butterworth. "How Public Is Public Radio? A study of NPR's guest list." *Extra!* (May 2004).

[19] *Forbes* magazine went as far as to actually sell the cover of its January 2014 issue to AT&T as part of the magazine's enthusiastic embrace of native advertising. Mike Shields. "Cover of Forbes Takes Native Ads to New Level." *Wall Street Journal.* (5 Jan 2015): B4.

[20] In his book *No Place to Hide*, Glenn Greenwald recounts how U.S. government officials sought to delay *The Guardian* from publishing the first story on NSA spying to come from the documents provided by Edward Snowden. As Greenwald writes, after consulting on a conference call with up to 12 U.S. officials all urging a delay in the paper's publishing, *The Guardian* informed the government that it was going to move forward with publication. As one official then sniped, "no normal journalistic outlet would publish this quickly without first meeting with us." Glenn Greenwald. *No Place to Hide: Edward Snowden, the NSA, and the U.S. Surveillance State.* (New York: Metropolitan Books, 2014): 68.

[21] So-called objectivity, Chris Hedges observes, "creates the formula of quoting establishment specialist or experts within the narrow confines of the power elite who

Off-the-Record Session

An editorial meeting seeing prominent *official sources* layout their vision for the coverage of various issues to enthralled members of the *respectable press*.[22]

Official Sources

The *government* officials dictating to members of the *free press* what the content of their *news* stories are to entail.

Old News

A blockbuster exposé on *government* corruption and criminality, which is to be studiously ignored and downplayed due to the fact that *we* already sort of knew that such crimes were occurring and nobody really seemed to care before, so, really, why care now?

O'Reilly Factor, The

America's most watched cable *news* program airing on *Fox News* and hosted by Bill O'Reilly. The historically important Bill O'Reilly rewards viewers of *The Factor* by nightly fusing fraudulent personal anecdotes onto hackneyed political analysis.[23]

---

debate policy numbers like medieval theologians. As long as one viewpoint is balanced by another, usually no more than what Sigmund Freud would term 'the narcissism of minor difference,' the job of the reporter is deemed complete. But this is more often a way to obscure rather than expose." Chris Hedges. "The Disease of Objectivity." In *Will The Last Reporter Please Turn Out The Lights: The Colapse of Journalism and What Can Be Done to Fix It.* Ed. By Robert W. McChesny and Victor Pickard. (New York: The New Press, 2011): 210-211.

[22] To take one case: Prior to announcing an escalation of the war against ISIS in Iraq and Syria in September 2014, President Obama held an off-the-record session at the White House with: "New York Times columnists David Brooks, Tom Friedman and Frank Bruni and editorial writer Carol Giacomo; The Washington Post's David Ignatius, Eugene Robinson and Ruth Marcus; The New Yorker's Dexter Filkins and George Packer; The Atlantic's Jeffrey Goldberg and Peter Beinart; The New Republic's Julia Ioffe; Columbia Journalism School Dean Steve Coll; The Wall Street Journal's Jerry Seib; and The Daily Beast's Michael Tomasky." Michael Calderone. "Obama Met Privately With Top Journalists Before ISIS War Speech." *Huffington Post.* (13 Sept 2014).

[23] In the wake of his mundane interview with President Obama prior to the 2014 Super Bowl, Bill O'Reilly proudly crowed: "that interview that I did is going to go down in journalistic history as what should be done." Dylan Byers. "Bill O'Reilly: Obama interview will go down in 'journalistic history.'" *Politico.* (6 Feb 2014).

PBS Newshour

The Public Broadcasting System's leading daily *television news* program. Or, just another public outlet putting *experts* on the air.[24]

Propaganda

All *news* reports conflicting the claims of *official sources*.

Pundit

Someone who practices a dogmatic adherence to official *orthodoxy* and is thusly rewarded by having her writings appear in prominent newspapers and magazines, her commentary heard on national radio programs, and her face seen on *televisions* across the country.

Ratings

That which determines what is fit to broadcast.[25]

Respectable Press

Those who shun *advocacy journalism* and instead *work* with *official sources* to strip any biasedly *un-American* historical context from their reports.[26]

---

[24] A 2010 study by the media watch group Fairness and Accuracy in Reporting stated that the *Newshour* "feature[s] sources drawn largely from a narrow range of elite white male experts." For example, of all think tank guests appearing on the *Newshour* over the course of the FAIR study, one half were from right leaning think tanks, with only 13% from left leaning institutions. Steve Rendall and Michael Morel. "Does NewsHour 'Help Us See America Whole'? A FAIR study of PBS's flagship news show." *Extra!* (Nov 2010).

[25] Tellingly, when questioned in April 2014 on whether CNN's around the clock coverage of missing Malaysian Airlines Flight 370 was driven by ratings, CNN anchor Don Lemon argued, "Part of our mission is to give the audience what they want." Obviously, such a perspective lends itself to the coverage of the salacious far more than the substantive. But if one is more concerned with delivering entertainment over actual news, then audience desires indeed become determinative. Josh Feldman. "Barbara Walters Grills Don Lemon on MH370: CNN Wouldn't Cover If 'Not for the Ratings.'" Mediaite. (14 April 2014).

[26] As David Edwards and David Cromwell write, "The job of mainstream journalism is to learn nothing from the past, to treat rare individuals motivated by compassion as rare fools deserving contempt." David Edwards and David Cromwell. *Newspeak in the 21ˢᵗ Century.* (New York: Pluto Press, 2009): 222.

RT

A *"propaganda* bullhorn" posing a challenge to the U.S. *government* akin to that posed by the *Islamic State.*[27]

Situation Room, The

CNN's premier daytime *news* program hosted by the veteran journalist Wolf Blitzer. Viewers of *The Situation Room* are treated to unabashed, old-fashioned *objective reporting*, where nothing is out of bounds for the *AIPAC* staffer-cum-newsman Blitzer.[28]

Special Correspondent

A child of privilege with dubious journalistic credentials, brought on board by a prominent *news* organization in order to cravenly curry favor with those in *power.*[29]

Spin

The wholehearted *truth* freed from the restraints of *reality*.

Sunday Morning Talk Show

A weekly confluence of political *power* and conventional wisdom featuring appearances by Senators John McCain and Lindsey Graham.[30]

---

[27] In April 2014, Secretary of State John Kerry attacked the Russian-funded English language RT news station as a "propaganda bullhorn." In a January 2015 interview with the *New York Times*, the newly-appointed chief of the U.S. Broadcasting Board of Governors (the body overseeing all U.S.-funded international media) stated, "We are facing a number of challenges from entities like Russia Today which is out there pushing a point of view, the Islamic State in the Middle East and groups like Boko Haram." See "'Propaganda bullhorn': John Kerry attacks RT during Ukraine address." RT.com. (25 April 2014); "Head of US state media put RT on same challenge list as ISIS, Boko Haram." RT.com. (23 Jan 2015).

[28] In the mid-1970s, Blitzer served as the editor of AIPAC's *Near East Report*.

[29] In 2011, NBC News hired Chelsea Clinton as a "special correspondent," despite her having no experience or training in journalism. It was reported in 2014 that NBC paid Clinton an annual salary of $600,000. Likewise, NBC News also employs Jenna Bush-Hager as a "special correspondent" for the *Today Show*. Dylan Byers and Maggie Haberman. "Chelsea Clinton paid $600K by NBC." *Politico*. (13 June 2014).

[30] A September 2014 analysis by the *New York Times* of the guests appearing on the five Sunday morning talk shows on CNN, ABC, CBS, NBC, and Fox News found McCain and Graham to top the list of most appearances since January 2009. McCain

Talk Radio

A time warp superimposing the *orthodox* opinions of 1950s white men onto the latest *news* of the day.

Talking Head

Someone appearing on *television* with extraordinarily little of substance to say on an impressive array of issues.

Trial of the Century

The court case – whichever one it is – currently being dissected ad nausea on *CNN*, *Fox News*, and *MSNBC*.

Voice of America

A U.S. *government*-funded international *news* organization seeking to counter the *propaganda* of *the world*'s assorted *freedom* haters by indoctrinating dispensable people in *American values*.

Washington Post

A paper comfortably resting on its laurels since the days of *Watergate*.

We Only Have a Minute, So Briefly…

Drop any attempt at providing informed analysis and just give me a *talking point* before we have to hear *a word from our sponsors*.

White House Correspondents' Association Dinner

A once a year gala held in *Washington* D.C., during which members of the *respectable press* openly fraternize with the nation's top *politicians*. That is, the one night of the year the two groups openly socialize in front of *television* cameras.[31]

---

came in first with 97 appearances. Graham was second with 85. "Sunday Talk Show Guests." *New York Times* The Upshot. (5 Sept 2014).

[31] Began in 1920 as a low-key affair, today the White House Correspondents' Association dinner has ballooned into a fusion of celebrity and political culture functioning, Mark Leibovich writes, as little more than "a multiday symbol of the city's self-intoxication." Leibovich. *This Town*, 135.

WikiLeaks

A *terrorist organization.*[32]

---

[32] In 2010, Rep. Peter King (NY) called on "Secretary of State Hillary Clinton to declare WikiLeaks a foreign terrorist organization." Michael O'Brien. "Republican wants WikiLeaks labeled as terrorist group." *The Hill.* (29 Nov 2010).

5. Justice for All

New High In U.S. Prison Numbers.

- Washington Post, *2008*[1]

In Financial Crisis, No Prosecutions of Top Figures.

- New York Times, *2011*[2]

Affluenza

A winning legal defense, seeing a defendant of a heinous *crime* use his formidable wealth and privilege to explain to the court that it is he who is the real victim. And though Lady Justice is blind, she's not deaf, and *money* talks.[3]

Ag-Gag

Laws which criminalize any unauthorized filming on *factory farms* by *whistleblowers* in a clearly noble attempt to protect the *privacy* rights of animals.[4]

Agent Provocateurs

FBI agents and informants. (See *Entrapment* below and *Foiled Terror Plot*, Chapter 12)

---

[1] N.C. Aizenman. "New High In U.S. Prison Numbers." *Washington Post*. (29 Feb 2008).

[2] Gretchen Morgenson and Louise Story. "In Financial Crisis, No Prosecutions of Top Figures." *New York Times*. (14 April 2011).

[3] In February 2014, a Texas judge sentenced Ethan Couch to just 10 years' probation after a drunk driving crash that killed four and left two others severely injured. Couch's defense team had argued that Couch, 16 at the time of the crash, was a victim of "affluenza." Similarly, Robert Richards IV, an heir to the DuPont family fortune, was in 2009 sentenced to probation for raping his three-year-old daughter. Richards eluded jail time after the judge deemed that he "wouldn't fare well in prison." Dana Ford. "Judge orders Texas teen Ethan Couch to rehab for driving drunk, killing 4." CNN. (6 Feb 2014); Jay Michaelson. "Delaware's Affluenza Case Affects Justice, Too." *The Daily Beast*. (1 April 2014).

[4] As of 2013, 15 so-called ag-gag bills had been introduced in 11 states: Arkansas, California, Indiana, Nebraska, New Hampshire, New Mexico, North Carolina, Pennsylvania, Tennessee, Wyoming, and Vermont. "Anti-Whistleblower Bills Hide Factory-Farming Abuses from the Public." Human Society of the United States. (25 March 2014).

Asset Forfeiture

The favored means of securing "little goodies" for *police* departments the nation over.[5]

Border Control

Federal agency tasked with *neutralizing* rock-throwing teenagers along the U.S.-*Mexico* border.[6]

Citizens Police Review Board

A toothless tiger.

Civil Disobedience

A childish stunt pulled off by narcissistic individuals craving more attention and likely more *handouts*.

Civil Rights Movement

A good movement, in retrospect, which, with racial harmony now firmly established, really ought to be relegated to the annals of *history*.

Crime

The supposed threat posed – mainly by poor men of color – to the property and life of *the 1%*.

---

[5] Asset forfeiture permits police agencies to seize private property they deemed to be involved in criminal activity. A 2014 *Washington Post* investigation put the value of seized assets nationwide dating from 2008 at $2.5 billion. Such assets, which are deemed guilty until proven otherwise, are then used by police agencies, as Brad Cates, a former director of the asset forfeiture program at the Justice Department, remarked, as "a free floating slush fund." No wonder, then, that during a September 2014 seminar offered to police departments on seizing property, Harry S. Connelly Jr., the city attorney of Las Cruces, NM, deemed seized assets "little goodies." See: Robert O'Harrow Jr. and Steven Rich. "Asset seizures fuel police spending." *Washington Post.* (11 Oct 2014); Shaila Dewan. "Police Use Department Wish List When Deciding Which Assets to Seize." *New York Times.* (9 Nov 2014).

[6] Since 2010, U.S. Border Patrol agents have shot and killed no less than 10 individuals along the U.S-Mexico border for allegedly lobbing rocks at agents or their vehicles. In one case, sixteen-year old Jose Antonio Elena Rodriguez was shot 10 times for allegedly throwing rocks at agents. At the time, Rodriquez was on the Mexican side of the 60 foot border fence near Nogales, Sonora, Mexico. In all, since 2010, Border Patrol agents have killed 27 individuals along the border. Vicki B. Gaubeca. "Why is U.S. Border Patrol Shooting Rock-Throwing Teenagers?" ACLU Blog of Rights. (13 March 2014).

Criminal

Someone – typically a poor man of color – the rest of *society* is permitted to openly hate.[7]

Crowd Control

The *police* tear-gassing, pepper-spraying, and baton-beating of individuals practicing *civil disobedience*.

Death Penalty

The ultimate *criminal* penalty, reflecting *America*'s Christian values; you know, an eye for an eye.[8]

Demographics Unit

A *police racial profiling* unit delicately rechristened for a *post-racial America*.[9]

Department of Justice

Federal department tasked with clandestinely scooping up the phone records of journalists – or *co-conspirators* – in an effort to bring *government whistleblowers* to *justice*.[10]

---

[7] "Criminals, it turns out," Michelle Alexander writes, "are the one social group in America we have permission to hate. In 'colorblind' America, criminals are the new whipping boys. They are entitled to no respect and little moral concern. Like the 'coloreds' in the years following emancipation, criminals today are deemed a characterless and purposeless people, deserving of our collective scorn and contempt. When we say someone was 'treated like a criminal,' what we mean to say is that he or she was treated as less than human, like a shameful creature." Michelle Alexander. *The New Jim Crow: Mass Incarceration in the Age of Colorblindness*. (New York: The New Press, 2012): 141.

[8] A 2014 report by Amnesty International found the U.S. executed the fifth most inmates in the world in 2013, killing a total of 39. The only nations executing more in 2013 were China, Iran, Iraq, and Saudi Arabia. "Death Sentences and Executions 2013." Amnesty International. (26 March 2014).

[9] New York City Police Department's "demographics unit," targeting the city's Muslim community for surveillance post 9/11, was formally disbanded in 2014. Matt Apuzzo and Joseph Goldstein. "New York Drops Unit That Spied on Muslims." *New York Times*. (15 April 2014).

[10] As part of an investigation into leaks attributed to a May 2012 Associated Press story, the Justice Department secretly obtained the records from more than 20 telephone lines (including personal phone numbers) of AP reporters and editors

Double Judgment

The use of a prior offense for which one has already served time to justify one's deportation. Once a *criminal* always a *criminal*, in other words – especially so if one is a foreign person of color.[11]

Drug Enforcement Agency – DEA

Federal agency responsible for ensuring *illegal drugs* aren't cutting too far into the market share of the nation's leading pharmaceuticals.

Entrapment

Creating *criminals* and *terrorists* in order to stop *criminals* and *terrorists*. Or, the primary means through which the *FBI* protects the *homeland* from the *menace* that is young *Muslim* men.[12] (See also, *Foiled Terror Plot*, Chapter 12)

Federal Bureau of Investigations – FBI

Federal agency long tasked with infiltrating, tracking, and generally harassing those working within the *antiwar movement*. After September 11, 2001, the FBI also has added the *entrapment* of *Muslims* to its portfolio.

---

from April and May 2012. Mark Sherman. "Gov't obtains wide AP phone records in probe." Associated Press. (13 May 2013).

[11] Double judgment, as *The Nation* notes, "applies not only to undocumented immigrants, but also to those with legal statuses, such as refugee or permanent residency status." JOMO. "Fighting Obama's Deportation Policies Without Papers – and Without Fear." *The Nation*. (24 April 2014).

[12] A 2011 *Mother Jones* investigation found the FBI employs upwards of 15,000 domestic spies, which have become instrumental in a spat of FBI stings that have accounted for all but a handful of the most high-profile domestic "terror plots" since 9/11. But as the *Mother Jones* piece explained, "FBI agents and informants target not just active jihadists, but tens of thousands of law-abiding people, seeking to identify those disgruntled few who might participate in a plot given the means and the opportunity. And then, in case after case, the government provides the plot, the means, and the opportunity.

"Here's how it works: Informants report to their handlers on people who have, say, made statements sympathizing with terrorists. Those names are then cross-referenced with existing intelligence data, such as immigration and criminal records. FBI agents may then assign an undercover operative to approach the target by posing as a radical. Sometimes the operative will propose a plot, provide explosives, even lead the target in a fake oath to Al Qaeda. Once enough incriminating information has been gathered, there's an arrest – and a press conference announcing another foiled plot." Trevor Aaronson. "The Informants." *Mother Jones*. (Sept/Oct 2011).

Felon

A label branded on individuals – typically poor men of color – in order to prevent them from voting, working, finding housing, and otherwise living the *American Dream*.[13]

Fusion Center

A collaboration bringing together state, local, and federal *law* enforcement officials, along with the *private sector* and the military, to share intelligence on all "suspicious" individuals (i.e., political *activists* and *Muslims*).[14]

Grand Jury

A secretive tribunal used to exonerate *peace officers* in their killings of unarmed men of color.

Illegal Drugs

A conduit through which to attain social control at home, while simultaneously providing a lucrative source of supplemental *CIA* funds.[15]

Jim Crow

A system of racial segregation – "separate but equal" – instituted in the U.S. South in the wake of the abolition of slavery. Jim Crow has today been made redundant in a *post-racial America* busily waging a *war on drugs*.

Joint Terrorism Task Force

Located in 103 cities nationwide, Joint Terrorism Task Forces bring together local, state, and federal agencies (including the military – *Posse Comitatus* is

---

[13] The National Sentencing Project reports that "an estimated 5.85 million Americans are denied the right to vote because of laws that prohibit voting by people with felony convictions," including "1 of every 13 African Americans." <http://www.sentencingproject.org/template/page.cfm?id=133>

[14] Michael German and Jay Stanley. "What's Wrong with Fusion Centers?" American Civil Liberties Union. (Dec 2007).

[15] As Gore Vidal remarked: "Drugs. If they did not exist our governors would have invented them in order to prohibit them and so make much of the population vulnerable to arrest, imprisonment, seizure of property, and so on." On the CIA and drugs, see "CIA," Chapter 9. Gore Vidal. *Perpetual War for Perpetual Peace: How We Got To Be So Hated.* (New York: Nation Books, 2002): 54.

negotiable in the *war on terror*, after all) in order to "provide one-stop shopping for information regarding terrorist activities."[16]

Judicial Activism

Any court decision which infringes upon the rights of *corporations*.

Justice

The prosecution and conviction of petty thieves, *criminals*, drug users, drug dealers, rapists, murderers, pedophiles, and other assorted *bad apples*. And conversely, the immunity conferred upon *presidents*, policymakers, *police*, military brass, and others of affluence complicit in *isolated incidents*, *tragic errors*, and *mistakes*.

Law

A system of rules manipulated and selectively enforced by thieving elites seeking to mask their grand larceny behind a shroud of respectability.

Law and Order

A popular political mantra used to signify one's desire to lock-up as many young minorities as overcrowded *prisons* will hold.

Mass Incarceration

The systemic jailing of persons of color and *others* of low socioeconomic status as part of the *war on drugs*.[17]

Mosque Crawler

A *police* informant tasked with moving from mosque to mosque in an attempt to recruit the foot soldiers necessary for *FBI terror plots*.

Mug Shot

A rather profitable extortion racket for the enterprising online *entrepreneur*.[18]

---

[16] "Protecting America from Terrorist Attack Our Joint Terrorism Task Forces." The Federal Bureau of Investigations. <www.fbi.gov>

[17] As of 2012, 2.2 million people were incarcerated in the U.S. <http://www.sentencingproject.org/template/page.cfm?id=107>

[18] A host of for-profit websites now publish virtually every mug shot taken in the U.S. The *New York Times* explains that these sites then go about turning a profit "by

No-Knock Warrant

A warrant allowing a *police SWAT Team* to quickly enter the premises of a highly dangerous, violent *criminal* without having to first announce their presence. Of course, because of the danger involved in fulfilling no-knock warrants against violent offenders, *police* departments often prefer to serve them against completely innocent individuals, thus prudently reducing the risk to the health and safety of their officers.[19]

Non-Prosecution Agreement

An agreement signed by a company under *criminal* investigation, in which the company agrees to make cosmetic changes it claims will mitigate any future wrongdoing in return for the dropping of all *criminal* charges. In other words, *justice* come to *Wall Street*.[20]

Parallel Construction

The *law* enforcement laundering of illegally obtained evidence, carried out by working backwards to build a parallel investigation in order to conceal the extralegal origins of the initial investigation.[21] A reminder that when it comes to enforcing the *law*, one must never be constrained by the *law*.

---

charging a fee to remove the image. That fee can be anywhere from $30 to $400, or even higher. Pay up, in other words, and the picture is deleted, at least from the site that was paid." David Segal. "Mugged by a Mug Shot Online." *New York Times*. (5 Oct 2013).

[19] As Radley Balko reported, at least 10% of New York City's 450 monthly no-knock raids in 2003 "were served on the wrong address, were served under bad information, or otherwise didn't produce enough evidence for an arrest." Radley Balko. *Rise of the Warrior Cop: The Militarization of America's Police Forces*. (New York: Public Affairs, 2013): 266.

[20] A 2005 report by the *Corporate Crime Reporter* found "that prosecutors have entered into twice as many non-prosecution and deferred prosecution agreements with major American corporations in the last four years (23 agreements between 2002 to 2005) than they have in the previous ten years (11 agreements between 1992 to 2001)." "Crime Without Conviction: The Rise of Deferred and Non Prosecution Agreements." *Corporate Crime Reporter*. (28 Dec 2005).

[21] According to a 2013 Reuters report, the Drug Enforcement Agency's Special Operations Unit works in tandem with the National Security Agency to funnel NSA intercepts "to authorities across the nation to help them launch criminal investigations of Americans." The report went on to note that, "law enforcement agents have been directed to conceal how such investigations truly begin – not only from defense lawyers but also sometimes from prosecutors and judges." John

Patrolling (Police)

Gallivanting through the streets on repurposed military vehicles.

Peace Officer

A gun-shooting, Taser-discharging, choke-holding, and baton-beating member of the *police*.

Police

Trigger-happy bounty hunters tasked with protecting the life, *liberty*, and *private property* of *corporations* and *the 1%* by working to corral and imprison all the undesirable and redundant elements of *society*.[22]

Police Brutality

Inconceivable lacking clear video evidence. And in that case, an *isolated incident*.

Police Shooting

The always justified use of lethal force by *police* officers.[23]

Posse Comitatus

Act passed in 1878 prohibiting the use of federal troops in domestic *law*

Shiffman and Kristina Cooke. "Exclusive: U.S. directs agents to cover up program used to investigate Americans." Reuters. (5 Aug 2013).

[22] As Lee Ballinger argues, "cops are modern day slave catchers, but with a broader racial mandate than then nineteenth century enforcers of fugitive slave laws." Lee Ballinger. "The Jury is Out: Class, Politics and the Justice System." *CounterPunch* Vol. 21 No. 1. (Jan 2014): 15.

[23] As the *Wall Street Journal* commented in a 2014 report on police killings: "It is nearly impossible to determine how many people are killed by the police each year." This is because law enforcement agencies are not actually required to report such killings. Indeed, a *Journal* analysis of 105 of the country's largest police agencies between the years 2007 and 2012 "found more than 550 police killings during those years were missing from the national [FBI] tally or, in a few dozen cases, not attributed to the agency involved." Of course, reported or not, nearly all police shootings are deemed to be justified. For example, reporting on FBI shootings, the *New York Times* found "from 1993 to early 2011, F.B.I. agents fatally shot about 70 'subjects' and wounded about 80 others — and every one of those episodes was deemed justified." See: Rob Barry and Coulter Jones. "Hundreds of Police Killings Uncounted in Federal Stats." *Wall Street Journal*. (3 Dec 2014): A1; Charlie Savage and Michael Schmidt. "The F.B.I. Deemed Agents Faultless in 150 Shootings." *New York Times*. (18 June 2013).

enforcement. Posse Comitatus does not apply to *fusion centers* or *joint terrorism task forces* (per the standard *war on terror* exemption to established *law*), and can otherwise be skirted by simply militarizing local *police* departments with surplus military equipment.[24]

Predictive Policing

The use of *just war*-tested mass surveillance and computer algorithm *technology* in the fight against *homeland* pre-*crime*.[25]

Preemptive Prosecution

Targeting hitherto innocent individuals, who, nonetheless, remain innately predisposed to committing violent acts (you know, *Muslims* and anti-*war activists*).[26]

---

[24] Since 1990, the U.S. military has distributed $4.2 billion worth of surplus military equipment to local police agencies. Michael Virtanen. "Spoils of war: Police getting leftover Iraq trucks." *Chicago Sun-Times*. (24 Nov 2013).

[25] Two California cities currently utilize predictive policing (Los Angeles and Santa Cruz). As a 2014 *LA Weekly* report on the Los Angeles Police Department's use of predictive policing noted: "LAPD's mild-sounding 'predictive policing' technique, introduced by former Chief William Bratton to anticipate where future crime would hit, is actually a sophisticated system developed not by cops but by the U.S. military, based on 'insurgent' activity in Iraq and civilian casualty patterns in Afghanistan.

Records obtained by L.A. Weekly from the U.S. Army Research Office show that UCLA professors Jeff Brantingham and Andrea Bertozzi (anthropology and applied mathematics, respectively) in 2009 told the Army that their predictive techniques 'will provide the Army with a plethora of new data-intensive predictive algorithms for dealing with insurgents and terrorists abroad.' In a later update to the Army, after they had begun working with LAPD, they wrote, 'Terrorist and insurgent activities have a distinct parallel to urban crime.'" Darwin Bond-Graham and Ali Winston. "Forget the NSA, the LAPD Spies on Millions of Innocent Folks." *LA Weekly*. (27 Feb 2014).

[26] Preemptive prosecution, Deepa Kumar writes "involves targeting innocent people who haven't actually done anything wrong. It includes a range of tactics such as the use of *agent provocateurs* to incite people to do things they otherwise would not to charge 'material support' for terrorists, which can be applied to something as innocuous as giving money to a charitable foundation." In a 2010 case of preemptive prosecution involving the targeting of anti-war activists, "the FBI raided the homes and offices of antiwar activists (including Caucasian US citizens) in Illinois, Minnesota, and North Carolina. They were given grand jury subpoenas on the grounds that they provided material support for terrorism." Deepa Kumar. *Islamophobia and the Politics of Empire*. (Chicago: Haymarket Books, 2012): 147, 149.

Presumption of Innocence

A privilege not to be granted to *government whistleblowers*.[27]

Prison

A low-cost factory manned by the human refuse generated by systemic *racism* and economic deterioration.[28]

Private Prison

An *optimizing prison*.[29]

Protect and Serve

Harass and kill.

Racial Profiling

A controversial policing tactic, in which one is targeted based solely on his or her race. Most *police* departments have outlawed racial profiling, and now just stop people based on an officer's prejudicial *fear*.

---

[27] Defending his administration's prosecution of Army whistleblower Chelsea Manning at a 2011 California fundraiser, President Obama remarked "He [Manning] broke the law." At the time, Manning had merely been charged, not yet convicted. MJ Lee and Abby Phillip. "Barack Obama on Bradley Manning: 'He broke the law.'" *Politico*. (22 April 2011).

[28] There are an estimated 1 million prison laborers in the U.S. As Chris Hedges reports, federal prisoners, making as little as $1.25 an hour, work to "produce the military's helmets, uniforms, pants, shirts, ammunition belts, ID tags and tents." They also labor "through subcontractors, for major corporations such as Chevron, Bank of America, IBM, Motorola, Microsoft, AT&T, Starbucks, Nintendo, Victoria's Secret, J.C. Penney, Sears, Wal-Mart, Kmart, Eddie Bauer, Wendy's, Procter & Gamble, Johnson & Johnson, Fruit of the Loom, Motorola, Caterpillar, Sara Lee, Quaker Oats, Mary Kay, Microsoft, Texas Instruments, Dell, Honeywell, Hewlett-Packard, Nortel, Nordstrom's, Revlon, Macy's, Pierre Cardin and Target." Chris Hedges. "The Prison State of America." *Truthdig*. (28 Dec 2014).

[29] The penetration of private corporations into public prisons through the outsourcing of services typically provided by prisons themselves leaves the distinction between a public and a private prison perhaps irrelevant. As Angela Davis writes, "public prisons have become so thoroughly saturated with the profit-producing products and services of private corporations that the distinction is not as meaningful as one might suspect." Angela Y. Davis. *Are Prisons Obsolete?* (New York: Seven Stories Press, 2003): 99-100.

Reasonable Fear

A *fear* felt by a *police* officer of an *imminent threat* justifying the use of deadly force. More precisely, a *fear* felt by a *police* officer upon encountering an unarmed young man of color.

Riot

A peaceful *protest* culminating in *police* orders to *stop resisting*.

Rule of Law

Rule of naked class *power*.

Sneak and Peak Warrant

Good guy breaking and entering.[30]

Solitary Confinement

A cruel and unusual punishment meted out to *criminals* (i.e., those who have come to sacrifice their rights to the protections of the Eighth Amendment by choosing to be *criminals*).[31]

Stop-and-Frisk

The *freedom* granted *peace officers* to randomly stop people of color at will, so to win the *war on drugs* and sustain the system of *mass incarceration*. In other

---

[30] Sneak and peak warrants allow law enforcement to enter and search a particular residence without having to ever inform the premise's owner of their search.

[31] Upwards of 80,000 individuals are held at any one time in solitary confinement in the U.S. As the Center for Constitutional Rights remarks on the practice: "Researchers have demonstrated that prolonged solitary confinement causes a persistent and heightened state of anxiety and nervousness, headaches, insomnia, lethargy or chronic tiredness, nightmares, heart palpitations, and fear of impending nervous breakdowns. Other documented effects include obsessive ruminations, confused thought processes, an oversensitivity to stimuli, irrational anger, social withdrawal, hallucinations, violent fantasies, emotional flatness, mood swings, chronic depression, feelings of overall deterioration, as well as suicidal ideation. Exposure to such life-shattering conditions clearly constitutes cruel and unusual punishment – in violation of the Eighth Amendment to the U.S. Constitution." "Torture: The Use of Solitary Confinement in U.S. Prisons." Center for Constitutional Rights. <http://ccrjustice.org/files/CCR-Factsheet-Solitary-Confinement.pdf>

words, that whole *protect and serve* mission put in practice.[32]

Stop Resisting

The demand issued to individuals cowering in self-defense as *peace officers* rain blows down upon their bodies.

Superpredator

A fictitious, ruthlessly dangerous juvenile male of color. Because of the non-existence of superpredators, all juveniles are to be treated as *criminals* and tried as adults.[33]

Supreme Court

Nine civil rights pioneers fighting to protect the rights of *corporations* and *small businesses* the nation over.

SWAT Team

Paramilitary *police* units first created in the late 1970s and now present in virtually every local *police* department in the United States.[34] Used primarily in the *war on drugs*, SWAT Teams are staffed by *police* officers looking to reignite the magic of their childhood by once again dressing up and playing soldier.

---

[32] In New York City alone, there were 532,911 stop-and-frisk stops in 2012. "Stop-And-Frisk 2012." New York Civil Liberties Union. (May 2013). <http://www.nyclu.org/files/publications/2012_Report_NYCLU_0.pdf>

[33] In the early 1990s, University of Pennsylvania professor John Dilulio Jr. coined the term "superpredator" to much media fanfare. As Dilulio wrote of the superpredator, "a new generation of street criminals is upon us – the youngest, biggest and baddest generation any society has ever known." Dilulio's "research" and hyperbole was then exploited by right-wing legislators in nationwide pushes for stiffer criminal penalties for youth offenders. Of course, the accompanying rise in juvenile crime rates Dilulio predicted to accompany the rise of the superpredator never materialized. The superpredator was a myth. A fact Dilulio himself was years later to publicly admit. Elizabeth Becker. "As Ex-Theorist on Young 'Superpredators,' Bush Aide Has Regrets." *New York Times*. (9 Feb 2001).

[34] 80% of American towns with a population between 25,000 and 50,000 had a SWAT team in 2005, up from 25.6% in 1984. Balko. *Rise of the Warrior Cop*, 308.

Too-Big-To-Jail

All bankers, financial titans, *politicians*, and policymakers complicit in *criminal* acts.[35]

Tough on Crime

The no holds barred approach to petty *crime* taken by the representatives of the inter-state *criminal* syndicates (see *Democrats* and *Republicans*) safely entrenched in elected offices the nation over.

Unlawful Assembly

Peaceful *protest*.

War on Drugs

A social control program targeting potentially rebellious persons of color, along with whites of low socioeconomic status, for *mass incarceration*.

Watergate

The closest a modern *president* has come – and most certainly ever will come – to actually having to account for his crimes. Of course, President Richard Nixon was ultimately saved by the wonderful little idea that when it comes to high crimes, it's always best to *look forward, not backwards*.

---

[35] As Attorney General Eric Holder commented on why no financial institutions faced criminal charges in the wake of the 2008 financial crisis, "It does become difficult for us to prosecute them when we are hit with indications that if you do prosecute – if you do bring a criminal charge – it will have a negative impact on the national economy, perhaps even the world economy." Quoted in: Jed S. Rakoff. "The Financial Crisis: Why Have No High-Level Executives Been Prosecuted?" *New York Review of Books* Vol. LXI, No. 1 (9 Jan 2014): 4-8.

6.   American Society

Our culture is based on two things: television and petroleum.

- *Joe Bageant*, Deer Hunting With Jesus[1]

Affirmative Action

See *Reverse Racism*.

American Culture

A witch's brew of militarism, *reality TV*, *celebrity* worship, nihilistic individualism, and assorted commercial kitsch.

Antidepressants

Tranquilizers prescribed to generally disenchanted individuals, who, absent such sedation, may just help to precipitate a full-blown *crisis in democracy* by coming to engage in dangerous levels of civic involvement.[2]

Bicycle

A child's toy not to be ridden once one reaches legal driving age.

Bossy

The demeanor of any woman in a position of authority over any man.

Branding

Melding an illusory experience onto a product. For businesses, necessary for sustaining *profitability* (see *Marketing*, Chapter 7). For *politicians*, necessary for

---

[1] Joe Bageant. *Deer Hunting With Jesus: Dispatches From America's Class War*. (New York: Three Rivers Press, 2007): 262

[2] Antidepressants are the most commonly prescribed drug in America, with sales totaling $14.6 billion by 2009. In 2008 alone, 164 million prescriptions were written for antidepressants, while upwards of 500,000 American children and adolescents were estimated to be taking some sort of antipsychotic drug. Jed Bickman. "How America's Shrinks Collude with Drug Industry In Turning America's Children into Zombies." *CounterPunch* Vol. 18 No. 12. (June 2011): 1-4; Berman. *Why America Failed*, 62.

attaining the highest office in the land (see *Change You Can Believe In*, Chapter 1). And for individuals, necessary for simply *making it*.

Celebrity

A highly coveted social status transforming one into a genuine object of public concern. All success is predicated upon attaining celebrity status, regardless of whether one is to become an object of public adulation or an object of public ridicule.[3]

Civil War

In the North, the conflict between the Northern and Southern states occurring from 1861 to 1865 that ended slavery. In the South, the *war* of Northern *aggression* fought over states' rights occurring from 1861 to present.[4]

Collective Memory

The collective amnesia of the *American public* when it comes to matters of U.S. *foreign policy*. Responsible for charming questions like: Why do they hate our *freedoms?*[5]

Community

An abolished place where people sharing similar interests and experiences once chose to interact with one another.

Consumer

Everyone. No one is be recognized as anything but a consumer.

Consumption

The source of all of life's pleasures and an imperative for perpetuating the

---

[3] As C. Wright Mills wrote, "all those who succeed in America…are likely to become involved in the world of celebrity." Today, however, the inverse is just as true: all those who are involved in the world of celebrity succeed in America. Mills. *The Power Elite*, 71.

[4] On the Civil War as very much living history in the American South, see: Tony Horwitz. *Confederates in the Attic: Dispatches from the Unfinished Civil War*. (New York: Vintage, 1999).

[5] As Morris Berman quips: "Cicero wrote that 'Not to know what happened before one was born is always to be child.' Most Americans don't seem to know what's happening during their own lifetimes." Morris Berman. *Dark Ages America: The Final Phase of Empire*. (New York: W.W. Norton & Company, 2006): 295.

American way of life. Also, the most patriotic of acts any *American citizen* can undertake at a time of *crisis.*[6]

Culture War

An inverted *class war* using issues like, abortion, gay marriage, guns, religion, sex, etc. as placeholders for class in a *society* which has no classes.[7]

Cyclist

An unpatriotic heretic menacing the *American way of life.*[8]

Depression

An integral part of *having it all.*[9]

Elitism

A disparaging term out of touch factions of the *power elite* levy at rival out of touch factions of the *power elite.*

---

[6] In the wake of the 9/11 attacks, President Bush urged Americans to "Get down to Disney World in Florida. Take your families and enjoy life, the way we want it to be enjoyed." And then, as recession loomed in 2007, Bush again pleaded with Americans, stating: "I encourage you all to go shopping more."

[7] On the devolution of class politics to culture wars, see: Thomas Frank. *What's The Matter With Kansas: How Conservatives Won The Heart of America.* (New York: A Holt Paperback, 2005).

[8] As Zack Furness writes of the media portrayal of bicyclists: "the everyday cyclist is either childish, eccentric, deviant, or in some way lacking the qualities necessary to either be, or become, a stereotypically successful and/or well-adjusted person (i.e., a responsible straight white guy with a job)." As one might expect, then, 69% of all trips of under one mile are taken in the U.S. by car. Zack Furness. *One Less Car: Bicycling and the Politics of Automobility.* (Philadelphia: Temple University Press, 2010): 113.

    As for the threat posed by cyclists to the American way of life (not to mention the rising surveillance state), Heidi Boghosian explains: "bicyclists represent a symbolic challenge to car culture. With fewer cars, not only would gas consumption plummet but insurance companies would lose profits; the state's income stream from registration fees, tags, titles, fuel-related costs, parking, and traffic tickets would wither. As in Amsterdam and other bicycle-friendly cities, people would interact more in quieter public spaces and would be unencumbered by tracking devices that may be built into automobiles." Boghosian. *Spying on Democracy, 38.*

[9] As Morris Berman writes: "The National Institute of Health estimates that more than 14 million Americans suffer from major depression every year, which one psychologist, Gary Greenberg, argues is actually a sane response to a crazy world." Berman. *Why America Failed,* 62.

Evolution

A controversial scientific theory repudiated by its troubled founder on his deathbed.[10]

Family Values

A public disdain, *fear*, and closeted jealousy of those choosing to form a family outside the confines of a *traditional marriage*.

Gated Community

A *power elite safe haven*, providing a fortified sanctuary from the unkempt hordes.[11]

God

A *free market* champion blessing the *exceptional nation* and always counted on to be found standing behind its *heroes* in their battles against evil *barbarians the world* over.

Greed

A necessary sin befalling the nation's otherwise purely altruistic *job-creators*. Necessary, that is, given that more wealth accrued at the top means all the more left to trickle down. (See *Trickle-Down Economics*, Chapter 7.)

Happiness

Possessing the latest must-have gadget.

Having It All

Working *flexible hours* to pay off *student debt*.

---

[10] Creationists like to tout the fact that Charles Darwin repudiated his theory of evolution on his deathbed, as if that somehow invalidates evolution. Of course, as to whether Darwin actually did in fact disavow his theory is of continuing dispute.

[11] Seemingly moving the concept toward its logical conclusion, the latest trend in gated communities is the development of private apocalypse bunkers. The *Wall Street Journal* reported in 2014 on one such "community" of luxury condominiums built in a renovated Kansas missile silo. Selling for upwards of $3 million apiece, each condo comes complete with "enough emergency food on hand to last up to five years." Of course, the complex is also buffeted by an electrified fence, and offers tenants "armored transportation if owners get to the local airport or anywhere within 400 miles of the silo." Liz Moyer. "For Sale: Renovated Luxury Condo; Can Withstand Nuclear Attack." *Wall Street Journal.* (10 Nov 2014): A1, A12.

Hero

A *good guy* soldier partaking in an industrial-sized slaughter of a *dispensable nation*'s *unpeople*.

Hollywood

Industry tasked with assuring the *American public* that although they belong to an *exceptional nation* that is *a global force for good*, they themselves remain fat, ugly, and old.

Home Entertainment System

A great advance in personalized digital entertainment. Conveniently configured in one's home, a home entertainment system renders all burdensome voyages out of the home and into the surrounding *community* to interact with others in search of entertainment to be utterly void.

Hoodie

A most ominous item of clothing, commonly donned by the *superpredator-*type. *Stand your ground* upon any encounter with an individual wearing a hoodie.[12]

Illegal Alien

An illegal foreign *free rider* (the worst kind of *free rider*) directly responsible for, well, whatever you like.

Intellectual

A pompous individual, most likely harboring *un-American* beliefs.

Intelligent Design

Creationism; or, a coherent counter-theory to the ramblings of a clearly troubled Charles Darwin.

---

[12] When speaking with dispatchers prior to shooting and killing Trayvon Martin on 26 February 2012, so-called neighborhood watchman George Zimmerman described Martin as "suspicious-looking," later clarifying that he "looks black" and is wearing a "grey hoodie."

Islamophobia

A *fear* and hatred of Islam and *Muslims* in no way attributable to the *global force for good*'s indiscriminate butchering of *bad guy Muslims*.

Legitimate Rape

A rape which results in no pregnancy due to a woman's ability to, you know, "shut that whole thing down."[13]

Long-Term Thinking

Too much of a hindrance to the short-term.

Luck

There is no such thing. One is born into privilege strictly on one's merits.

Making It

Achieving a recognizable level of material and social status. Becoming, in other words, a *celebrity*.

Mass Shooting

A ritualized act in which a lone gunman in possession of a high powered military assault rifle randomly targets individuals gathered in a public place (typically, a school or *shopping mall*). Mass shootings are to be briefly grieved, then forgotten.

Me

The most important brand in *the world*.

Megachurch

A place where the faithful flock to relish in both the word of *God* and his most important gift: the *free market*.[14]

---

[13] In 2012, the Republican candidate for Senate in Missouri, Todd Aikin, defended his staunchly anti-choice position by arguing that cases of rape resulting in pregnancy are "really rare." "If it's a legitimate rape," Aikin claimed, "the female body has ways to try to shut that whole thing down." John Eligon and Michael Schwirtz. "Senate Candidate Provokes Ire With 'Legitimate Rape' Comment." *New York Times*. (19 Aug 2012).

[14] As Jeff Sharlet writes of the melding of gospel and free market ideology common to megachurches: "They are building aisles and aisles in which everyone can find

National Collegiate Athletic Association – NCAA

A multi-billion dollar sports association offering unpaid internships for aspiring professional athletes.[15]

National Football League – NFL

America's most popular sport, luring large *American* audiences with regular gladiatorial shows each Fall featuring young men violently slamming their heads together until they irreparably damage their brains.

No Angel

An unarmed black teen shot dead by a *peace officer*.[16]

Patriarchy

An antiquated system of male dominance, which today endures solely in the troubled minds of hairy legged man-haters, deeply resentful that they have failed to lock down a man, take his name in marriage, and bear his offspring.

Philanthropy

Hush *money*. For as Balzac asserted, behind every great fortune there lies a great *crime*.

Porn

Virtual reality's wildly popular and increasingly hip rendering of "sex." Of

---

something, but behind it all a single corporate entity persists, and with it a [free market] ideology." Jeff Sharlet. *The Family: The Secret Fundamentalism at the Heart of American Power*. (New York: Harper Perennial, 2008): 313.

[15] Despite raking in billions in merchandise, ticket sales, and TV deals, the NCAA strictly prohibits athletes from receiving any compensation outside of school scholarships and small living stipends. Such a system, seeing coaches and administrators pulling down six and seven figure salaries off the revenues generated by the athletes, has, as the journalist Taylor Branch remarked, the "unmistakable whiff of the plantation." Taylor Branch. "The Shame of College Sports." *The Atlantic*. (Oct 2011).

[16] In an August 2014 *New York Times* profile of Michael Brown, the unarmed 18-year old black teen shot dead earlier that month by Ferguson, Missouri police, John Eligon referred to Brown as "no angel." John Eligon. "Michael Brown Spent Last Weeks Grappling With Problems and Promise." *New York Times*. (24 Aug 2014).

course, "sex" here being the commodification of women as disposable sex objects existing solely for the solitary gratification of men.[17]

Positive Thinking

The knowledge that one can change one's lot in life through the sheer *power* of optimism. So, rent rising? Think happy thoughts. Lost your job? Smile wider. Diagnosed with terminal cancer? Well, maybe if you weren't always so negative…[18]

Post-Racial America

November 4, 2008 – present.

Processed Food

The industrial assemblage of salt, sugar, and fat into various food-like substances constituting the *American* diet.[19]

Professional Sports

A bulwark of any strong *democracy*, providing an escape and sense of purpose to devoted fans, not to mention a safely productive outlet for one's time and energy.[20]

---

[17] The U.S. porn market is estimated at $13 billion annually (trumping the revenue from Hollywood movies), with the overwhelming majority of porn users being men. Thus, as Gail Dines notes of contemporary pornography: "In porn, sex is the vehicle by which men are rendered all powerful and women all powerless; and for a short time a man gets to see what life would look like if only women unquestionably consented to men's sexual demands." Gail Dines. *Pornland: How Porn Has Hijacked Our Sexuality*. (Boston: Beacon Press, 2010): 47, 63.

[18] On the perils of positive thinking and positive psychology, see: Barbara Ehrenreich. *Bright-Sided: How the Relentless Promotion of Positive Thinking Has Undermined America*. (New York: Metropolitan Books, 2009).

[19] On the industrialization of the American diet, see: Moss. *Salt, Sugar, Fat*.

[20] Of course, sports do provide a needed escape in a society where one is conditioned to believe any sort of political engagement is fruitless. As Noam Chomsky remarked on the general phenomenon: "When I'm driving, I sometimes turn on the radio and I find very often that what I'm listening to is a discussion of sports. These are telephone conversations. People call in and have long and intricate discussions, and it's plain that quite a high degree of thought and analysis is going into that. People know a tremendous amount. They know all sorts of complicated details and enter into far-reaching discussion about whether the coach made the right decision yesterday and so on. These are ordinary people, not professionals, who are applying

Public Transportation

A wholly *inefficient* and *un-American* form of transportation unnecessarily clogging city roads and inhibiting the free flow of personal cars.

Race-Baiter

One who refuses to accept that the U.S. is now a *post-racial society*, and instead seeks to sow discord by constantly bringing up the legacies of *American racism*.

Racism

Discrimination based on the color of one's skin. Racism officially ended in *America* following the election of Barack Obama to the presidency, which ushered forth the official beginning of a *post-racial America*.

Rape Culture

A culture both permitting and fostering a climate conducive to rape and sexual *violence*. Of course, rape culture cannot be said to be endemic to *American society* as a whole, as most rapes occurring in the U.S. aren't really even "legitimate" in nature.[21] (See *Legitimate Rape*.)

---

their intelligence and analytic skills in these areas and accumulating quite a lot of knowledge and, for all I know, understanding. On the other hand, when I hear people talk about, say, international affairs or domestic problems, it's at a level of superficiality that's beyond belief...I think that this concentration on such topics as sports makes a certain degree of sense. The way the system is set up, there is virtually nothing people can do anyway, without a degree of organization that's far beyond anything that exists now, to influence the real world. They might as well live in a fantasy world, and that's in fact what they do." Noam Chomsky. "What the World is Really Like: Who Knows It – and Why" in *The Chomsky Reader*. (1983). <http://www.chomsky.info/books/reader02.htm>

[21] As Robert Jensen explains what America's rape culture looks like: "more than half of college women interviewed in one study reported being victims of some level of sexual aggression. More disturbing, only 27 percent of women whose experience met the legal definition of rape labeled themselves as rape victims. And perhaps even more disturbing, 47 percent of the men who had committed rape said they expected to engage in a similar assault in the future, and 88 percent of men who reported having committed an assault that met the legal definition of rape were adamant that they had not committed rape. We live in a culture in which the sex-domination nexus is so tight that victim and victimizer alike often do not recognize the violence in acts that the society has deemed violent enough to be illegal. That's a rape culture." Robert Jensen. *Getting Off Porn: Pornography and the End of Masculinity*. (Boston: South End Press, 2007): 48-49.

Reality

A corrosive form of negativity and the greatest obstacle to *making it*. The impediments of reality are best overcome through *positive thinking*.

Reality TV

The filtering of *reality* through the medium of *television* in order to cleanse it of all its negatively pessimistic connotations.

Religious Fundamentalism

A strict adherence to opaque and primitively non-Christian (i.e., Islamic) religious beliefs and doctrines.

Religious Liberty

The *freedom* to openly discriminate against those homosexual heathens.[22]

Reverse Racism

The hiring of highly qualified persons of color over less qualified white men.[23]

Reverse Sexism

Any un-ironic musings on modern-day *patriarchy*.

---

[22] In 2014, the state legislatures in both Arizona and Mississippi passed "religious liberty" laws permitting businesses to discriminate against the LGBT community based on religious beliefs. In early 2015, Arkansas and Indiana both passed into law similarly constructed measures.

[23] As Mike King remarks, reverse racism is "a concept that is only intelligible when we have erased history, social structure and power. In an imagined nation that has no history, and a postmodern society that has no structural forces, everyone has 'identity politics' and everyone can position themselves as a victim. In this milieu, claims of 'reverse racism' in relation to affirmative action have been somewhat successful because the cultural and political terrain is now defined by a total absence of an analysis that looks at the legacies of white supremacy and their contemporary structures.

"It is on this ahistorical and astructural landscape that declining white wages and a cornucopia of scapegoats have produced this emerging racial formation of aggrieved whiteness – a politicized white identity politics. This stretches beyond pronouncements of a 'post-racial' society, to one where the language of discrimination, racism, and oppression is not erased, but politically inverted. What has been produced is a policial [*sic*] subject that is materially and historically absurd in-itself, yet nonethless [*sic*] a current historical agent-for-itself – the 'racialized white victim.'" Mike King. "The White Victim Charade on Parade: The Very Real Politics of Postmodern White Nationalism." *CounterPunch*. (17 March 2014).

Self-Interest

The only interest ever worth protecting.

Selfie

A photograph of the single most important person in *the world* (*Me*) taken by the single most important person in *the world* (*Me*).

Sexism

Discrimination based on one's sex. Of course, great strides have been made in *American society* to eliminate the lingering ills of sexism, with straight men, for one, no longer having to *fear* much in the way of unwarranted prejudice for simply being a member of the superior sex.

Sharia Law

The religious *law* of Islam. Sharia translates as Islamic *law*, meaning Sharia *law* translates as Islamic *law law*. Needless to say, such a redundant *law* is clearly a burgeoning threat to *Middle America*.[24]

Shopping Mall

A giant *happiness* emporium. Also, a frequent site of *mass shootings*.

Slut

A woman advocating for greater access to affordable birth control.[25]

Slut Shaming

The noble task embarked on by great men of conscience, who take it upon themselves to publicly remind irresponsible women that when it comes to *sexual assault*, sexual harassment, and *legitimate rape*, it's imperative that women come to accept *personal responsibility*.

---

[24] Faced with the clear and present danger of creeping Sharia, eight states – Alabama, Arizona, Kansas, Louisiana, North Carolina, Oklahoma, South Dakota, and Tennessee – have passed laws banning "Sharia law."

[25] In 2010, Rush Limbaugh called then-Georgetown law student Sandra Fluke a "slut" and a "prostitute" for testifying before Congress in favor of birth control being covered under health plans provided by religious institutions.

Smart Phone

A *NSA* individualized mobile tracking beacon.[26]

Social Media

A *branding* platform for brand *Me*.

Society

There is no such thing.[27]

Sport Utility Vehicle – SUV

A fully mobilized *gated community* for the on the go, *fear*-stricken *American* suburbanite.[28]

Stand Your Ground

A *law* allowing one to kill a young person of color without having to *fear* the hardships of incarceration.

Super Bowl

A pseudo-national holiday celebrating the two great *American* loves: *violence* and *consumption*.

Supporting the Troops

The national obligation to stand behind the troops by placing patriotic bumper stickers and magnetic flags on one's car.

---

[26] As Julia Angwin puts it, "our cell phones are the world's most effective tracking devices." Julia Angwin. *Dragnet Nation: A Quest for Privacy, Security, and Freedom in a World of Relentless Surveillance*. (New York: Times Books, 2014): 141.

[27] The words of British Prime Minister and neoliberal heroine Margaret Thatcher.

[28] As Stephen Graham notes, SUVs are "carefully designed and marketed to exploit and perpetuate fears of the Other, the ghetto, while at the same time providing reassurance and patriotic symbolism for 'homeland' suburbanites who find themselves experiencing a new kind of war, in which vague and unknowable threats might lurk everywhere and anywhere, threatening to strike at any time. Add to this, SUVs have been shaped to tap powerfully into American cultural tropes of rugged individualism, the frontier existence, and the mastery of nature through technology." Stephen Graham. *Cities Under Siege: The New Military Urbanism*. (New York: Verso, 2011): 315.

Sustainability

Polluting the environment and depleting natural resources. Sustainability is really for everyone – from *BP* to *Monsanto*.[29]

Technology

The savior of the human race. And failing that, maybe just the savior of all that really matters: *the exceptional nation*.[30]

Television

An escape masquerading as an experience, which functions to implant the images of a selective *reality* in one's mind necessary for sustaining optimum levels of *consumption*.[31]

Thug

A derogatory term useful for whites too civilized to use the N-word in the context of a *post-racial America*, yet still wanting to disparage a man of color.[32]

---

[29] Virtually every major corporation in the chemicals or resources extraction industry now produces glossy reports touting their purported "sustainability." Monsanto even refers to itself as "a sustainable agriculture company."

[30] "Given our disadvantage in numbers," U.S. Defense Secretary Harold Brown remarked in 1980, "our technology will save us." Quoted in: Franklin Spinney. "Why Is This Handbook Necessary?" in *The Pentagon Labyrinth: 10 Short Essays to Help You Through It.* (Washington D.C.: Center for Defense Information, 2011): 7.

[31] "By the age of 75," Aric Sigman reports, "most of us will have spent more than twelve-and-a-half years of 24-hour days doing nothing but watching pure television." All the more disturbing, given the brainwashing effect of television. As Sigman explains, "within 30 seconds of turning on the television, our brain becomes neurologically less able to make judgments about what we see and hear on the screen. Our brain treats incoming information uncritically. Our brain waves switch to predominantly alpha waves, indicating an unfocused, receptive lack of attention." Aric Sigman. *Remotely Controlled: How Television is Damaging Our Lives.* (London: Vermillion, 2005): 2, 93.

[32] In the wake of an emotional, trash talking post-game interview following the NFL's 2014 NFC championship game, critics came to label Seattle Seahawk Richard Sherman a "thug." But as Sherman later noted when asked to reflect back on the firestorm his interview created, particularly the use of "thug" directed at him: "The only reason it bothers me is because it seems like it's the accepted way of calling somebody the N-word nowadays. Because they know." Barry Petchesky. "Richard Sherman Explains What People Mean When They Call Him A 'Thug.'" Deadspin. (22 Jan 2014).

Traditional Marriage

The internment of one man and one woman in a loveless, lifetime bond for the twin purposes of property transaction and procreation.

United We Stand

A bumper sticker placed on the vehicles of patriotic *Americans* as a show of support for the *war* – whatever *war* it is we're fighting now.

Urban Renewal

Swapping *inner city residents* for hipsters.

Veteran

A prop to be dressed up and rolled out for parades, sporting events, and political rallies, then promptly relegated once more to the rewarding life of post-warrior abandonment. (See also, *Department of Veteran Affairs*, Chapter 1 and *Army of One*, Chapter 11.)

Video Games

Childhood skill development for the nation's future fleet of *drone* pilots.[33]

Violence

The preferred *American* method of communication.

Virtual Reality

The only truly tolerable *reality*. After all, virtual reality allows one to experience *reality* without actually having to experience it at all. All of which is thanks to man's best friend and last *hope*: *technology*.[34]

---

[33] As Stephen Graham notes, "The newest Predator control systems from the arms maker Raytheon deliberately use the 'same HOTAS [hands on stick and throttle] system' as a video game uses. Raytheon's UAV designer argues that there is 'no point in re-inventing the wheel. The current generation of pilots was raised on the [Sony] PlayStation, so we created an interface that they will immediately understand'. Added to this is the fact that many of the latest video games depict the very same armed UAVs as those by the US forces in assassination raids." Graham. *Cities Under Siege*, 215.

[34] "For Americans," Sheldon Wolin writes, "the greatest triumph of virtual reality is war, the great unexperienced reality...War is an action game, played in the living room, or a spectacle on a screen, but, in either case, not actually experienced. Ordinary life goes on uninterruptedly: work, recreation, professional sports, family

War on Christmas

A popular motif appearing annually from October through December on *Fox News*.[35]

White Privilege

The *freedom* to *stand your ground*.

---

vacations. After 9/11 terrorism becomes another virtual reality, experienced only through its re-created images, its destructiveness (= wonders) absorbed through the spectacle of the occasional and hapless terrorist put on public display." Wolin. *Democracy Inc.*, 13.

[35] In December 2014, Fox News' Bill O'Reilly declared victory in the "War on Christmas." "I won the War on Christmas!" O'Reilly crowed. "It's over, we won." Catherine Taibi. "Bill O'Reilly Declares Victory In 'War On Christmas' Once Again." *Huffington Post.* (18 Dec 2014).

Part 2:

Free-Enterprise

...the principle of really existing free market theory is: free markets are fine for you, but not for me.

- *Noam Chomsky, 1996*[1]

I've abandoned free-market principles to save the free-market system.

- *President George W. Bush, 2008*[2]

---

[1] Noam Chomsky. "Free Market Fantasies: Capitalism in the Real World." Address delivered at Harvard University. (13 April 1996).
<http://www.chomsky.info/talks/19960413.htm>
[2] Quoted in: Frank. *Pity the Billionaire*, 56.

7.   The American Free-Enterprise System

The whole world should adopt the American system. The American system can survive in America only if it becomes a world system.

-    *President Harry Truman, 1947*[1]

Arms Sales

A *government jobs* program (the lone acceptable *government jobs* program) working to deliver all the latest in U.S. defense industry hardware to all the international *good guys*.[2]

Asset Backed Securities

This is for the good people on *Wall Street*, and only the good people on *Wall Street*, to know.

Asset Price Inflation

See *Bubble*.

Austerity

The shrinking of *government* down to a size where it can be safely lured into the bathtub and drowned.[3]

Auto Bailout (2008)

The federally administered *neutering* of the *competitiveness* inhibiting United Auto Workers *union*.[4]

---

[1] Quoted in: Jan Nederveen Pieterse. *Globalization or Empire*. (New York: Routledge, 2004): 131.

[2] Foreign weapons sales by the U.S. totaled $66.3 billion in 2011, "or more than three-quarters of the global arms market." Thom Shanker. "U.S. Arms Sales Make Up Most of Global Market." *New York Times*. (26 Aug 2012).

[3] As the influential anti-tax crusader Grover Norquist once declared, "Our goal is to shrink government to the size where we can drown it in a bathtub."

[4] As Sheldon Wolin remarks on the particularly harsh terms of the federal auto bailout in regards to the UAW: "Under the terms of the bailout, the government –

Bank Bailout

The rescue of insolvent private banks with public funds; that is, the means through which *Wall Street* firms maintain their *profitability*.

Bank Stress Test

An examination of a private bank's balance sheet by *government* regulators working to assess when to administer the next infusion of public funds.

Bubble (Financial)

The artificial inflation of asset prices (i.e., financial instruments), which although appearing to many of the *smartest people in the room* as if they are to continue rising indefinitely, ultimately come to crash with the inevitable popping of the bubble.[5]

Business Cycle

Bubble recklessly inflated → *bubble* catastrophically pops → repeat.

Capitalism

An economic system based on the public financing of ruggedly individualistic private *corporations*. Or, the greatest, most *efficient* economic system ever created, which is irreversible and not to be questioned; unless, of course, one hates *freedom*.

---

or as it was said 'the taxpayers' – lent GM $50 billion. The union, which had also been forced to buy a 55 percent share in Chrysler, now had to draw upon its pension fund to purchase 17.5 percent of the shares of GM. The union further agreed to a wage freeze and pledged not to strike. In return it received representation on the corporation's governing board but with the proviso that its shares would not bring voting rights. The workers' union also agreed to accept the loss of several thousand jobs of its members." Wolin. *Democracy Inc.*, xvi.

[5] The continual inflation of financial bubbles has become endemic to the global capitalist system and its imperative for ever expanding growth. As Fred Magdoff and John Bellamy Foster note: "In the twenty years between the 1987 stock market crash and the Great Financial Crisis indications of serious difficulties included: the massive savings and loan bank (thrift) debacle of the late 1980s; the 1992 bursting of the Japanese asset/price bubble; the 1994 Mexican financial crisis; the Asian financial crisis of the late 1990s; the collapse of the Long Term Capital Management in the same period; and the 2000 dot-com crash." Fred Magdoff and John Bellamy Foster. "Stagnation and Financialization: The Nature of the Contradiction." *Monthly Review* Vol. 66 No. 1. (May 2014): 8.

Capitalist

Someone who embraces the fact that working people are but a means to the end of realizing ever-greater *profits*.

Carbon Trading

The harnessing of *market forces* in the fight against *climate change*. Establishing a set price on carbon and then enabling it to be traded and sold, carbon trading is championed as an innovative approach to reducing greenhouse gas emissions within the parameters of a *free market* system. Of course, whether such a scheme actually reduces carbon emissions, or merely encourages further emissions, is irrelevant.[6] The important thing is that carbon trading opens a whole new avenue for profiteering. And that ought to be enough to get even a *climate skeptic* to embrace *climate change*.

Chicago School

Economic school of thought made famous by University of Chicago economist Milton Friedman. Adhering to a monetarist doctrine, the Chicago School champions *free market principles* (*privatization*, *deregulation*, and social spending cuts) as being inseparable from economic *development* and *democracy*. Of course, if there happens to be an excess of *democracy* conspiring to shackle the market, *democracy* will most certainly have to be shoved aside in order to set the market free. In other words, *democracy* will need to be destroyed before it is saved.[7]

Collateralized Debt Obligation

This is for the fine folks on *Wall Street*, and only the fine folks on *Wall Street*, to know.

---

[6] Carbon trading hasn't been show to actually reduce carbon emission. As the blog Climate & Capitalism remarks on the European Union's Emissions Trading Scheme: "it doesn't reduce greenhouse gases, subsidizes the worst polluters, and locks in the fossil fuel economy." See "Carbon trading has failed: scrap the ETS now." Climate & Capitalism. <http://climateandcapitalism.com/2013/02/08/carbon-trading-has-failed-scrap-the-ets-now/>

[7] Having first failed to break through the Keynesian consensus in the U.S., it took the bloody 1973 coup in Chile before the Chicago School adherents – Pinochet's "Chicago Boys" – could finally come to implement their radical reforms in practice. See Naomi Klein. *The Shock Doctrine: The Rise of Disaster Capitalism*. (New York: Picador, 2007): 91-120.

Colonialism

A particularly crude form of Western exploitation and wealth extraction no longer in vogue in the enlightened age of *structural adjustment*.

Commodity

A disposable item. (See *Associates*, *Partners*, and *Team Members*, Chapter 8.)

Competitiveness

The ability of employers to slash wages and benefits, while also skirting environmental and safety standards, in order to keep pace with foreign competitors.[8]

Creative Destruction

The dynamic ability of the *capitalist* system to create wealth and *opportunity* out of the ashes of destruction. For example, bomb a country's infrastructure into dust and *voila*, you've got a creatively profitable *opportunity* for *American small businesses*.[9]

---

[8] The prioritizing of "competitiveness" over all else has become so hegemonic that even union leaders have come to embrace the mantra. As UAW President Bob King explained the beleaguered union's philosophy in early 2014, "Our philosophy is, we want to work in partnership with companies to succeed…With every company that we work with, we're concerned about competitiveness." Mike Elk. "After Historic UAW Defeat at Tennessee Volkswagen Plant, Theories Abound." *In These Times* Working Blog. (15 Feb 2014).

[9] As Maximilian Forte notes, securing business deals for American corporations topped the agenda of U.S. diplomats soon after the 2011 U.S. intervention in Libya. Forte writes, "just as the Libyan government began to crumble after six months of continuous NATO bombings of its troops and civilian brigades, the U.S. immediately rushed in to secure business opportunities, especially the kinds from which they had been blocked before. As battles raged in Sirte in late September 2011, U.S. Ambassador Gene Cretz returned to Tripoli…and he immediately 'participated in a State Department conference call with about 150 American companies hoping to do business with Libya.' Which kinds of business opportunities most occupied Cretz? Infrastructure….Cretz added: 'If we can get American companies here on a fairly big scale, which we will try to do everything we can to do that, then this will redound to improve the situation in the United States with respect to our own jobs.'" Maximillian Forte. *Slouching Towards Sirte: NATO's War on Libya and Africa*. (Montreal: Baraka Books, 2012): 61.

Credit

The only means through which to afford all the grandeurs of the *American way of life*.

Credit Card

A payment card allowing heavily indebted *Americans* to service outstanding credit card payments.

Credit Default Swap

This is for the caring souls on *Wall Street*, and only the caring souls on *Wall Street*, to know.

Creditors

See *Wall Street*.

Crisis (Economic)

An *opportunity* to remove any built-up accumulations of *democracy*.[10]

Crony Capitalism

A corrupt form of *capitalism*, where one's success is based <u>solely</u> on one's relationship to those in positions of *power*. As opposed to actually existing *capitalism*, where one's success is based <u>largely</u> on one's relationship to those in positions of *power*.

Davos

An annual celebration for *the world*'s elite organized by the World Economic Forum and held in the exclusive Switzerland resort town of Davos. An *opportunity*, then, for all *the world's smartest people in the room* to climb aboard their private jets and head for the plush confines of Davos in order to address grave issues like *climate change*.[11]

---

[10] As Naomi Klein notes on the use of economic crises: "if an economic crisis hits and is severe enough – a currency meltdown, a market crash, a major recession – it blows everything else out of the water, and leaders are liberated to do whatever is necessary (or said to be necessary) in the name of responding to a national emergency. Crises are, in a way, democracy-free zones – gaps in politics as usual when the need for consent and consensus do not seem to apply." Klein. *The Shock Doctrine*, 175.

[11] Upwards of 500 private jets ferried the world's elite to Davos in late January 2015, where climate change was near the top of the agenda. Eric Holthaus. "Hundreds of

Debt

An indispensable social construction, necessary in order to ensure a free people are kept in a permanent state of servitude to the high priests of finance.

Debtors

See *American People*, Chapter 1.

Deindustrialization

The shifting of domestic industrial capacity to more profitable locations overseas. The social problems associated with the *American* process of deindustrialization (namely, the creation of a surplus population of redundant *labor*) were ultimately resolved with the implementation of *mass incarceration* accompanying the escalation of the *war on drugs*.

Department of Commerce

Department of *Competitiveness*.

Department of Treasury

Department tasked with ensuring the *profitability* of *Wall Street* firms, primarily through the execution of *bank bailouts*.

Derivatives

This is for *God*'s chosen people on *Wall Street*, and only *God*'s chosen people on *Wall Street*, to know.

Developed Economy

A matured *capitalist* economy found in the *West*. Serving as a beacon of *hope* for those stuck in the *undeveloped world*, such an economy is marked by stagnated *growth*, widening *economic inequality*, and generalized social *crisis*.

Development

Colonialism → *imperialism* → *humanitarian interventionism* → *structural adjustment* → *poverty* → social *crisis*.

Private Jets Delivered People to Davos. Also, It's Climate Change Day at Davos." *Slate*. (23 Jan 2015).

Dollar, the

The global reserve currency and financial pillar of the *American Empire*. Any threat from a *next Hitler* to dislodge the dollar from its perch as *the world*'s reserve currency cannot to be tolerated.[12]

Dow Jones Industrial Average

The lone acceptable harbinger of national economic health.

Economic Inequality

The gap between the rich and the poor. The larger the better, considering it can only help to encourage all the slothful *free riders* to *work* just a little harder.[13]

---

[12] As the world's reserve currency, the dollar is used internationally to purchase oil. This in turn requires (a) that oil consuming states possess large dollar reserves in order to purchase oil, and (b) that oil producing states flush with petrodollars recycle them back through either American financial institutions, or the U.S. defense industry through the purchase of American arms. Christopher Doran argues that it was the Iraqi threat posed to the dollar – namely, an initiative to start selling its oil in euros – that led the U.S. to target Iraq in 2003. Similarly, Horace Campbell argues that the preservation of both the euro and dollar as dominant world currencies contributed to NATO's 2011 intervention into Libya. See Christopher Doran. *Making the World Safe For Capitalism: How Iraq Threatened The US Economic Empire And Had To Be Destroyed.* (London: Pluto Press, 2012); Horace Campbell. *Global NATO and the Catastrophic Failure in Libya: Lessons for Africa in the Forging of African Unity.* (New York: Monthly Review Press, 2013).

[13] In their path breaking 2009 book, *The Spirit Level*, British researchers Richard Wilkinson and Kate Pickett tirelessly document the link between economic inequality and a host of societal maladies, from poor physical and mental health, to substandard educational performance and increased levels of violence. What's perhaps most striking about their findings is that economic inequality not only comes to hurt the economically disadvantaged, but nearly all elements of a society. As Wilkinson and Pickett explain in regards to link between economic equality and physical health: "It's worth repeating that health disparities are not simply a contrast between the ill-health of the poor and the better health of everybody else. Instead, they run right across society so that even the reasonably well-off have shorter lives than the very rich. Likewise, the benefits of greater equality spread right across society, improving health for everyone – not just those at the bottom. In other words, at almost any level of income, it's better to live in a more equal place." Richard Wilkinson and Kate Pickett. *The Spirit Level: Why Greater Equality Makes Societies Stronger.* (New York: Bloomsbury Press, 2010): 84.

Economic Innovation

Creating machines to replace irksome rights- and wage-demanding employees.

Economic Recovery

The recuperation in value of elite portfolios in the wake of a bursting *bubble*.

Economics

An academic disciple used to provide a guise of scientific legitimacy to political decisions aimed at ensuring the poor are kept in their proper place.

Efficient

Any individualized *consumption*. For example, on a street of 12 private houses, the presence of 12 privately owned lawn mowers, 12 privately owned washing machines, and 24-plus privately owned cars. *There is no alternative* to the efficient ways of *capitalism*.

Emerging Markets

The *Third World* markets to which *job-creators* turn in pursuit of cheap *labor* and increased *profits*.[14]

Federal Reserve (The Fed)

The U.S. Central Bank. More precisely, a privately owned bank holding no real reserves.[15] The Fed, as it is often called, is tasked with overseeing the

---

[14] As Lenin remarked: "As long as capitalism remains what it is, surplus capital…will be used for the purpose of increasing those profits by exporting capital abroad to the backward countries…the necessity for exporting capital arises from the fact that in a few countries capitalism has become 'over-ripe' and…capital cannot find 'profitable' investment." V.I. Lenin. *Imperialism: The Highest Stage of Capitalism.* (New York: International Publishers, 1988): 63.

[15] As Ellen Brown explains: "Although the Federal Reserve is commonly called the 'Fed,' confusing it with the U.S. government, it is actually a private corporation. It is so private that its stock is not even traded on the stock exchange. The government doesn't own it. You and I can't own it. It is owned by a consortium of private banks, the biggest of which are Citibank and J.P. Morgan Chase Company…As for keeping 'reserves,' Wright Patman decided to see for himself…Patman wrote: 'The cash, in truth, does not exist and never has existed. What we call 'cash reserves' are simply bookkeeping credits entered upon the ledgers of the Federal Reserve Banks and then passed along through the banking system…*It* [the Fed] *doesn't get money, it creates it.*

U.S. monetary system, ensuring while doing so that the nation's financial institutions – and only the nation's financial institutions – are fully protected from *market forces*.[16]

Financial Collapse of 2007-08

A global *recession* brought on by an *entitlement culture* and a few *bad apples* on *Wall Street*.

Financial Fraud

See *Financial Innovation*.

Financial Innovation

All the latest swindles, cons, and Ponzi schemes developed by the *smartest people in the room*.

Financialization

A reoccurring elite wet dream, wherein financial elites make *money* off nothing but more *money*, completely detached from the *real economy* and the unpleasantness thus entailed; specifically, having to compensate costly workers.

Free-Enterprise System

Capitalism, yet free from any of *capitalism*'s more negative connotations.[17]

When the Federal Reserve writes a check for a government bond *it does exactly what any bank does, it creates money, it created money purely and simply by writing a check…The Federal Reserve, in short, is a total money-making machine.*" Ellen H. Brown. *The Web of Debt: The Shocking Truth About Our Money System – The Slight of Hand That Has Trapped Us in Debt And How We Can Break Free.* (Baton Rouge: Third Millennium Press, 2007): 24-25.

[16] As William Greider puts it, for the Fed, "rescuing a major financial institution [is] in the public interest, but government bailouts for other kinds of private enterprises [is] wrong." William Greider. *Secrets of the Temple: How the Federal Reserve Runs the Country.* (Simon and Schuster Inc.: New York, 1987): 192.

[17] In 2010, the Texas Board of Education passed a deeply reactionary social studies curriculum, part of which saw the replacement of "capitalism" with "free-enterprise system" throughout course textbooks. As one Board of Education member stated, "Let's face it, capitalism does have a negative connotation. You know, 'capitalist pig!'" James C. McKinley Jr. "Texas Conservatives Win Curriculum Change." *New York Times.* (12 March 2010).

Free Market

God's greatest gift to mankind.

Free Market Principles

The notion that being *God*'s gift, the *free market* is not to be altered, tampered with, or questioned in any way. After all, as the *free market* prophet Milton Friedman noted, "underlying most arguments against the free market is a lack of belief in freedom itself."[18]

Free Trade

Ensuring *investor rights* are protected across borders.

Free Trade Agreement

The ceding of national *sovereignty* to the proprietors of *small businesses* – foreign and domestic.

Full Employment

The point at which everyone both able and willing to *work* is employed. In no way ideal, due to the burdens the accompanying rise in worker wages would come to place on *competitiveness*.

Globalization

Imperialism rebranded for a post-*history* epoch. (See *End of History*, Chapter 1).

Great Recession

The prolonged *recession* following the *financial collapse of 2007-08*. Really not much of a big deal, outside of a bunch of self-entitled whiners. (See *Occupy*, Chapter 1.)

Gross National Product – GDP

The lone acceptable measure of national success, with success being a 3% or more annual increase in GDP – forever and ever.

Growth

That which must be maintained and expanded on a finite plant in perpetuity.

---

[18] Milton Friedman. *Capitalism and Democracy*. (Chicago: University of Chicago Press, 2002): 7.

High Frequency Trading

This is for the philanthropic minded on *Wall Street*, and only the philanthropic minded on *Wall Street*, to know.

Imperialism

Creating a world after one's own image – by the barrel of a gun…or the lens of a *drone*.[19] Either way, one would always be wise to use *globalization* in lieu of imperialism when seeking to gain status within *respectable circles*.

Inefficient

The sharing of goods and resources.

Inflation

That which must always be guarded against, considering it has the potential to substantially reduce the value of the *debt debtors* will ultimately come to repay to financial institutions. Swelling the ranks of the *unemployed* is thus always a much more preferable policy objective to inflation.

Intellectual Property Rights

The rights ensuring there are no *free riders* when it comes to things like expanding creativity or sharing life-saving medical drugs.

International Monetary Fund – IMF

An international (wink-wink) financial institution, which works to ensnare *Third World* countries in a web of *debt* and dependency – er, that is, ensnare them in *freedom* and *prosperity*.[20] (See also, *Structural Adjustment*, *Washington Consensus*, and *World Bank*.)

Investment Climate

The degree to which *labor* has been beaten into submission in any particular locale.

---

[19] "In a word, it [the bourgeoisie] creates a world after its own image." Karl Marx and Frederick Engels. *The Communist Manifesto*. (New York: International Publishers, 2009): 13.

[20] John Perkins has labeled the IMF, of which the U.S. maintains a controlling influence over, a "colonizing tool." John Perkins. *The Secret History of the American Empire: The Truth About Economic Hit Men, Jackals, and How to Change the World*. (New York: Plume, 2007): 167

Investor Rights

Corporate Rights.

Invisible Hand

The hand clenched tightly around the throat of *labor*.

Keynesianism

Economic doctrine advanced by the British economist John Maynard Keynes, which asserts that *crises* can be avoided through *government deficit* spending aimed at stimulating aggregate demand. Of course, in our brave new *world* lacking in alternatives, Keynesianism is now officially null and void.

Labor Theory of Value

A rather sacrilegious and downright insulting theory, suggesting that the source of wealth is not educated and sophisticated *job-creators*, but rather the horde of dim-witted workers.

Laissez-Faire

The purified, natural state of an economy, existing completely free from any *government meddling*.[21]

Main Street

Wall Street's unwitting co-signer.

Market-Based Reforms

The unleashing of greater *market forces*.

Market Failure

Why, *God*'s gift is infallible.

---

[21] "There is nothing natural about laissez-faire," Karl Polanyi wrote; "free markets could never have come into being merely by allowing things to take their course... laissez-faire itself was enforced by the state[...]The road to the free market was opened and kept open by an enormous increase in continuous, centrally organized and controlled [state] intervention." Karl Polanyi. *The Great Transformation: The Political and Economic Origins of Our Time*. (Boston: Beacon Press, 2001): 145-146.

Market Forces

The impersonal forces apolitically brought to negatively bear on the lives of everyone not of *the 1%*.

Marketing

The absolutely vital process of conning *consumers* into purchasing items they neither need nor want.[22]

Mass Unemployment

A necessary – useful, even – means through which runaway worker wages are reined in and uppity workers disciplined.

Middle-Out/Middle-Class Economics

Doctrine championed by *American liberals* as being a *radical* break from *trickle-down economics*. By targeting polices toward benefiting the *middle class*, Middle-Out Economic adherents assert the benefits will then come to, well, maybe sort of trickle down to the poor?

Military-Industrial Complex

The largest private defense contractors and their favored elements within the *Pentagon*, who collectively come together to forge a suitably profitable national defense strategy.[23]

---

[22] As John Bellamy Foster writes, "the United States in 2005 spent over $1 trillion, or around 9 percent of GDP, on various forms of marketing." John Bellamy Foster. "The Ecology of Marxian Political Economy." *Monthly Review* Vol. 63 No. 4. (Sept 2011).

[23] With such interests guiding U.S. "defense" policy, it is no wonder American leaders (regardless of party) are so quick to call for military interventions in crises around the world. As Franklin Spinney helps explain of the imperative of war in sustaining the military-industrial complex: "Continuing small wars (or the threat thereof) are essential for the corporate component of the MICC [the military-industrial-congressional-complex]; these companies have no alternative means to survive. Although they now make up a very substantial part of America's much diminished industrial base, they cannot convert to civilian production. Many of them tried and failed; they simply do not have the marketing, managing, engineering and manufacturing skills to compete successfully in global commercial markets." Spinney. "Why Is This Handbook Necessary?" 4.

Military Keynesianism

The limited application of Keynesian principles to worthy *government* programs, as deemed worthy by the *military-industrial complex*.

Miracle Economy

A foreign economy which has managed to thoroughly discipline *labor*.

Modernization

Stripping workers of all previously won gains (in wages, hours, seniority, workplace safety, etc.).

Sentence Example: To overcome stagnating rates of *growth*, the economy must see continued modernization.

Monetarism

Economic doctrine which claims *crises* can be mitigated by regulating the supply of *money* in circulation, rather than through wasteful *freedom*-impairing *government* spending, á la all *Keynesianism* measures applied outside the realm of *defense spending*.

Monetary Measures

Adjusting interest rates in order to contain *inflation* and ration *money* to the advantage of large *corporations* and the most affluent.

Monopoly

The ultimate goal of every *competitiveness* loving *job-creator*.

Moral Hazard

A situation in which one person or firm determines the level of risk to assume, while *others* are left to bear the costs. Public expenditures on those lacking in *personal responsibility* are a moral hazard. Public expenditures on overleveraged *Wall Street* firms are a moral imperative.

Mortgage-Backed Securities

This is for prophets on *Wall Street*, and only the prophets on *Wall Street*, to know.

Nationalization

That which must never be spoken.

Natural Rate of Unemployment

A rate of unemployment deemed necessary to keep the twin economic threats of *inflation* and *labor* in check.

Negative Externality

An economic term connoting a spillover effect wherein a third party is negatively affected by a transaction, but is not compensated. A more pleasant way of recognizing the fact that you and your neighbors dying from that coal dust blowing over the neighborhood from the rundown storage site down by the docks aren't going to be getting anything other than a premature death from that lucrative coal trade.

Neoliberalism

Hegemonic economic doctrine advocating a return to *free market principles* as the only alternative. (See *There Is No Alternative*.)

Newly Industrialized Economies

The collection of upstart nations posing a potential threat to *American* business interests. Newly industrialized economies are thus to be kept under the tightest of surveillance.[24]

North American Free Trade Agreement – NAFTA

The 1994 *free trade agreement* signed by the U.S., *Canada*, and *Mexico*. The trade

---

[24] We know from the NSA documents leaked by Edward Snowden that the U.S. has targeted commercial interests in newly industrialized economies, including Brazil's state oil company Petrobras, and the Chinese telecommunications company Huawei. In fact, as the *New York Times* reported, the NSA's spying on Huawei in particular was undertaken in part to expand the NSA's reach of commercial targets by exploiting "Huawei's technology so that when the company sold equipment to other countries — including both allies and nations that avoid buying American products — the N.S.A. could roam through their computer and telephone networks to conduct surveillance and, if ordered by the president, offensive cyberoperations." David Sanger and Nicole Perlroth. "N.S.A. Breached Chinese Servers Seen as Security Threat." *New York Times*. (22 March 2014).

pact has unequivocally demonstrated that nothing works quite like *free trade* in cleansing an economy from any glut of good *jobs*.[25]

Oil

A highly valuable global *commodity* owned wholly by the U.S. and exchangeable in both blood and *American dollars*. (See *Carter Doctrine*, Chapter 9.)

Open Markets

Foreign markets *American small businesses* are able to freely exploit without first requiring the assistance of the *U.S. military*.

Peace Dividend

The availability of more public funds occurring due to a reduction in *defense spending* resulting from the end of the *Cold War (old)*. The peace dividend was obviously a dire threat to the health of the *American* economy and was therefore revoked in 2001, soon after that year's *new Pearl Harbor*.

Peak Oil

The idea that at a certain point world *oil* production will reach its maximum, after which time it will enter into a terminal decline. Of course, the pessimists and *fear* mongers championing the notion of peak oil have been proven wrong by the recent *revolution* of drilling techniques allowing for the extraction of shale *oil* for ever and ever.[26] (See *Hydraulic Fracking*, Chapter 1.)

---

[25] The Economic Policy Institute reported that by 2010, "682,900 good U.S. jobs" had been eliminated due to NAFTA. Moreover, in Mexico, much the same as the U.S., wages have flat lined since NAFTA came into effect. As Noam Chomsky quipped on the trade deal: "NAFTA is a remarkable success: it's the first trade agreement in history that's succeeded in harming the populations of all three countries involved. That's quite an achievement." Robert E. Scott. "NAFTA's Legacy: Growing U.S. Trade Deficits Cost 682,900 Jobs." Economic Policy Institute. (17 Dec 2013); Noam Chomsky. *Rogue States: The Rule of Law in World Affairs*. (Cambridge, MA: South End Press, 2000): 99.

[26] As Edward Morse, the Global Head of Commodities Research at Citi Bank, writes in praise of the fracking boom, what he deems to be "a good thing for the world": "Forget peak oil production; given a combination of efficiency gains, environmental concerns, and substitution by natural gas, what is foreseeable is peak oil demand." Edward Morse. "Welcome to the Revolution: Why Shale Is the Next Shale." *Foreign Affairs* Vol. 93 No. 3 (May/June 2014): 3.

Pollution

But a meager price to pay for the splendors of endless *growth*.

Private Property

A sacred shrine to the private *liberty* embedded within the *free-enterprise* system, which is to be kept off and never trespassed upon.

Private Sector

The economic sphere comprised of the nation's *small businesses*. Also, the only sector of the economy that creates *jobs* and thus must be referenced in every *jobs* related speech and proposal. Granting too much deference here is simply not possible.

Privatization

The solution to everything. Really. (See Chapter 3 Reforming Education.)

Productivity

An increase in worker output; necessary so that *job-creators* can *downsize* and increase their *profitability*.[27]

Profitability

The ability of *job-creators* to squeeze greater *productivity* out of their dwindling *associates*.

Profits

That which makes *the world* go round.

Progress

The realization of economic *growth*.

Public Sector

The economic sphere enriching the parasitic, fat cat *bureaucrat*. (Although is there any other kind of *bureaucrat*?) The public realm, furthermore, is not a

---

[27] "To be a productive worker is therefore not a piece of luck, but a misfortune." Karl Marx. *Capital Vol. 1*. (New York: Penguin, 1992): 644.

source of job creation. Hence, one must refrain from any mention in job related speeches or proposals.

Quantitative Easing – QE

A *monetary measure* in which the *Fed* endeavors to increase the *money* supply and lower interest rates through the mass purchase of securities. Put more simply, re-inflating the *bubble*. (See also, *Business Cycle*.)

Real Economy

The sector of the economy where real products are made and real services delivered. The real economy is for the benighted commoners just too daft to partake in the sophisticated craft found on *Wall Street*.

Recession

A time for *shared sacrifice*.

Reserve Army of Labor

An army of unemployed workers wielded by *job-creators* in their long quest to contain the scourge of rising wages and vanquish once and for all the *tyranny* of *direct democracy* in the workplace.

Road to Serfdom

The road traveled once the *state* takes it upon itself to do anything more than nothing in the economic realm.[28]

Securities and Exchange Commission – SEC

Federal agency tasked with ensuring *Wall Street* penthouses and their occupants remain safe, secure, and utterly undisturbed.[29]

---

[28] "Road to Serfdom" being the title of the 1944 book written by neoliberal economist F.A. Hayek. Despite the insistence from Hayek's modern day adherents that any state intervention automatically sends one on the path to serfdom, Hayek himself saw at least a limited role for the state. As Hayek wrote, "In no system that could be rationally defended would the state just do nothing…the prevention of fraud and deception (including exploitation of ignorance), provides a great and by no means yet fully accomplished object of legislative activity." F.A. Hayek. *The Road to Serfdom: Text and Documents: The Definitive Edition*. (London: The University of Chicago Press, 2007): 88.

[29] During March 2014 remarks coming as part of his retirement party, SEC trial lawyer James Kidney observed that the SEC has become "an agency that polices the

Service Economy

The fun, fast-paced, flexible economy of the future, promising exciting employment opportunities in multiple dead-end, low-wage fields.

Shorting

A financial term describing the practice where one sells a borrowed security one doesn't actually own in the *hope* that the price will be driven down, at which point the security can be rebought and returned to the owner with the price difference kept as *profit*.

Investment tip: Short the *American Dream* and the *Middle Class*.

Smartest People in the Room

Biggest assholes in the room.

Social Mobility

The former ability to move up the socioeconomic ladder. All such movement has ground to a halt over the past 30 years, as too many *Americans* in the preceding generation appear to have achieved textbook success in the *pursuit of happiness*.

Sound Economics

Tax relief for the rich, *austerity* for the *undeserving poor*, and fat *government* contracts for the defense establishment.

Speculation

Soundly investing in the *profitability* of human misery.[30]

---

broken windows on the street level and rarely goes to the penthouse floors." "On the rare occasions when enforcement does go to the penthouse," Kidney continued, "good manners are paramount. Tough enforcement, risky enforcement, is subject to extensive negotiation and weakening." Kidney went on to chastise his superiors, who he claimed "were more focused on getting high-paying jobs after their government service than on bringing difficult cases." Robert Schmidt. "SEC Goldman Lawyer Says Agency Too Timid on Wall Street Misdeeds." *Bloomberg.* (7 April 2014).

[30] The global spike in food prices and the accompanying riots seen in 2008, for instance, are widely seen to have been the result of commodity speculation in

Stagnation

A prolonged flat lining of economic *growth* to be overcome by greater *financialization* and a further disciplining of *labor*.[31]

Stock Market

An elite-run gaming casino.

Structural Adjustment

The siphoning of wealth from the developing *world* via the imposition of an *IMF* imposed *austerity* regime attached to an *IMF* loan. The price, in other words, of *independence*.[32]

Structural Unemployment

Unemployment occurring due to long-term economic trends; for instance, the coming of age of a workforce inculcated within an *entitlement culture*.

---

agricultural futures markets, which were deregulated in 2000 after intense lobbying from banks. See Frederick Kaufman. "How Goldman Sachs Created the Food Crisis." *Foreign Policy.* (27 April 2011).

[31] Greater financialization does not, in fact, help to resolve stagnation. As John Bellamy Foster and Robert McChesney write, "rather than overcoming the stagnation problem, this renewed financialization will only serve at best to put off the problem, while piling on further contradictions, setting the stage for even bigger shocks in the future." John Bellamy Foster and Robert McChesney. *The Endless Crisis: How Monopoly-Finance Capital Produces Stagnation and Upheaval from the USA to China.* (New York: Monthly Review Press, 2012): 30.

In terms of the disciplining of labor, the impacts on the U.S. working class have been particularly severe. As Fred Magdoff and John Bellamy Foster note: "The effects of the Great Recession and the Great Stagnation have thus only served to worsen the conditions associated with the loss of worker power under the prolonged attack on labor. There are a number of important trends occurring simultaneously in this respect – (1) the decline of employment, (2) erosion of health associated with job loss, (3) wage stagnation, (4) growth of the working poor, (5) increased exploitation of labor on the job, and (6) the drop in the labor share of income." Fred Magdoff and John Bellamy Foster. "The Plight of U.S. Workers." *Monthly Review* Vol. 65 No. 8. (Jan 2014): 7.

[32] In April 2014, the pro-Western Ukrainian Prime Minister Arseny Yatseniuk deemed a deeply unpopular IMF aid package to his country, requiring the doubling of gas prices and the slashing of wages and pensions, to be "the price of independence." Natalia Zinets, Richard Balmforth and Paul Ingrassia. "Ukraine PM says will stick to austerity despite Moscow pressure." Reuters. (5 April 2014).

Systemic Risk

An innocuous byproduct of *financialization*.

There Is No Alternative – TINA

The necessarily internalized belief that there is no alternative to *capitalism* generally, and neoliberal *capitalism* in particular.

Too-Big-To-Fail

The most profitable business model ever devised.

Trickle-Down Economics

Economic doctrine that asserts giving tax breaks to those at the top of the income hierarchy will ultimately come to benefit those below, as the largesse given to the elite will eventually come to trickle down. And if not, no matter, as it's probably only a matter of time before each of us (okay, just *Me*) comes to join the moneyed elite anyway.[33]

Troubled Asset Relief Program – TARP

This is for the intelligent and good looking people on *Wall Street*, and only the intelligent and good looking people on *Wall Street*, to know.

Undeveloped Economy

An economy not fully privatized and not yet fully penetrated by Western *multinational corporations*.

Undeveloped World

The collection of nations patiently awaiting *development* from *American corporations*, or at least *liberation* from the *global force for good*.

---

[33] Consider that one survey, for example, found a remarkable 40% of Americans believe they are either already in the top 1% of income earners or will be there "soon." Another survey found a more measured outlook, but even then 31% of Americans were still found saying it "was 'very' (10 percent) or 'fairly' (21 percent) likely that they would 'ever be rich.'" See Michael J. Graetz and Ian Shapiro. *Death by a Thousand Cuts: The Fight Over Taxing Inherited Wealth*. (Princeton: Princeton University Press, 2005): 119; Hacker and Pierson. *Winner-Take-All Politics*, 153.

U.S. Military

The entity tasked with ensuring the full faith and *credit* of the *American dollar* since the day in 1972, when the U.S. went off the gold standard, *Washington* having preferred from there forth to support the *dollar* with a fixed amount of force rather than a fixed amount of gold.

Wall Street

The nation's *power* capital and place of toil for those, in the words of *Goldman Sachs* CEO Lloyd Blankfein, "doing God's work."[34]

War

The lifeblood of the *American* economy. As President George W. Bush noted, "The best way to revitalize the economy is war. The United States has grown stronger with war. All the economic growth of the United States has been encouraged by the various wars."[35]

Washington Consensus

The set of policy conditions promoted by the *IMF* and *World Bank*; specifically, that the *undeveloped world* ought to relinquish its national wealth to the *West* in exchange for various forms of Western imposed human misery.

World Bank

A world bank (wink-wink) tasked with strengthening U.S. corporate interests abroad and bolstering the leverage of the indispensable nation in international affairs.[36]

---

[34] Matt Phillips. "Goldman Sachs' Blankfein on Banking: 'Doing God's Work.'" *The Wall Street Journal* Market Beat Blog. (9 Nov 2009).

[35] Attributed to Bush by Argentine President Nester Kirchner. *South of the Border.* Dir. Oliver Stone. (2009).

[36] John Perkins, a self-proclaimed former economic hit man (EHM) working on behalf of American corporate interests, explains how the World Bank really functions. As Perkins writes: "We [EHM] channeled funds from the Bank and its sister organizations into schemes that appeared to serve the poor while primarily benefitting a few wealthy people. Under the most common of these, we would identify a developing country that possessed resources our corporations coveted (such as oil), arrange a huge loan for that country, and then direct most of the money to our own engineering and construction companies – and a few collaborators in the developing country. Infrastructure projects, such as power plants, airports, and

World Social Forum

An annual meeting held by global *civil society* groups. The World Social Forum bills itself as an alternative to the World Economic Forum, claiming that a better *world* is possible. Of course, a better *world* is not possible, as there exists no alternative to that promoted each year in *Davos*. (See *There Is No Alternative*.)

World Trade Organization – WTO

International body working, via *free trade*, to stuff the private coffers of Western *multinational corporations* with the public wealth of lesser nations.

---

industrial parks, sprang up; however, they seldom helped the poor, who were not connected to electrical grids, never used airports, and lacked the skills required for employment in industrial parks. At some point we EHMs returned to the indebted country and demanded our pound of flesh: cheap oil, votes on critical United Nations issues, or troops to support ours someplace in the world, like Iraq." Perkins. *The Secret History of the American Empire*. 2-3.

8.　Corporations and Their Associates

You work three jobs?...Uniquely American, isn't it? I mean, that is fantastic that you're doing that.

- *President George W. Bush, speaking to a single mother of three, 2005*[1]

Amazon

The Frederick Taylor ("corporations are people, my friend")[2] of the ecommerce age.[3]

American Federation of Labor-Congress of Industrial Workers – AFL-CIO

The largest *organized labor* federation in the United States, existing to spinelessly deposit member dues into the *campaign* coffers of anti-*union*, pro-business *Democrats*.

Associate

A low-wage worker.

---

[1] *The Wit and Anti-Wisdom of George W. Bush: A Hysterical Historical Timeline.* (Naperville, Ill.: Sourcebooks, Inc., 2006): 162.

[2] The words of 2012 Republican presidential nominee Mitt Romney.

[3] Simon Head details Amazon's dystopian labor management as follows: "Amazon's system of employee monitoring is the most oppressive I have ever come across and combines state-of-the-art surveillance technology with the system of 'functional foreman,' introduced by [Frederick] Taylor in the workshops of the Pennsylvania machine-tool industry in the 1890s. In a fine piece of investigative reporting for the London Financial Times, economics correspondent Sarah O'Connor describes how, at Amazon's center at Rugeley, England, Amazon tags its employees with personal sat-nav (satellite navigation) computers that tell them the route they must travel to shelve consignments of goods, but also set target times for their warehouse journeys and then measure whether targets are met.

"All this information is available to management in real time, and if an employee is behind schedule she will receive a text message pointing this out and telling her to reach her targets or suffer the consequences." Simon Head. "Worse than Wal-Mart: Amazon's sick brutality and secret history of ruthlessly intimidating workers." *Salon.* (23 Feb 2014).

AT&T

A *government* informant.[4]

Bank of America

A compulsive liar.[5]

Blue-Collar

A line of *work* where one is physically ground down to dust in lieu of *retirement*.

Boeing

A thriving extortionist.[6]

Bourgeoisie

An outdated term for those today known as *job-creators*.

British Petroleum – BP

An innovative conservationist championing a bold plan to increase the extraction of hydrocarbons as a means of achieving environmental "restoration."[7]

---

[4] As the *Washington Post* reported in August 2013, "The National Security Agency is paying hundreds of millions of dollars a year to U.S. companies for clandestine access to their communications networks, filtering vast traffic flows for foreign targets in a process that also sweeps in large volumes of American telephone calls, e-mails and instant messages." According to the *Post*, AT&T "charges $325 to activate surveillance of an account and also a daily rate of $5 or $10, depending on the information gathered. For providing the numbers that have accessed cell towers, meanwhile, AT&T charged $75 per tower." Craig Timberg and Barton Gellman. "NSA paying U.S. companies for access to communications networks." *Washington Post*. (29 Aug 2013).

[5] In sworn statements submitted as part of a 2013 civil lawsuit against Bank of America, six former bank employees and one contractor asserted that "Bank of America's mortgage servicing unit systematically lied to homeowners, fraudulently denied loan modifications, and paid their staff bonuses for deliberately pushing people into foreclosure." As former loan-level representative Simone Gordon claimed in her affidavit: "we were told to lie to customers." David Dayen. "Bank of America whistle-blower's bombshell: 'We were told to lie.'" *Salon*. (18 June 2013).

[6] In 2013, Washington State gave Boeing an $8.7 billion tax break, the largest in U.S. history, after Boeing threatened to move production of its 777X jet out of state. Pat Garofalo. "Boeing's Corporate Tax Blackmail." *US News*. (13 Nov 2013).

[7] On its website, on the very same page no less, BP touts its efforts to restore the Gulf of Mexico to an environmental state not seen since prior to the Deepwater

Capital

That which conjures the *labor* chocking *invisible hand*.

Capital-Labor Accord

An informal post-*Good War* pact in which business submitted to rising wages and greater unionization in exchange for *labor*'s help in ensuring continued corporate *profitability*. The accord fell apart during the *stagnation* of the 1970s, but remains alive and well in the minds of *American labor* leaders, who so adorably *hope* "to persuade business leaders to work in partnership" once again.[8]

Card Check

An expedited means through which employees can brazenly mock *democracy* and hasten the rise of *tyranny*.[9]

Chief Executive Officer – CEO

Someone who is, on average, 331 to 774 (or so) times more talented than any *associate* or *team member*.[10]

Clopening

A treasured perk of working *flexible hours*, wherein a retail *associate* gets to experience the adrenaline rush of closing late one night and opening mere hours later the very next morning.[11]

Horizon rupture, while also crowing over a planned $4 billion investment in further drilling in the Gulf. See <http://www.bp.com/en/global/corporate/gulf-of-mexico-restoration.html>

[8] The words of former SEIU President Andy Stern. Andy Stern. *A Country That Works: Getting America Back on Track*. (New York: Free Press, 2006): 37.

[9] An alternative to traditional National Labor Relations Board sanctioned secret ballot elections (which are fraught with numerous employer friendly power imbalances), card check allows for employees to sign simple authorization cards in an effort to join a union. And then once 50% or more employees sign such cards, an employer becomes required to recognize the union.

[10] As a 2014 AFL-CIO report noted: "In 2013 the CEO to worker pay ratio was 331:1 and the CEO to minimum wage worker pay ratio was 774:1." "Executive Paywatch: High-Paid CEOs and the Low-Wage Economy." AFL-CIO. (2014). <http://www.aflcio.org/Corporate-Watch/Paywatch-2014>

[11] As the *New York Times* notes, in the U.S. no "national or state labor law or regulation governs the intervals between shifts." Thus the increasing prevalence of clopening cases like Ramsey Montanez, who "struggles to stay alert on the mornings that he returns to his security guard station at 7 a.m., after wrapping up a 16-hour

Collective Bargaining

The means through which workers collectively negotiate over pay and *work* conditions with their employer. In the *private sector*, a threat to *competitiveness*; in the *public sector*, a threat to *fiscal responsibility*.

Corporate Merger

A corporate marriage enabling each smitten spouse to finally cut ties with all redundant, inheritance-draining offspring (or *associates*).

Corporate Social Responsibility

Lipstick on a pig.

Corporations

People. (See *Citizens United*, Chapter 1.)

Department of Labor

Federal department tasked with ensuring *American* workers never come to hinder the *competitiveness* of *American small businesses*.

Downsize

Fire *associates*.

Efficiencies

Gains in *profits* achieved through aggressive *downsizing*.

Entrepreneur

An endeavoring *job-creator*.

Entrepreneurial Spirit

The inner huckster to be found within every aspiring *entrepreneur*.

Executive Compensation

The just reward for *wage theft*, *pension* slashing, *downsizing*, and *outsourcing*.

---

double shift at 11 p.m. the night before." Steven Greenhouse. "In Service Sector, No Rest for the Working." *New York Times*. (21 Feb 2015).

Factory Farm

A place where *enhanced interrogation techniques* are used on livestock in an effort to extract actionable *profits*.

Family Farm/Farmers

Colossal agribusiness conglomerates.

Flexible Hours

Hours allowing an employee the fun and *freedom* of never being able to know one's *work* schedule week in and week out. In addition, the hours allowing an employer the fun and *freedom* of keeping employee hours below those requiring the provision of costly benefits.

Fulfillment Center Associate

Amazon warehouse worker.

General Electric – GE

Just a deserving bloke on the dole.[12]

General Motors (Old)

A serial killer.[13]

---

[12] From 2008 to 2012, GE paid no federal taxes, while receiving $12.7 billion in tax subsidies. GE accrues such benefits from something called the "active financing exception." As Citizens for Tax Justice explains, "This tax break allows financial companies (GE has a major financial branch) to pay no taxes on foreign (or ostensibly foreign) lending and leasing, apparently while deducting the interest expenses of engaging in such activities from their U.S. taxable income." Robert S. McIntyre, Matthew Gardner, and Richard Phillips. "The Sorry State of Corporate Taxes: What Fortune 500 Firms Pay (or Don't Pay) in the USA And What they Pay Abroad – 2008 to 2012." Citizens for Tax Justice. (Feb 2014): 15.

[13] After discovering a defect in vehicle ignition switches in 2001, which caused affected vehicles to unexpectedly shut off and air bags to fail, GM set upon a cover-up, viewing a fix to the affected vehicles, estimated in 2005 to be between $2 and $5 per vehicle, as too cost prohibitive. It is estimated that up to 300 people may have been killed in GM vehicles in which air bags failed to deploy. Shannon Jones. "Evidence mounts of cover-up of deaths related to GM ignition defect." World Socialist Web Site. (17 March 2014).

General Motors (New)

No relation to the serial killer with the same name.[14]

Golden Parachute

Proof that even failure pays better atop the corporate ladder.

Goldman Sachs

Place of *work* for both future and former *U.S. Treasury* officials.[15]

Google

The person who knows the most about you.[16]

Guest Worker

A guest who is expected to do all the taxing chores, express thanks for having the *opportunity* to do all those chores, and then promptly leave before wearing out her welcome.

Halliburton

A well-connected individual benefiting from a topnotch accounting department that can always be counted on to round up.[17]

---

[14] In April 2014, GM sought to freeze litigation related to the company's faulty ignition switches, arguing that the "new" GM (created after the company's 2009 bankruptcy restructuring) cannot be held financially liable for actions that occurred under the "old" GM.

[15] Both Clinton-era Secretary of Treasury Robert Robin and Bush-era Secretary of Treasury Hank Paulson came to the Treasury after an extended career at Goldman. In fact, a 2010 CBS News investigation on the revolving door between Goldman and government found "at least four dozen former employees, lobbyists or advisers at the highest reaches of power both in Washington and around the world," fifteen of whom spent time at Treasury. CBS Investigates. "Goldman Sachs' Revolving Door." CBS News. (8 April 2010).

[16] As Julia Angwin, author of *Dragnet Nation*, remarked, "Google has everything. They have every map you've ever looked at. They have every, you know, search. They have your email content." Amy Goodman. "Dragnet Nation: Do Google, Facebook Know More Private Info Than NSA and Soviet-Era Secret Police?" *Democracy Now!* (2 April 2014).

[17] Since 1995, according to the Project on Government Oversight, Halliburton (Vice President Dick Cheney's former company) has racked up $997.5 million in

Hedge Fund

A high-end gambling ring with a most agreeable tax rate.[18]

Hidden Unemployment

A state of unemployment not counted in official data because one has stopped actively looking for *work*. In other words, the long favored means of "lowering" the official unemployment rate.

Human Capital

An employee as viewed through a corporate prism.

Human Resources – HR

The personnel department within a firm meant to dissuade any latent employee interest in forming or joining a *labor union*. Why, after all, would one ever want to discuss workplace issues with a complete outsider, like some *union thug*, when one has the ability to have an open and honest dialogue with corporate's HR rep?

Independent Contractor

An employee unworthy of *health care* or other benefits.[19]

Intern

The ideal worker: cheap, lacking in rights, and eager to please.[20]

---

misconduct related to government contracts. "Federal Contractor Misconduct Database: Halliburton." POGO.

[18] Hedge fund managers, earning an income classified as a "capital gain," typically pay a tax rate of only 15%.

[19] The package delivery company FedEx is particularly notorious for its liberal use of the "independent contractor" label. In fact, in 2014, the Ninth Circuit Court of Appeals ruled the company had for years intentionally mislabeled 2,300 of its ground delivery drivers. By doing so, "FedEx avoided health care, workers compensation, paid sick leave and vacation, retirement and more. FedEx made drivers pay for their uniquely FedEx branded trucks, FedEx branded uniforms, and FedEx scanners. Plus, fuel, insurance, tires, oil changes, maintenance, even workers compensation coverage." Robert Wood. "FedEx Misclassified Drivers As Independent Contractors, Rules Ninth Circuit." *Forbes.* (27 Aug 2014).

[20] Up to 50% of interns in the U.S. are either paid below the minimum wage or not paid at all, helping American businesses save as much as $2 billion annually. Moreover, given the increasing importance of landing an internship for one's career advancement, the prevalence of unpaid positions (as well as those internships which

Job-Creator

An *American* messiah benevolently creating *jobs* out of a sheer moral imperative.

JPMorgan Chase

A compulsive gambler.[21]

Labor

A constant strain on *profits*, and thus the one thing all *job-creators* would much prefer to do without.

Labor Discipline

Instilling sufficient levels of *fear* throughout the workforce over things like getting fired; necessary so that *job-creators* will come to have the docile, productive, and low-cost *labor force* needed for maximizing *profits*.

Labor Flexibility

The *freedom job-creators* need to *outsource* and *downsize* at will in order to enhance *profitability*.

Labor Force

The total combination of *associates* and their unemployed counterparts who

---

actually charge a fee) serves to effectively price out all but the most affluent – or those at least willing to take on staggering debt – from the most desired white-collar jobs. As Ross Perlin explains, "many internships, especially the small but influential sliver of unpaid and glamorous ones, are the preserve of the upper-middle class and the super-rich. These internships provide the already privileged with a significant head start that pays professional and financial dividends over time, as boosters never tire of repeating. The rich get richer or stay rich, in other words, thanks in part to prized internships, while the poor get poorer because they're barred from the world of white-collar work, where high salaries are increasingly concentrated." Rose Perlin. *Intern Nation: How to Earn Nothing and Learn Little in the Brave New Economy.* (New York: Verso, 2012): 162.

[21] In May 2012, JPMorgan revealed it had lost $2 billion on a hedging bet went awry. Despite this, coming in addition to record fines in 2013, JPMorgan CEO Jaime Dimon received $18.5 million worth of restricted stock as a 2013 bonus – amounting to a 74% pay hike from 2012. Chris Isidore. "JPMorgan's Dimon gets 74% pay hike despite legal woes." CNN Money. (24 Jan 2014).

have remarkably not yet succumbed to utter despair and still actively seek employment.

Labor Movement

According to the bumper sticker, the folks that brought you the weekend. In other words, an entirely antiquated movement, seeing that we've got the weekend now.[22]

Labor Strike

A total inconvenience to *consumers*.[23]

Lean Production

A production system seeking to achieve constant improvements in *productivity* by working to unlock employee knowledge in order to eliminate all "waste" (i.e., employees) in the production process.[24]

Leisure Time

The time awarded to those who have worked sufficiently hard – and only those who have worked sufficiently hard. That is, *the 1%*.[25]

---

[22] Although meant as a show of solidarity with organized labor, the "unions brought you the weekend" meme actually plays into the reactionary attack that unions are somehow incompatible with the modern economy.

[23] The labor strike as consumer inconvenience is a dominating feature of the mainstream media coverage of labor. As Christopher Martin argues, because the media assumes a consumer orientation, "organized labor is almost always portrayed as an impediment for the consumer, either by adding costs to goods, making poor-quality products, or (via strikes or inefficiencies attributed to labor) delaying the instant gratification of consumer goods and services." Christopher Martin. *Framed! Labor and the Corporate Media.* (Ithaca: ILR Press, 2004): 53.

[24] As Kim Moody writes: "Waste, in this definition not only includes excessive parts, mistakes, or buffers, but excessive labor. 'Waste' is discovered by removing resources without reducing production. Can a job previously done by five workers be done in the same or even less time by four? When one phase of production is tightened up those that follow in sequence must also be re-calibrated." Kim Moody. *US Labor in Trouble and Transition: The Failure of Reform From Above, The Promise of Revival From Below.* (New York: Verso, 2007): 29-30.

[25] The U.S. ranks among one of the most overworked societies among developed nations, with the U.S. appearing near the bottom of OECD nations in terms of leisure time available for the average worker. "Work-Life Balance." OECD Better Life Index. <http://www.oecdbetterlifeindex.org/topics/work-life-balance/>

Lockheed Martin

An inept airplane designer with a lucrative passion for designing wholly inoperable replicas of actual combat ready fighter jets. (See *F-35 Joint Strike Fighter*, Chapter 11.)

Low-Wage Job

The future of employment, with the future being now for most.[26]

Micro-Entrepreneurs

The *associates* of the *on-demand work* industry.

Microsoft

Another *government* informant.[27]

Minimum Wage

A wage allowing one to simultaneously enjoy the thrills of both *work* and *poverty*.[28]

Monsanto

Our new infallible Creator.

---

[26] In 2009, the U.S. had the highest percentage of workers working in low-wage jobs of any OECD member country. Bonnie Kavoussi. "U.S. Has Highest Share Working In Low-Wage Jobs, OECD Says." *Huffington Post*. (16 April 2012).

[27] As *The Guardian* reported, "Microsoft helped the NSA to circumvent its encryption to address concerns that the agency would be unable to intercept web chats on the new Outlook.com portal." Moreover, the report continues, Microsoft "worked with the FBI this year [2013] to allow the NSA easier access via Prism to its cloud storage service SkyDrive, which now has more than 250 million users worldwide; Microsoft also worked with the FBI's Data Intercept Unit to 'understand' potential issues with a feature in Outlook.com that allows users to create email aliases. In July last year [2012], nine months after Microsoft bought Skype, the NSA boasted that a new capability had tripled the amount of Skype video calls being collected through Prism." Glenn Greenwald, Ewen MacAskill, Laura Poitras, Spencer Ackerman and Dominic Rushe. "Microsoft handed the NSA access to encrypted messages." *The Guardian*. (11 July 2013).

[28] Under the current federal minimum wage of $7.25/hour, even a fulltime worker (40 hours per week for 52 weeks a year) would earn a wage under the federal poverty line for a family of two or more.

Multinational Corporations

Cosmopolitan people.

National Labor Relations Board – NLRB

National regulatory body tasked with overseeing the crushing of *organized labor* by *small businesses*.

Nonprofit Organization

Intern purgatory.[29]

Occupational Safety and Health Administration – OSHA

Federal agency tasked with ensuring that the *competitiveness* of *small businesses* is never obstructed by arduous inspections of workplace safety.[30]

On-Demand Work

A type of flexible employment offering workers the *freedom* to only do the *jobs* they like, when they like…for the substandard pay they have no choice but to accept.[31]

---

[29] As one nonprofit worker explained to the journalist Ross Perlin, "The way the field works now…is you can go on any job site – Idealist, Charity Jobs, Relief Web – and you'll see there's never entry-level positions advertised, because there are no entry-level positions. They're getting [often unpaid] interns to do them." Perlin. *Intern Nation*, 121.

[30] OHSA's ability to effectively monitor workplace safety is severely hamstrung by its meager funding. As journalist Mike Elk notes, "There are only 2,218 inspectors at both the federal and state level who inspect workplace safety to cover 7.5 million workplaces employing more than 130 million workers. That's one inspector for every 57,984 workers. At this rate, OSHA can inspect a workplace on average once every 129 years and state OSHA inspectors could inspect one every 67 years." Safety, it appears, is just not compatible with the imperative of employers to remain "competitive." Mike Elk. "Why Is Earth Day So Much More Popular Than Workers Memorial Day?" *In These Times* Working Blog. (29 April 2011).

[31] Take, for example, the on-demand work car service Uber. Uber is widely celebrated across the political spectrum (former Obama White House official David Plouffe heads the company's policy and strategy team) as a pioneering company offering its on-demand workers unprecedented flexibility at respectable compensation levels. Indeed, according to an Uber funded study, its drivers average $19 an hour. But by not classifying their drivers as "employees," Uber is able to not only outsource costs like health insurance, auto insurance, and general vehicle maintenance onto drivers, it is also able to dictate fare rates to workers not protected

Optimization

Getting ever fewer workers to generate ever greater *profits*.

Organized Labor

Obsolete and irrelevant.

Outsourcing

The firing of *associates* in order to increase *competitiveness* by employing cheaper *labor* found abroad.

Partner

A low-wage worker.

Pension

In the *public sector*, the thing that must be cut in the name of *fiscal responsibility*. In the *private sector*, the thing that must be cut in the name of *profitability*.

Permatemp

Someone who is forever temporarily employed.

Prison Labor

The next best thing to an unpaid *intern*.[32]

Proletariat

Outdated term for those who are today known as *associates*, *partners*, and *team members*.

---

by most labor laws. As one Uber driver described how this shakes out for the average driver, "basically you're in a service industry job making $8 to $10 per hour and getting clobbered on the depreciation of your vehicle." Lauren Webber and Rachel Emma Silverman. "On-Demand Workers: 'We Are Not Robots.'" *Wall Street Journal.* (28 Jan 2015): B7.

[32] The wages of the roughly 1 million incarcerated workers in the U.S. are nothing short of scandalous. In New Jersey, for instance, as Chris Hedges reports, "a prisoner made $1.20 for eight hours of work – yes, eight hours of work – in 1980 and today makes $1.30 for a day's labor. Prisoners earn, on average, $28 a month. Those incarcerated in for-profit prisons earn as little as 17 cents an hour." Hedges. "The Prison State of America." *Truthdig.*

Race to the Bottom

The lowering of taxes, gutting of regulation, and slashing of wages in an attempt to lure businesses in the *hope* of creating more *jobs*. Known within the corporate board room as the *race to the top*.

Rationalization

Maintaining current *productivity* levels while still *downsizing*.

Replacement Worker

A worker willing to betray his *God*, his country, his family, and his class just to help a *job-creator* through some tough times.[33]

Retirement

That which is no longer in the cards for *the 99%*.[34]

Right-to-Work

The right to *work*…for less – less *union* interference and less superfluous pay. Not to be confused with the right to employment, which doesn't exist.

Sanctity of Contract

The notion that parties entering into a contract must honor their obligation under that contract. Sanctity of contract cannot be tampered with when it comes to executive bonuses, because, well, sanctity of contract. When it comes to worker *pensions*, however, sanctity of contract must obviously yield to the imperative of *fiscal responsibility*.

Scab

See *Replacement Worker*.

---

[33] Scab: "a traitor to his God, his country, his family and his class." (Jack London's "The Scab.")

[34] As Jessica Bruder reports: "Nearly 7.7 million Americans sixty-five and older were still employed last year [2013], up 60 percent from a decade earlier. And while 71 percent of Americans aged fifty to sixty-five envision retirement as 'a time of leisure,' according to a recent AARP survey, only 17 percent anticipate that they won't work at all in their later years." Jessica Bruder. "The End of Retirement: When you can't afford to stop working." *Harper's*. (Aug 2014): 29.

Skilled Labor

White, formally educated workers.

Small Businesses

All NASDAQ and Dow Jones listed *corporations*.

Solidarity

An affront to *American values*.

Team Member

A low-wage worker.

Temp Agency

An agency working to round up desperate, easily exploited individuals and deliver them to large *corporations* for the purpose of ongoing contingent *labor* under the false pretense that such *work* will eventually lead to something fulltime.

Temporary Employment

A permanent state of provisional employment, providing employers a cost effective solution to the burdens associated with actually having to hire benefit demanding full-time employees.[35]

Troublemaker

Someone bent on destroying the "fast, fun, and friendly" workplace environment by seeking to bring in a *money*-hungry *union*.[36]

---

[35] "Every year," a ProPublica investigation notes, "a tenth of all U.S. workers finds a job at a staffing agency," with many temps having "worked for the same company for as long as 11 years, never getting hired on full-time." The obvious allure of hiring "temporary" employees being that it "insulates the host companies from workers' compensation claims, unemployment taxes, union drives and the duty to ensure that their workers are citizens or legal immigrants. In turn, the temps suffer high injury rates, according to federal officials and academic studies, and many of them endure hours of unpaid waiting and face fees that depress their pay below minimum wage." Michael Grabell. "The Expendables: How the Temps Who Power Corporate Giants Are Getting Crushed." ProPublica. (27 June 2013); Michael Grabell. "U.S. Lags Behind World in Temp Worker Protections." ProPublica. (24 Feb 2014).
[36] An internal anti-union video produced by the retailer Target, and leaked in early 2014, stressed to Target "team members" that a union is just another business

Underemployment

A state in which a worker holds a part-time *job*, yet seeks full-time employment; or, when a worker has a full-time *job*, albeit one in which she is overly qualified.[37] Strictly speaking, underemployment is the clearly deserved fate of those lacking a proper *work* ethic.

Unemployed

A sign of deep personal failure; namely, that one is a lazy waste of a human being.

Union

A coalition of workers organizing through the *job* in an attempt to subvert *democracy* and ruin corporate *competitiveness*.

Union Thug

A *law* abiding, dues paying member of a *labor union*.

Unskilled Labor

Non-formally educated workers of color.

Verizon

Just another snitch on the *government*'s payroll.[38]

Wage Labor

Legalized prostitution.

---

looking for their money, which also threatens Target's "fast, fun, and friendly" work environment. Ucilia Wang. "Why Target's anti-union video is no joke." *The Guardian.* (31 March 2014).

[37] Over 20 million Americans, as of early 2014, were either unemployed or underemployed, with recent college graduates especially prone to underemployment. A 2013 poll, for instance, found that more than 40% of recent college graduates considered themselves underemployed. Patricia Reaney. "Youth Employment: Recent U.S. College Graduates Disillusioned, Underemployed Says Poll." Reuters. (30 April 2013).

[38] Like AT&T, Verizon charges the government fees to access its customers' personal data. Timberg and Gellman. "NSA paying U.S. companies for access to communications networks." *Washington Post.*

Wage Restraint

Keeping the insatiable *greed* of *labor* at bay.

Wage Theft

The deliberate withholding of wages from any particularly languid employees as a motivational ploy, intended as a means to inspire just a little more effort on the job.[39]

Wal-Mart

A philanthropist thanklessly providing a much-needed supplemental source of income for the nation's *Medicaid* enrollees and *food stamp* recipients.[40]

White-Collar

A line of *work* where it pays dividends (literally) to break the *law*.

Work

A mostly empty drudgery all must endure in order to fulfil the *patriotic* duty of buying every latest expendable product one has been programed by *marketing* to want.

Working Class

All those who earn their living without deriving their wealth from controlling the *labor* of others. A non-existent class in the U.S., given that the nation is a class devoid *society*.

---

[39] A 2009 study of 4,387 low-wage workers in Chicago, Los Angeles and New York City "found that the typical worker had lost $51 the previous week through wage violations, out of average weekly earnings of $339. That translates into a 15 percent loss in pay." A total of 68% of those surveyed reported some sort of wage theft in the previous work week. Steven Greenhouse. "Low-Wage Workers Are Often Cheated, Study Says." *New York Times.* (1 Sept 2009).

[40] Wal-Mart employees – or "associates" – comprise the largest single group of food stamp recipients and Medicaid enrollees in state after state. In Ohio, for example, "Wal-Mart had more employees or household members on food stamps (14,684) or Medicaid (14,056) than any other company in the state" as of 2013. In Missouri, 1,555 Wal-Mart employees were found to be enrolled in the state's Medicaid program in 2009, with 3,040 additional employee dependents enrolled. For a state by state breakdown, see: <http://www.goodjobsfirst.org/corporate-subsidy-watch/hidden-taxpayer-costs>

Part 3:
America's World

...the United States of America will remain the greatest force for freedom that the world has ever known.

- *President Barak Obama, 2014*[1]

US the biggest threat to world peace in 2013 – poll.

- *RT headline*[2]

---

[1] Barack Obama. "Remarks by the President at MacDill Air Force Base." Whitehouse.gov. (17 Sept 2014).
[2] "US the biggest threat to world peace in 2013 – poll." RT.com. (2 Jan 2014).

9. American Diplomacy

Peace is no longer serious; only war is serious.

- *C. Wright Mills*, The Power Elite[1]

A Change in the Government

A *good guy coup d'état.*[2]

A Receding Tide of War

A fleeting interlude occurring between the last and next *war*, for a receding tide always gives way to a rising one.[3]

A War of No More Than Five Months

A *war* that begins in earnest five months after the initial invasion of *American* forces.[4]

A War that Pays for Itself

A $3 trillion *war*; or, more precisely, the *Iraq war*.[5]

---

[1] C. Wright Mills. *The Power Elite*, 206.

[2] The day after the April 2002 U.S.-supported coup d'état against the government of Hugo Chavez in Venezuela, White House spokesperson Ari Fleischer claimed what had occurred in Venezuela was "a change in the government," brought about, Fleisher stated, after "the Venezuelan people expressed their right to peaceful protest." Press Briefing by Ari Fleischer. (12 April 2002).

[3] Over the course of 2011 and early 2012, President Obama repeatedly remarked in reference to the Iraq war that, "the tide of war is receding." Yet, by September 2014, Obama was announcing the redeployment of American troops to Iraq, along with a campaign of U.S. aerial bombardment.

[4] When asked during a 2002 interview how long a war with Iraq might last, then-Secretary of Defense Donald Rumsfeld responded, "I can't tell you if the use of force in Iraq today will last five days, five weeks or five months, but it won't last any longer than that." "Rumsfeld: No World War III in Iraq." CNN. (15 Nov 2002).

[5] As Paul Wolfowitz stated prior to the Iraq war, "We're dealing with a country [Iraq] that can really finance its own reconstruction, and relatively soon." Yet as Joseph Stiglitz and Linda Bilmes calculate, the total monetary cost of the Iraq war for American taxpayers is liable to be near $3 trillion, an estimate which they acknowledge is conservative. See Joseph Stiglitz and Linda Bilmes. *The Three Trillion*

Acts of Genocide

A *genocide* no *global force for good* can be bothered with.[6]

Administration

The *regime* holding *power* in *Washington*.

Adventurism

The inherently reckless deployment of military force abroad by any of *the world's dispensable nations*.

Afghanistan War

A *mistake*.

Aggression

The use of military force or threat of force against *American* interests.

Ambassador of the United States

A duly rewarded presidential campaign contributor.[7]

America's Pacific Century

The 21st century – *China* be damned.[8] (See also, *Pivot to Asia*.)

Dollar War: The True Costs of the Iraq Conflict. (New York: W. W. Norton & Company, 2008).

[6] During the 1994 genocide in Rwanda, the U.S. State Department refused to classify the killings as a genocide, instead claiming that there were "acts of genocide" occurring in Rwanda. The fear in the U.S. government was that the use of the word "genocide" unqualified would generate a public demand for some sort of U.S. intervention against the pro-Western Rwandan Patriotic Front. See Edward Herman and David Peterson. *Enduring Lies: The Rwandan Genocide in the Propaganda System, 20 Years Later*. (Evergreen Park, IL: The Real News Books, 2014).

[7] As of early 2014, 23 serving ambassadors appointed by President Obama were also campaign bundlers (those who raise at least $500,000 for a political candidate). Campaign bundler and Obama's pick to become the U.S. ambassador to Norway, George Tsunis, was forced to concede in a congressional hearing that he couldn't actually identify the country's major political parties. Meanwhile, Obama's pick for ambassador to Argentina, Obama bundler Noah Bryson Mametat, admitted in a 2014 hearing that he had never actually been to Argentina. Max Fisher. "This very telling map shows which U.S. ambassadors were campaign bundlers." *Washington Post*. (10 Feb 2014).

[8] Originally coined by then-Secretary of State Hillary Clinton in 2011, America's Pacific Century, as Clinton asserted, is to be achieved through "harnessing Asia's

Ancient History

Any *mistakes*, no matter how recent, committed by the *exceptional nation*.[9]

Another Cuba

The primal *fear* underlying U.S. policy throughout *America's backyard* since 1959.

Apartheid

The one word never to be uttered in the same sentence as the *lone democracy in the Middle East*; unless one is a raving *anti-Semite*.

Arab Spring

Both a threat to *stability* (*Bahrain*, *Egypt*, Tunisia) and a most useful *pretext* for *protecting civilians* (*Libya*, *Syria*).

Aspirations

The desire of all foreign people to one day be *liberated* by the *U.S. military*.

Atrocities

The use of *counterinsurgency* and *pacification* tactics by *rogue states*.

Bad Actor

A foreign head of *state* both capable and willing to contest the will of *Washington*.

---

growth and dynamism." Hillary Clinton. "America's Pacific Century." *Foreign Policy*. (11 Oct 2011).

[9] In early 2014, Secretary of State John Kerry, speaking of Russia, asserted on both *Meet the Press* and *Face the Nation*, "You just don't in the 21st century behave in 19th century fashion by invading another country on completely trumped up pretexts." Of course, this was the same John Kerry who 10 years prior voted to authorize the use of force against Iraq on "completely trumped up pretexts." So was Kerry questioned on his wanton hypocrisy by the respectable Sunday talk show hosts? Was it noted that Kerry was perhaps not exactly a paradigm of moral authority when it comes to admonishing the violation of a nation's sovereignty? Of course not. After all, by 2014, the Iraq war was "ancient history." And so Kerry was free to play the voice of supreme moral authority. And anyone daring to say anything to the contrary was assuredly "stuck in history" – ancient history, to be precise.

Bad Guys

Whoever it is that is currently being bombed and shot at by the U.S. and its *partners*.

Barbarians

Those committing *war crimes* without the use of *cruise missiles* and *drones*.

Barbarism

The use of *asymmetric warfare* against a *full spectrum dominance* aspiring *mistake*- and *isolated incident*-prone *global force for good*.

Beheading

A barbaric act necessitating that *something must be done*…unless committed by *good guys*. In that case, more of a local matter of *justice*.[10]

Bellicose Rhetoric

The provocative claims made by *rogue state hardliners* that any *U.S. military* attack will face resistance.

Blowback

The bountiful harvest of *American foreign policy*.

Boots on the Ground

The deployment of U.S. ground troops to a *rogue state* as part of a future *mistake*.

Carter Doctrine

The formal declaration, first articulated by President Jimmy Carter, that all

---

[10] While the beheadings of two American journalists by Islamic State fighters in the late summer of 2014 were used to gin up support for an American bombing campaign within Iraq and Syria, American ally and coalition member Saudi Arabia was simultaneously beheading prisoners at a brisk pace to the conspicuous silence of American political and media figures. Indeed, in the month of August 2014 alone, Saudi Arabia beheaded 19 individuals. "Rights group says surge in Saudi beheadings." Al Jazeera English. (21 Aug 2014).

Middle Eastern *oil* is the sovereign property of the U.S. *government*.[11] (See also, *Oil*, Chapter 7 and *Middle East*, Chapter 10.)

Central Intelligence Agency – CIA

The *president*'s own private army, responsible for conducting *targeted killings* and implementing *regime change* abroad with the funds and friends it accrues through securing the safe passage of *illegal drugs* into *American inter cities*.[12]

Chaos

The inability of U.S. forces to establish *stability* in a foreign land.

Chemical Weapons

A particularly heinous and savage munition no napalm-spraying, *white phosphorous*-shelling, or *depleted uranium*-discharging nation could ever stand to see deployed.

CIA Asset

A *CIA* adopted and sponsored drug-running, peasant-murdering, and/or dissident-torturing goon.

Civil Unrest (Bad)

Hooliganism engineered by a *bad actor* in a land hungry for *democratization*.

Civil Unrest (Good)

A political awakening in a hitherto *authoritarian* land.

---

[11] As President Carter stated in his 1980 State of the Union Address: "An attempt by any outside force [excluding the U.S., of course] to gain control of the Persian Gulf region [i.e., its oil] will be regarded as an assault on the vital interests of the United States of America, and such an assault will be repelled by any means necessary, including military force." Jimmy Carter. "State of the Union Address 1980." JimmyCarterLibrary.gov. (23 Jan 1980).

[12] As Chalmers Johnson remarked on the relationship between the CIA and the modern American president: "The CIA belongs as much to the president as the Praetorian Guard once belonged to the Roman emperors." [Johnson. *Nemesis*, 95.] On the CIA's role in the illicit narcotics trade, see: Alfred McCoy. *The Politics of Heroin: CIA Complicity in the Global Drug Trade*. (Chicago: Lawrence Hill Books, 2003); Alexander Cockburn and Jeffrey St. Clair. *Whiteout: The CIA, Drugs and The Press*. (New York: Verso, 1999).

Civilized Society

A *society* that fights its *wars* with advanced weaponry in faraway lands, all the while maintaining solid social cohesion at home by ensuring its disheveled masses keep to their proper place; that is, along *society*'s margins – out of sight and out of mind.

Clash of Civilizations

Old fashioned imperial conflicts renamed for an age of *globalization.*

Client State

A subordinate, junior member of the *international community.*

Coalition (of the Willing)

A military alliance of *democracy* promoters generally comprised of the U.S., its most loyal European lackeys, and the medieval monarchies of the Gulf.

Coercive Diplomacy

Prepositioning troops for the eventual invasion of a *rogue state.*[13]

Cold War (Old)

A most glorious victory won by *Ronald Reagan* for *freedom* over *tyranny,* which helped usher forth the *end of history.*

Cold War (New)

Fighting to keep a revisionist *Russia* from resurrecting *history.*

Collateral Damage

The killing of innocent civilians in military operations. Regrettable, but what are you going to do? Ground the *drones* and shelve the bombs? Don't be ridiculous. Instead, just avoid having to even acknowledge any measure of

---

[13] Coercive diplomacy being the "diplomatic" track the Bush administration set for dealing with Iraq prior to its 2003 invasion. As President Bush recalled in his memoir: "Coercive diplomacy with Iraq consisted of two tracks: One was to rally a coalition of nations to make clear that Saddam's defiance of his international obligations was unacceptable. The other was to develop a credible military option that could be used if he failed to comply. These tracks would run parallel at first. As the military option grew more visible and more advanced, the tracks would converge." George W. Bush. *Decision Points.* (New York: Crown, 2010): 230.

regret by denying and concealing all occurrences. And if that fails, just dole out some blood *money* to shut the locals up.[14]

Color Revolution

A U.S.-funded *regime change* operation seeking to manufacture and control an indigenous *popular uprising.* Look for color revolutions to "organically" appear in resource-rich or geopolitically important *states.*[15]

Constructive Engagement

The sustained capitulation by a foreign *government* to the demands issued forth from *Washington.*

Containment

A *Cold War (old)* era doctrine stipulating that the interests of all but *exceptional nations* were to be kept within their national borders.[16] (For containment in the modern context see: *Cold War (New)* and *Pivot to Asia.*)

---

[14] A 2013 report by *The Nation* magazine found that, "the Pentagon disbursed more than $30 million in condolence payments in Afghanistan and, mainly, Iraq from 2003 through 2006." Nick Turse. "Blood Money: Afghanistan's Reparations Files." *The Nation.* (19 Sept 2013).

[15] As Eva Golinger remarks on "color revolutions": "The recipe is always the same. Student and youth movements lead the way with a fresh face, attracting others to join in as though it were the fashion, the cool thing to do. There's always a logo, a color, a marketing strategy. In Serbia, the group OTPOR, which led the overthrow of Slobodan Milosevic, hit the streets with t-shirts, posters and flags boasting a fist in black and white, their symbol of resistance. In Ukraine, the logo remained the same, but the color changed to orange. In Georgia, it was a rose-colored fist, and in Venezuela, instead of the closed fist, the hands are open, in black and white, to add a little variety.

"Colored revolutions always occur in a nation with strategic, natural resources: gas, oil, military bases and geopolitical interests. And they also always take place in countries with socialist-leaning, anti-imperialist governments. The movements promoted by US agencies in those countries are generally anti-communist, anti-socialist, pro-capitalist and pro-imperialist." Eva Golinger. "Colored Revolutions: A New Form of Regime Change, Made in the USA." *Global Research.* (5 March 2014).

[16] American policy against the Soviet Union, as George Keenan argued in a 1940s *Foreign Affairs* article written under the pseudonym Mr. X, ought to be one "of firm containment, designed to confront the Russians with unalterable counterforce at every point where they show signs of encroaching upon the interest of a peaceful and stable world." Mr. X (George Keenan). "The Sources of Soviet Conduct." *Foreign Affairs.* (July 1947).

Coup D'état

A grave breech of democratic norms coming via an unconstitutional seizure of *power*...unless such a seizure of *power* is carried out by a cabal of pro-*Washington* elites promising to serve U.S. interests. In that case, the proper terminology is something more along the lines of *a change in the government*. And if such a seizure of *power* were to occur in, say, a *state* receiving large amounts of *U.S. military* aid, well, who's to say exactly what the proper terminology would be.[17]

Credibility

That which must be preserved through the dropping of *American* bombs.[18]

Crimes against Humanity

Fighting, resisting, or otherwise seeking to deny the inevitable worldwide march of *American* imposed *freedom* and *democracy*.

Cuban Embargo

The over 50 year punishment levied on the Cuban people for (1) having the nerve to overthrow a *strongman* in *America's backyard* and (2) having the audacity to live in a *rogue state*.

---

[17] Following the 2013 coup in Egypt, the U.S. refused to publicly deem the ousting of President Mohamed Morsi as such, in order to continue providing the Egyptian military with aid. As State Department spokesperson Jen Psaki stated: "The law does not require us to make a formal determination...as to whether a coup took place, and it is not in our national interest to make such a determination." Julian Pecquet. "Obama administration won't label toppling of Egypt's Morsi a coup." *The Hill*. (26 July 2013).

[18] As Noam Chomsky remarks on the use of "credibility" in mainstream discourse as the raison d'être for U.S. military adventurism: "a rogue superpower [i.e., the U.S.] must maintain 'credibility': failure to respect its power carries sever penalties. The concept is evoked regularly in justification of state violence. The regular appeal to 'credibility' was the only plausible argument advanced for the preference for war over other means in the case of Kosovo in early 1999; the standard cover phrase was 'credibility of NATO,' but no one believed that it was the credibility of Belgium or Italy that had to be established in the minds of potentially disobedient elements." And so it was, then, that we were treated in 2014 to the public laments of former Defense Secretary Leon Panetta, who fretted over President Obama's failure to bomb Syria a year prior over President Assad's supposed use of chemical weapons, which Panetta declared had "damaged U.S. credibility." See Chomsky. *Rogue States*, 6; Justin Sink. "Panetta: Obama's 'red line' on Syria damaged US credibility." *The Hill*. (7 Oct 2014).

Defending Freedom

Defending the commercial interests of U.S. *corporations* abroad, along with any foreign elites diligently servicing such interests.

Defensive Weapons

Offensive weapons.[19]

Defiant

A foreign *state* refusing to partake in *constructive engagement*.

Democracy Promotion

Footing the bill for the cadre of aspiring *imperfect leaders* in a geopolitically important nation who are sure to engage in *good governance* once in *power*. (See also, *Color Revolution*.)

Democratization

Democracy promotion overseen by *boots on the ground*.

Department of State

The junior partner to the *Pentagon* in the crafting of *American foreign policy*.

Destabilization

Any developments which precipitate a waning of U.S. influence in a particular region or *state*.

Deterrence

Both the accumulation of vast stocks of nuclear weapons and a pattern of behavior demonstrating a willingness to actually deploy such weapons. The United States possesses an unrivaled measure of deterrence. (See *Hiroshima* and *Nagasaki*, Chapter 11.)

---

[19] In February 2015, the *New York Times* reported the U.S. was on the verge of delivering "defensive weapons" to the coup government in Kiev to use against pro-Russian federalist rebels in eastern Ukraine. Included under the "defensive weapons" umbrella: "anti-armor missiles, reconnaissance drones, armored Humvees and radars that can determine the location of enemy rocket and artillery fire." Michael Gordon and Eric Schmitt. "U.S. Considers Supplying Arms to Ukraine Forces, Officials Say." *New York Times*. (1 Feb 2015).

Dictator

A bad *strongman* (e.g., *Russia*'s Vladimir Putin, *Syria*'s Bashar al-Assad).

Diplomacy

Building *coalitions* for a *preventive* or *preemptive war*.

Diplomatic Isolation

The indignity of being frozen out by both the lone indispensable nation and the *lone democracy in the Middle East*.

Dirty War

A *war* for when *war fatigue* at home won't permit the implementation of a *no-fly zone* or even *limited strikes*.

Disarming

The removing of arms from a foreign *state* by the *U.S. military*.

Dispensable Nations

The bombing targets and firing ranges comprising the assorted *homelands* of the *global force for good*'s *collateral damage*.

Domino Theory

A *Cold War (old)* theory postulating that the fall of one *state* to *communism* would led to a chain reaction causing neighboring states to also fall to *communism*.   The Domino Theory is today seen to have been a rather misguided policy, responsible in part for the failed U.S. *intervention* into Vietnam.[20] And so with the Domino Theory now fully discredited, the far more enlightened *American* planners of today have come to realize that it is not, in fact, *communism* that spreads as a contagion necessitating U.S. *interventions* around *the world*, but rather *terrorism*. For if *terrorism* were to gain a foot hold in *Afghanistan*, for instance, it would led to a chain reaction – akin,

---

[20] As no less than former Defense Secretary Robert McNamara was to later reflect on the Domino Theory's role in leading the U.S. to escalate the conflict in Vietnam, "We were wrong. But we had in our minds a mindset that led to that action." *The Fog of War: Eleven Lessons from the Life of Robert S. McNamara*. Dir. Errol Morris. (2003).

you might even say, to a toppled line of dominos – leading neighboring *states* to succumb to *terrorism* as well.[21]

Emerging International Norm

Every unilateral action taken by a *state* with an unwavering belief in its own divine brilliance.

Enlightened Leadership

Foreign leaders who willfully acquiesce to the fact that *liberal democracy* is the last stage of human political development.

Escalation

Any response taken to U.S. *provocations*.

Ethnic Cleansing

A most grievous breach of *international law* no *Manifest Destiny* decedent supporters of the *lone democracy in the Middle East* can ever let stand.

Evil Empire

The vanquished Soviet Union – an empire wholly different from the benign *American Empire* of the present day.

Failed State

The end product of a successful *humanitarian intervention*. (See *Libya*, Chapter 10.)

Force for Stability

The alliance forged between the *democracy* promoters in *Washington* and their favorite medieval monarchy.[22]

---

[21] Of course, the Domino Theory remains very much alive in regards to American strategic thinking on Russia as well. As a Domino Theory channeling Zbigniew Brzezinski warned after Russia annexed Crimea in early 2014: "If Ukraine is crushed while the West is simply watching, the new freedom and security in bordering Romania, Poland and the three Baltic republics would also be threatened." Zbigniew Brzezinski. "What is to be done? Putin's aggression in Ukraine needs a response." *Washington Post.* (3 March 2014).

[22] Remarking on the death of Saudi King Abdullah bin Abdulaziz in January 2015, President Obama asserted: "I always valued King Abdullah's…convictions. One of

Foreign Aid

See *Arms Sales*, Chapter 7.

Free and Fair Election

The *victory* – legitimate or not – of an *American* favored candidate in a foreign election.

Freedom Fighter

A *CIA*-funded fighter.

Freedom of Action

The *liberty* bequeathed to an *exceptional nation* to bomb, strafe, and pillage anywhere it chooses, at any time it likes, for any reason it fabricates.

Geneva Conventions

The set of rules governing all lesser nations in the humanitarian treatment of *war*.

Genocide

A usefully hollow word employed to sufficiently demonize the *bad guys* in order to send the *American people* into the *war* frenzy needed for the next *just war*.[23]

---

those convictions was his steadfast and passionate belief in the importance of the U.S.-Saudi relationship as a force for stability and security in the Middle East and beyond." President Barack Obama. "Statement by the President on the Death of King Abdullah bin Abdulaziz." Whitehouse.gov. (22 Jan 2015).

[23] As Edward Herman and David Peterson thoroughly document in their book *The Politics of Genocide*, the term "genocide" in Western discourse has been so repeatedly contorted in the service of political expediency as to lose all meaning. For instance, the U.S. print media invoked "genocide" a mere 13 times when discussing the 1,000,000 estimated Iraqis killed in the U.S.-U.K. war and occupation launched in 2003. In comparison, the same media invoked the term "genocide" 323 times in relation to Kosovo Albanians and 1,172 times in relation to Darfur, despite the substantially reduced casualty figures in relation to Iraq, estimated at 4,000 and 300,000 respectfully. As Herman and Peterson conclude, "The Western establishment rushed to proclaim 'genocide' in Bosnia-Herzegovina, Rwanda, Kosovo, and Darfur, and also agitated for tribunals to hold the alleged perpetrators accountable. In contract, its silence over the crimes committed by its own regimes against the peoples of Southeast Asia, Central America, the Middle East, and Sub-

Genocide Denial

Rationalizing the systemic crimes of a "good" empire as merely a series of disjointed *mistakes*, *tragic errors*, and *isolated incidents*.[24]

Giving a Nation a Chance for Democracy

Tearing a nation's social fabric asunder through a ruthless blitzkrieg and prolonged military *occupation*.[25] (See also, *Planting the Seeds of Democracy*.)

Global Leadership

That which is exhibited by every position taken by the U.S. in world affairs.

Good Governance

The proper adherence to *Washington* diktats by foreign capitals.

Good Guys

Those justifiably bombing and shooting the *bad guys*.[26]

Gulf War (1991)

Prelude to the eminently more profitable *Iraq war*. (See also, *Desert Storm*, Chapter 11.)

Saharan Africa is deafening. *This* is the 'politics of genocide.'" Edward Herman and David Peterson. *The Politics of Genocide.* (New York: Monthly Review Press, 2010): 112.

[24] Again, as Herman and Peterson argue: "The inability of any sector of the U.S. establishment to recognize fully that the human and material destruction of Southeast Asia and the Middle East are the consequence, not of accident, much less error, but of deliberate policies that produced this result, ranks among the greatest intellectual and moral failures in U.S. history. If the phrase *genocide denial* has any validity, we find it here, in the standard practice of the richest and most well-educated classes in the world." *Ibid*, 111.

[25] Speaking in mid-2014, as Iraq splintered under the weight of Islamic rebel advances and sectarian political divisions, President Obama reflected back on the U.S. occupation and boldly asserted, "We gave Iraq the chance to have an inclusive democracy." Michael Martinez. "Obama: 'Won't be a military solution' if Iraqi political structure not fixed." CNN. (20 June 2014).

[26] In late July 2014, CNN reported that U.S. intelligence had detected the use of ballistic missiles by the Ukrainian government against federalist rebels in the country's east. But as CNN's Barbara Star went on to note, a U.S. official "said it is not clear if the United States will show satellite imagery of the Ukrainian firings 'because these are the good guys.'" "CNN 2014 07 29 Ballistic missiles Ukraine." YouTube. (29 July 2014). <https://www.youtube.com/watch?v=y9-8KvtfjZA>

Hard Power

The use of coercion and military force to achieve one's objectives in foreign affairs. In a word, *American foreign policy*.

Hardliner

Any member of a foreign *regime* not cowered by U.S. threats of *regime change*.

Hostilities

A level of engagement by U.S. forces far in excess of merely toppling a foreign *regime* through a sustained *campaign* of bombing and strafing.[27]

Human Rights

A threat to *free trade* and just generally a rather onerous burden to the exceptional.[28]

Human Rights Abuses

The heinous crimes of *rogue states*. That is, things like denying their citizens access to clean water,[29] racially discriminating against their minority

---

[27] In order to skirt the restrictions of the War Powers Act in regards to its 2011 intervention in Libya, the Obama administration claimed that flying bombing missions over Libya didn't actually constitute "hostilities," thus necessitating no measure of congressional approval.

[28] As William Blum writes: "Under the Clinton administration, in 1996, a United Nations-sponsored World Food Summit affirmed the 'right of everyone to have access to safe and nutritious food.' The United States took issue with this, insisting that it does not recognize a 'right to food.' Washington instead championed free trade as the key to ending the poverty at the root of hunger, and expressed fears that recognition of a 'right to food' could lead to lawsuits from poor nations seeking aid and special trade provisions.

"The situation did not improve under the administration of George W. Bush. In 2002, in Rome, world leaders at another UN-sponsored World Food Summit again approved a declaration that everyone had the right to 'safe and nutritious food.' The United States continued to oppose the clause, again fearing it would leave them open to future legal claims by famine-stricken countries." William Blum. *America's Deadliest Export: Democracy – The Truth About US Foreign Policy and Everything Else*. (New York, Zed Books, 2013): 129-130.

[29] In June 2014, a group of United Nations experts publicly deemed the Detroit Water and Sewerage Department's water shut-offs to residents unable to pay their bills (affecting upwards of 30,000 Detroit residents) to be an "affront to their human rights." "Widespread water shut-offs in US city of Detroit prompt outcry from UN rights experts." UN News Centre. (25 June 2014).

populations,[30] or subjecting foreign nationals and citizens alike to political assassination.[31]

Human Rights Watch

An international *human rights* organization proudly joined at the hip with *Washington*, thus ensuring its righteous condemnations are always strategically and selectively levied upon *bad actors* and *rogue states*.[32]

Humanitarian Aid

The bare minimum amount of humanitarian relief needed to create the necessary cover for a covert intelligence or military operation.[33]

---

[30] As the vice chairman of the UN Committee on the Elimination of Racial Discrimination told reporters in August 2014, "Racial and ethnic discrimination [in the U.S.] remains a serious and persistent problem in all areas of life from de facto school segregation, access to health care and housing." Stephanie Nebehay. "U.N. urges U.S. to stop police brutality after Missouri shooting." Reuters. (29 Aug 2014).

[31] See "Killing One's Own People" and the accompanying footnote.

[32] In a May 2014 letter to Human Rights Watch, two Nobel Peace Prize Laureates and over 100 scholars called on the organization to live up to its supposed independence and close the revolving door between the organization and the U.S. government. As an example of the cozy relationship between HRW and the U.S. government, the letter noted: "HRW's Washington advocacy director, Tom Malinowski, previously served as a special assistant to President Bill Clinton and as a speechwriter to Secretary of State Madeleine Albright. In 2013, he left HRW after being nominated as Assistant Secretary of State for Democracy, Human Rights & Labor under John Kerry.

"In her HRW.org biography, Board of Directors' Vice Chair Susan Manilow describes herself as 'a longtime friend to Bill Clinton' who is 'highly involved' in his political party, and 'has hosted dozens of events' for the Democratic National Committee.

"Currently, HRW Americas' advisory committee includes Myles Frechette, a former U.S. ambassador to Colombia, and Michael Shifter, one-time Latin America director for the U.S. government-financed National Endowment for Democracy. Miguel Díaz, a Central Intelligence Agency analyst in the 1990s, sat on HRW Americas' advisory committee from 2003-11. Now at the State Department, Díaz serves as 'an interlocutor between the intelligence community and non-government experts.'" See: "Nobel Peace Laureates to Human Rights Watch: Close Your Revolving Door to U.S. Government." *AlterNet*. (12 May 2014).

[33] To take but one recent example, the U.S. military and CIA used American humanitarian relief missions into the Pakistani Kashmir region in the wake of the devastating 2005 earthquake to covertly advance Washington's strategic aims in the region. As the *New York Times'* Mark Mazzetti writes: "Billions of dollars of international aid poured into Pakistani Kashmir, and almost immediately a stream of

Humanitarian Crisis

Either a *crisis* directly threatening the interests and well-being of well-to-do *good guys*, or one threatening random *unpeople* that, nonetheless, may be exploited to advance the interests of well-to-do *good guys*.

Humanitarian Intervention

A shrewdly rebranded colonial crusade.[34]

Imperfect Leader

A despotic *strongman* on the U.S. take.

In the Last Throes

An insurgency on the verge of forcing *liberating American* forces into a hasty retreat.[35]

Independence

A nation's move into the *American* orbit after its elites manage to wrest themselves free from the *tyranny* of their *public opinion*.

Instability

The governing of territory by *states* outside the *international community*.

Insurgents

Bad *rebels* (e.g., the Vietcong, the Taliban).

American military helicopters crossed the border from Afghanistan to deliver humanitarian aid…But the Americans were not just on a mercy mission. In the months after the earthquake, the CIA used the relief effort in Kashmir to slip covert officers into the country without the ISI's [Pakistan's Inter-Services Intelligence] knowledge. The American spies adopted covers of various civilian professions." Mark Mazzetti. *The Way of the Knife: The CIA, a Secret Army, and a War at the Ends of the Earth.* (New York: Penguin Press, 2013): 164-165.

[34] As Alexander Cockburn remarked on NATO's 2011 "humanitarian intervention" in Libya, the assault will go down in history as little more than "an old-fashioned colonial smash-and-grab." Alexander Cockburn. "Libya: An Old-Fashioned Colonial Smash-and-Grab." *The Nation.* (27 June 2011).

[35] As Vice President Dick Cheney declared of the Iraqi insurgency in mid-2005, "I think they're in the last throes, if you will, of the insurgency." "Iraq insurgency in 'last throes,' Cheney says." CNN. (20 June 2005).

Internal Aggression

The locals' use of force against U.S. *boots on the ground.*

International Community

Those voting with the U.S. at the *United Nations* and joining its *coalitions.*

International Law

The internationally accepted rules governing *states* in their relations with other *states.* In no way applicable to those within the *international community.*

International Pariah

A *state* never voting with the U.S. at the *United Nations* and never joining one of its *coalitions.*

Intervention

The best means for solving complex international problems when undertaken by the U.S. A troubling breach of *international law* likely to only compound problems when undertaken by a more *dispensable nation.*

Iran-Contra Affair

An *isolated incident.*

Iraq War

A *mistake.*

Killing One's Own People

The premeditated and *criminal* butchery of innocent citizens at the hands of their own *government.* Not to be confused with the U.S. *campaign* of *targeted killings,* which just happens to include the killing of *American citizens.*[36]

---

[36] A 2011 Justice Department memo justifies killing Americans abroad with drones as long as they constitute an "imminent threat," with what constitutes an "imminent threat" left to the judgment of "informed, high-level official of the U.S. government." See "Lawfulness of a Lethal Operation Directed Against a U.S. Citizen Who is a Senor Operational Leader of Al-Qa'ida or an Associated Force." Department of Justice White Paper. (2011).
<http://msnbcmedia.msn.com/i/msnbc/sections/news/020413_DOJ_White_Pa per.pdf>

Korean War

A forgotten *mistake*.

Liberated

All lands falling under the occupation of U.S. forces.

Liberation

The raining down of "Made in the USA" stamped ordinances.

Limited Strikes

A prudent rebranding of *shock and awe* for a time of heightened *war fatigue*.[37]

Lone Democracy in the Middle East

A U.S.-armed *Apartheid state*. (See *Israel*, Chapter 10.)

Lost

Any nation or region which successfully repels liberating U.S. forces, eschews *Washington* diktats, and consequently develops into a bona fide *anti-access environment*. Contemplating whether the U.S. has lost any particular country is of constant angst within the *Washington foreign policy* establishment; for to

---

[37] When the Obama administration sought to sell a war wary public on a military campaign against Syria in 2013, it was repeated ad nauseam that such strikes would be "limited" in nature. As Secretary of State John Kerry sought to assure, any attack would be an "unbelievably small, limited kind of effort." Yet despite the public avows of a "limited strike," the White House was actually contemplating a much wider campaign behind the scenes. As Seymour Hersh later reported, in the days before President Obama pulled back under pressure from the top military brass, the list of targets within Syria had mushroomed from a "limited strike" into a "monster strike." As one source relayed to Hersh: "'Every day the target list was getting longer…The Pentagon planners said we can't use only Tomahawks to strike at Syria's missile sites because their warheads are buried too far below ground, so the two B-52 air wings with two-thousand pound bombs were assigned to the mission. Then we'll need standby search-and-rescue teams to recover downed pilots and drones for target selection. It became huge.' The new target list was meant to 'completely eradicate any military capabilities Assad had', the former intelligence official said. The core targets included electric power grids, oil and gas depots, all known logistic and weapons depots, all known command and control facilities, and all known military and intelligence buildings." Seymour Hersh. "The Red Line and the Rat Line." *London Review of Books.* (6 April 2014).

have lost something is to sadly acknowledge that *work* still remains in fulfilling the dreams of *full spectrum dominance*.[38]

Lost All Legitimacy

A foreign leader failing to bow with the proper measure of deference to *Washington*.

Low-Intensity Conflict

Any conflict in which no *Americans* perish. Foreign casualty numbers are irrelevant in gauging conflict intensity.

Making the Economy Scream

Torpedoing the economy of a *dispensable nation* in order to protect *freedom* and *democracy* from the foolish electoral whims of dispensable people.[39] (See also, *Sanctions*.)

Meddling

Interfering in the internal affairs of a *state* the U.S. is currently occupying.[40]

---

[38] Recent countries and regions the U.S. foreign policy establishment has fretted over having "lost": Afghanistan, Crimea, Egypt, Iraq, Libya, South America, and Yemen, to name but a few.

[39] In 1970, following the election of the socialist Salvador Allende to the presidency of Chile, the U.S., fearing "another Cuba" in the southern cone of "America's backyard," moved to restore "freedom" and "democracy" to Chile. To set about doing so, President Richard Nixon and Secretary of State Henry Kissinger ordered CIA Director Richard Helms to "make the [Chilean] economy scream." The idea being that if the Chilean economy could be brought to its knees, the Chilean people would come to their senses, see their mistake in voting in a socialist, and ultimately rise up to restore "democracy." And in turn, Chile could thus be returned to the "free world." And indeed, after three years spent making the economy scream, Washington was eventually able to help guide the right-wing General Augusto Pinochet to power through a September 11 (the other September 11), 1973 coup. And through Pinochet's iron grip on power, it was assured there would be no "new Cuba" in Chile. See "CIA Activities in Chile." Central Intelligence Agency Library. (10 Sept 2000). <https://www.cia.gov/library/reports/general-reports-1/chile/index.html>

[40] The official outrage in Washington over so-called Iranian "meddling" in Iraq during the U.S. occupation was a pervasive theme running through U.S. media coverage of the war. Consider the following sample of headlines: "Growing concerns in Baghdad about Iranian meddling" (*Christian Science Monitor*, 2004); "General Reports Spike in Iranian Activity in Iraq " (*Washington Post*, 2006); "Iran still

Menace

Any foreign *state* threatening *stability*.

Military Coup

A particularly bad sounding *coup d'état* used to make your run-of-the-mill *good guy* coup sound just a bit more palatable.[41]

Military Option

The only option serious policymakers will ever consider.

Mischief

The *foreign policy* of *states* outside the *international community*.

Mission Accomplished

Igniting a conflagration destined to immolate thousands of *heroes* and hundreds of thousands of *others*.[42]

Mission Creep

The slow rollout of a military *campaign*, occurring in piecemeal due to a dangerous case of *war fatigue* afflicting the politically immature *American public*.

Mistake

A *criminal war* of *aggression* gone sour, leaving a distressingly *war fatigued* public in its wake.

---

meddling in Iraq, U.S. says" (*Los Angeles Times*, 2007); "Bush Declares Iran's Arms Role in Iraq Is Certain" (*New York Times*, 2007); "U.S. official has new evidence of Iranian meddling in Iraq" (CNN, 2008). A similar sample referring to U.S. "meddling" in Iraq cannot be found.

[41] Following the 2009 coup in Honduras, the U.S. – not wanting to deem the illegal removal of Honduran President Manuel Zelaya an unqualified "coup," which would have required the severing of U.S. aid to the new pro-Washington regime – claimed that what had taken place was indeed a coup, but U.S. funds could still legally flow to the coup regime in Tegucigalpa because it did not constitute a "military coup." Robert Naiman. "WikiLeaks Honduras: State Dept. Busted on Support of Coup." *Huffington Post*. (29 Nov 2010).

[42] Draping a "Mission Accomplished" banner across the USS *Abraham Lincoln* in May of 2003 was one of the few mistakes President Bush admitted to in his memoir. Yet for Bush, the mistake, much as the photo op, was superficial in nature. As Bush wrote of the incident: "Our stagecraft had gone awry. It was a big mistake." Bush. *Decision Points*, 257.

Mob

Those protesting against U.S. interests abroad.[43]

Moderate

Any foreign pro-U.S. official or fighter – nonviolent, violent, it doesn't matter.

Nation Building

Pulverizing a nation's infrastructure and institutions in order to profitably remake them in our own image. Emphasis on profitably. (See *Creative Destruction*, Chapter 6.)

National Endowment for Democracy

The *CIA*'s Trojan horse.[44]

---

[43] A December 2013 NPR story on Ukraine described pro-Western protesters occupying government buildings in Kiev as "protesters." An April 2014 NPR story on pro-Russian protesters occupying government buildings in Luhansk and Kharkiv in Eastern Ukraine described the occupiers as a "mob." "How Does The NPR Distinguish 'Protesters' From 'Mobs'?" MoonofAlabama.org. (8 April 2014).

[44] The National Endowment for Democracy, as William Blum writes, functions as a CIA Trojan horse. As Blum explains the organization's history: "The NED was set up in the early 1980s under President Reagan in the wake of all the negative revelations about the CIA in the second half of the 1970s [...]

"The idea was that the NED would do somewhat overtly what the CIA had been doing covertly for decades, and thus, hopefully, eliminate the stigma associated with CIA covert activities.

"It was a masterpiece. Of politics, of public relations and of cynicism. Thus it was that in 1983, the National Endowment for Democracy was set up to 'support democratic institutions throughout the world through private, nongovernmental efforts'. Notice the 'nongovernmental' – part of the image, part of the myth. In actuality, virtually every penny of its funding comes from the federal government, as is clearly indicated in the financial statement in each issue of its annual report. NED likes to refer to itself as an NGO (non-governmental organization) because this helps to maintain a certain credibility abroad that an official US government agency might not have. But NGO is the wrong category. NED is a GO.

"Allen Weinstein, who helped draft the legislation establishing NED, was quite candid when he said in 1991: 'A lot of what we do today was done covertly 25 years ago by the CIA.' In effect, the CIA has been laundering money through NED." William Blum. *Rogue State: A Guide to the World's Only Superpower*. (Monroe: Common Courage Press, 2005): 238-239.

National Security

The ability to secure the *vital national interests*.

National Security Council

The council tasked with helping *presidents* determine things like: What *regime* should be changed next? What people are in need of *shock and awe*? What *terrorist* shall be marked for the next *targeted killing*? And on that last account, what *American*?

Nationalism

A dangerously naïve idea, positing that the natural resources of *dispensable nations* actually belong to *dispensable nations*.

Nationalist

A demagogic threat to *freedom* who must be *deposed*.

Next Hitler, the

A charismatic and stubbornly independent leader of a foreign *state* currently subjected to *coercive diplomacy* from *Washington*.

No Boots on the Ground

The deploying of a small enough number of *boots on the ground* that *Americans* will neither notice nor care.[45]

---

[45] In the lead-up to the 2011 NATO bombing of Libya, for example, President Obama unequivocally stated: "I also want to be clear about what we will not be doing. The United States is not going to deploy ground troops into Libya." By the end of March 2011, though, the *New York Times* was able to report that teams of CIA officers had been working on the ground in Libya for weeks, helping to select bombing targets for NATO planes. And by August, even the Pentagon was admitting that American troops were, indeed, on the ground in Libya. A little over a year later, upwards of 500 American troops were officially revealed to be on the ground in Libya, training Libyan Special Forces. But by that time, of course, the American media had moved on from Libya. The focus was instead on the assurances from Washington that no boots were going to be on the ground in Syria. See: President Barack Obama. "Remarks by the President on the Situation in Libya." Whitehouse.gov (18 March 2011); Mark Mazzetti and Eric Schmitt. "C.I.A. Agents in Libya Aid Airstrikes and Meet Rebels." *New York Times.* (30 March 2011); Justin Fishel. "U.S. Boots on the Ground in Libya, Pentagon Confirms." FoxNews.com.

No Civilian Deaths

The killing of a certain number of *unpeople* that garners a public reaction equivalent to the killing of no civilians at all.[46]

No-Fly Zone

A *war*, but waged by a Nobel Peace Prize laureate with the purest of intentions.[47]

Non-Governmental Organization – NGO

A *government* agency doing all sorts of unscrupulous things abroad that are probably best thought of as being "independent" from the U.S. *government*. (See *National Endowment for Democracy*.)

Non-Lethal Military Aid

Lethal military aid diligently relabeled to accommodate a weak stomached public.

(12 Sept 2011); Eric Schmitt. "U.S. to Help Create an Elite Libyan Force to Combat Islamic Extremists." *New York Times*. (15 Oct 2012).

[46] In late June 2011, then-President Obama's chief counterterrorism adviser John Brennan claimed that American drones hadn't killed a civilian in Pakistan for nearly a year. As Brennan stated, "nearly for the past year there hasn't been a single collateral death because of the exceptional proficiency, precision of the capabilities that we've been able to develop." The Bureau of Investigative Journalism later reported that up to 45 civilians had been killed by U.S. drones from August 2010 till the day Brenan claimed no civilian deaths had occurred in the previous year. But that fact seemed not to matter; nobody seemed to care – except, of course, for those 45 slaughtered innocents in Pakistan and their families. But in the U.S., they're all unpeople. And as long as unpeople are knocked off bit by bit, who's to notice or really care? It's really like it doesn't even happen. So, no civilian deaths, as Brennan would say. See Chris Woods. "US claims of 'no civilian deaths' are untrue." The Bureau of Investigative Journalism. (18 July 2011).

[47] As Secretary of Defense Robert Gates commented as the U.S. debated imposing a "no-fly zone" over Libya in 2011: "Let's just call a spade a spade. A no-fly zone begins with an attack on Libya to destroy the air defenses. That's the way you do a no-fly zone. And then you can fly planes around the country and not worry about our guys being shot down. But that's the way it starts." David E. Sanger and Thom Shanker. "Gates Warns of Risks of a No-Flight Zone." *New York Times*. (3 March 2011): A12.

Nonproliferation

The movement to decommission all nuclear warheads not under the control of the *U.S. military.*

Occupation

The *democratization* of a foreign people.

On the Table

The *military option* (nuclear weapons and all).

Others

The nameless, faceless *unpeople* killed alongside our *heroes.*[48]

Our Kind of Guy

See *Strongman.*[49]

Partners

Those helping to put a decidedly more local looking face on the *American liberation* of a faraway land and people.

Pathway to Democracy

A one-way path leading *states* away from any alternative political systems and toward the promised land of *liberal democracy.*

Pax Americana

See *Peace.*

Peace

The realization of U.S. *full spectrum dominance.*

---

[48] Israeli soldiers, of course, are counted amongst our "heroes." As a *McClatchy* newspaper headline read during the July 2014 Israeli war on Gaza: "13 Israeli soldiers, 70 Others killed." Trita Parsi. Twitter. (22 July 2014). <https://twitter.com/tparsi/status/491782872987348992>
[49] "Our kind of guy" being the Clinton administration's chosen description for Indonesian dictator Suharto. See Chomsky. *Rogue States*, 23.

Peace Process

The U.S. brokered negotiations between *Israel* and the *Palestinians*, during which the wholly impartial U.S. dictates *Israel's* terms to *Palestinians* – take it or leave it.

Peaceful Protesters

Pro-U.S. *agent provocateurs*, rioters, and general hooligans seeking to overthrow a *rogue state regime* through the deployment of street *violence*.

Pivot to Asia

The military *containment* of *China*.[50]

Planting the Seeds of Democracy

Shocking and awing one's way to killing hundreds of thousands of *unpeople*.[51] (See also, *Giving a Nation a Chance for Democracy*.)

Political Solution

A solution to be sought only once the much more profitable *military option* has been fully exhausted.

Popular Uprising

Any uprising in a foreign country led and controlled by pro-*American* elites.

Power Projection

Sending U.S. aircraft carriers to the very edge of *anti-access environments* in order to visibly threaten *rogue states* with *preemptive war*.

Preemptive War

A *war* launched in order to hasten an inevitable future *war*. In the most famous instance, the U.S. was forced to launch a preemptive war against *Iraq* in 2003 after being faced with the imminent impossibility of a mushroom

---

[50] As James Lyons, an ex-commander of the U.S. Pacific Fleet remarked in 2008, "operation tactics used against the former Soviet Union [i.e., containment] should be applied against China." Quoted in: Mahdi Darius Nazemroaya. *The Globalization of NATO*. (Atlanta: Clarity Press, 2012): 263.

[51] As President Bush declared, "The reason we are in Iraq is to plant the seeds of democracy so they flourish there and spread to the entire region of authoritarianism."

cloud rising over New York City in the wake of a nuclear attack from the non-nuclear *Iraq*.

Pretext

Regrettably, that which must be sought in a nominally democratic country prior to the launch of the next *just war*. (See *Protecting Civilians*.)

Preventive War

A deadly and destructive *war* waged to prevent the horrors of a deadly and destructive *war* from ever occurring.

Projecting Strength

Leveling threats of military attack against militarily inferior *states*.

Protecting Civilians

Protecting our corporate interests by *deposing* a *bad actor* in a *rogue state*. (See *Operation Falcon Freedom*, Chapter 11 and *Libya*, Chapter 10.)

Provocation

The *power projection* or *projecting of strength* by those outside the *international community*.

Quagmire

Something that looks a lot like the Donald Rumsfeld-led *wars* in *Afghanistan* and *Iraq*, but isn't. After all, as Rumsfeld assured the public in July of 2003, "I don't do quagmires."[52]

Realpolitik

The practice of international affairs based on *power* and material interests, rather than idealism. *American foreign policy* planners always shun realpolitik, choosing to instead base policy solely on the principles of *democracy* and *freedom*.

Rebels

Good *insurgents* (e.g., Libyan anti-Gaddafi fighters, Syrian anti-*regime* fighters).

---

[52] "DoD News Briefing - Secretary Rumsfeld and Ambassador Bremer." Defense.gov. (24 July 2003).

Red Line Threat

A military ultimatum issued by an *American politician* seeking to appear *muscular.*[53]

Refugees

A byproduct of the *freedom* agenda.[54]

Regime

An *administration* in a *state* outside the *international community.*

Regime Change

Fixing the electoral mistakes of people in *dispensable nations.*

Regime Loyalists

All *insurgents* fighting against U.S. forces at a moment in which it is not politically viable to acknowledge the existence of an insurgency.[55]

Reparations

The legal and moral obligation for those with *criminal responsibility.*

Repression

The denial by the *next Hitler* of his people's *aspirations.*

---

[53] In his first term alone, President Obama issued "red line" threats to both Iran and Syria. And he came precariously close to authorizing military strikes against Syria in 2013, after the Syrian government's purported use of chemical weapons, a red line for Obama. Obama's "red line" threat against Syria, however, is widely seen to have been a result of an off-the-cuff comment, rather than deliberated strategy. Nonetheless, it still led the U.S. to the precipice of war, for no other reason, it appears, than that Obama needed some way to save face.

[54] A 2009 report by the United Nations Refugee Agency reported that half of all refugees worldwide at the time were displaced by the U.S. wars in Iraq and Afghanistan. But, seeing that civilians under attack by American forces are unpeople, the refugees from Iraq and Afghanistan received scant attention from an American press corps clearly too enamored with and embedded within the forces of "Shock and Awe." "2008 Global Trends: Refugees, Asylum-seekers, Returnees, Internally Displaced and Stateless Persons." United Nations Refugee Agency. (16 June 2009). <http://www.unhcr.org/4a375c426.html>

[55] "Regime loyalists" being Donald Rumsfeld's favored term for Iraqi insurgents battling American forces.

Responsibility

In no way applicable to the truly exceptional.[56]

Responsibility to Protect

The obligation to cloak imperial projects in the *liberal* guise of humanitarianism.

Restoration of Democracy

The toppling of an elected *government* by a U.S. supplied and funded military junta.[57]

Restraint

For a foreign *state*, the refusal to use force against attacking U.S. forces. For the U.S. and *Israel*, the use of military force short of deploying thermo-nuclear weapons.

Revisionist Power

A *state* (*Russia*) failing to grasp the *God*-given right of *American* planners to stop *history* and realize global *full-spectrum dominance*.[58]

Rogue Nukes

Any nuclear weapon not under the control of the *U.S. military*, or the control of an allied *state*.

Rogue State

A *state* shunned by the *international community* due to its independent *foreign policy*.

---

[56] As Islamic rebels marched toward Baghdad in mid-2014, and while Libya remained marred in turmoil three years after NATO's intervention, Secretary of State John Kerry boldly declared that, "The United States of America is not responsible for what happened in Libya, nor is it responsible for what is happening in Iraq today." See "Kerry: US 'not responsible' for crisis in Iraq, Libya." RT.com (22 June 2014).

[57] Secretary of State John Kerry defended the 2013 coup by the Egyptian military by arguing the army was "restoring democracy." Michael R. Gordon and Kareem Fahim. "Kerry Says Egypt's Military Was 'Restoring Democracy' in Ousting Morsi." *New York Times*. (1 Aug 2013).

[58] In late 2014, U.S. Secretary of Defense Chuck Hagel decried what he deemed the threat from a "revisionist Russia." Chuck Hagel. U.S. Department of Defense. (15 Oct 2014). <http://www.defense.gov/Speeches/Speech.aspx?SpeechID=1894>

Rotten Apple

A *state* afflicted with the contagion of true *self-determination*. (See *Cuba*, Chapter 10.)

Saber-Rattling

The testing of military defenses by a *state* militarily encircled by the *global force for good*.

Safe Haven

The reason the *just war* must continue indefinitely, lest the *terrorists* gain a sanctuary.

Sanctions

A politically expedient alternative to *war*,[59] entailing the collective punishment of people living in a *rogue state*. Sanctions are charitably imposed as an inducement for the sanctioned to finally come to realize their *aspirations* and rise up and overthrow their despotic leaders.[60]

Save

Destroy.[61]

---

[59] In reality, economic sanctions are not really an alternative to war, but in fact an act of war. What other word is there for the deliberate torpedoing of a foreign economy? Furthermore, far from working as an alternative to an actual shooting war, sanctions often serve as a prelude to an escalated confrontation. Indeed, it is one of Washington's favorite strategies: sanction today, invade tomorrow. Sanctions, for instance, were imposed on Iraq for decades prior to the 2003 U.S. invasion. In fact, in the Iraq case, sanctions appear to have been imposed in part to weaken Iraqi defenses prior to the eventual U.S. invasion.

[60] The record of sanctions actually working as their advocates loudly claim is a rather barren one. See Robert A. Page. "Why Economic Sanctions Do Not Work." *International Security* Vol. 22 Issue 2. (Aug 1997): 90-136.

[61] As one U.S. Major famously stated in 1968 to the journalist Peter Arnett, while stationed in Vietnam: "It became necessary to destroy the town to save it." Of course, the "destroy to save" line lingers to this day. For instance, as the U.S. Air Force bombarded the Syrian Kurdish town of Kobani under siege from Islamic militants in October 2014, the front page of the *Wall Street Journal* declared with no irony: "U.S.-Led Coalition Bombards City in Effort to Save It." *Wall Street Journal.* Vol. CCLXIV No. 89. (14 Oct 2014).

Secret War

A *war* the *free press*, after consultations with *official sources*, decides ought not to be revealed to the notoriously fickle *American public*.

Sectarian Violence

Violence no liberator shall take any measure of *responsibility* for.

Self-Determination

The right of all peoples to rule themselves in a manner fully in alignment with the interests of the U.S.

Slam Dunk Case

The intelligence case for *a war that pays for itself*.[62]

Soft Power

The use of *strategic communications* to get others to want what you want in foreign affairs. A nice idea, but certainly not as viscerally satisfying as *hard power*.

Sovereign

A *state* under the occupation of at least 130,000 *liberating* U.S. forces.[63]

---

[62] In late 2002, CIA Director George Tenet assured President Bush that the evidence of Iraqi weapons of mass destruction was a "slam dunk case." Of course, Tenet's confidence in the intelligence case against Iraq no doubt stemmed from that fact that he was cooking the intelligence to strictly adhere to White House policy. "As the invasion of Iraq drew closer," the *New York Times'* James Risen reported, "an attitude took hold among many senior CIA officials that war was inevitable – and so the quality of the intelligence on weapons of mass destruction didn't really matter." And in any regard, Tenet evidently didn't really care all that much whether he really had a slam dunk case or not. As Tyler Drumheller, the chief of the European Division in the CIA's Directorate of Operations remarked later, "I think Tenet believed that they would find WMD when they got to Iraq and that nobody would remember these questions [over the quality of the intelligence]." In 2004, Tenet was duly rewarded for his work in manipulating intelligence with a Presidential Medal of Freedom. See James Risen. *State of War: The Secret History of the CIA and the Bush Administration.* (New York: Free Press, 2006): 112-113.

[63] On June 28, 2004, Iraq was declared "sovereign." At the time, over 130,000 U.S. combat troops were stationed in the country. On a note delivered to him at the

Sovereignty

The right of *states* to exercise independent authority over their recognized territory. *States* running afoul of the whims of the *exceptional nation* sacrifice all rights to sovereignty.

Special Relationship

The relationship between the United States and the United Kingdom; specifically, London's willingness to strictly adhere to *Washington's* line.

Stability

The maintenance of *American* economic and military dominance abroad, achieved via *democratization* and the active support of foreign *strongmen*.

Stabilization

Deploying *boots on the ground.*

State Sponsor of Terror

Any *state* actively aiming to advance its own *vital national interests* in direct opposition to the interests of *Washington.*

Striking Hard at a Decisive Moment

Providing vital material support for the systematic *good guy* slaughter of *bad guys.*[64]

Strongman

Good *dictator* (e.g., the Jordanian and Saudi kings).

NATO summit in Istanbul informing him of Iraq's "sovereignty," President Bush scribbled, "let freedom reign." Bush. *Decision Points*, 359.

[64] Following a failed 1965 coup attempt by junior Indonesian military officers, the Indonesian military, under the leadership of General Suharto, launched a bloody campaign against the Indonesian Communist Party, which the military leadership claimed to be behind the aborted coup. To help assist the hunt for Indonesian communists, American diplomats "systematically compiled a comprehensive list of 'Communists' operatives, from top echelons down to village cadres, and turned over as many as 5,000 names to the Indonesian army, which hunted those person down and killed them." As Robert Marten, a former member of the U.S. Embassy's political section in Jakarta later reflected: "I probably have a lot of blood on my hands, but that's not all bad. There's a time when you have to strike hard at a decisive moment." Blum. *Killing Hope*. 194.

Stuff Happens

The looting of a nation's cultural relics post *American liberation*.[65]

Surgical Strike

The use of a *Hellfire missile* as a surgeon's scalpel.[66]

Targeted Sanctions

Your regular collectively punishing *sanctions* sensibly qualified to accommodate the *responsibility to protect* age of *humanitarian interventions*.[67]

Targeting Civilians

Any *rogue state*'s use of military force.

Territorial Integrity

A pillar of *international law*, holding a *state*'s *sovereignty* to be sacred. But being a principle of *international law*, a respect for territorial integrity is accordingly only applicable to those outside the *international community*, as those within the vaunted community of nations are obviously "not going to be restricted by borders."[68]

Tragic Error

Any large-scale *criminal* misdeed by *American* forces finding its way into the press.

---

[65] As Secretary of Defense Donald Rumsfeld remarked on the looting of Baghdad (minus the U.S. protected Oil and Interior Ministries) in the wake of the U.S. invasion in 2003, "stuff happens."

[66] In 2010, then-counterterrorism advisor to President Obama, John Brennan, stated the administration's counterterrorism approach was to be surgical in its precision. "In all our efforts," Brennan claimed, "we will exercise force prudently, recognizing that we often need to use a scalpel, not a hammer." John Brennan. "Remarks by Assistant to the President for Homeland Security and Counterterrorism John Brennan at CSIS." Whitehouse.gov (26 May 2010).

[67] As *The Guardian* reported in 2012 on the "targeted sanctions" levied at Iran, "millions of lives are at risk in Iran because western economic sanctions are hitting the importing of medicines and hospital equipment." Saeed Kamali Dehghan. "Iran sanctions 'putting millions of lives at risk.'" *The Guardian*. (17 Oct 2012). See also, Ben Schreiner. "Sanctioning Iran: Punishing Defiance." *CounterPunch*. (8 Jan 2013).

[68] The words of Benjamin Rhodes, President Obama's deputy national security adviser, when speaking in August 2014 on the U.S. military strategy against Islamist rebels in both Iraq and Syria. Peter Baker and Michael D. Shear. "U.S. Weighs Direct Military Action Against ISIS in Syria." *New York Times*. (22 Aug 2014).

Troop Surge

The throwing of good *money* after bad.

Troop Withdrawal

The transition from the foreign deployment of hundreds of thousands of combat troops to the foreign deployment of hundreds of thousands of *military advisors*.

Tyrant

See *Dictator*.

Unilateralism

A doctrine advocating the use of *state power* abroad without first garnering the support or participation of other *states*. *American foreign policy* is often deemed to be unilateral in nature. This is incorrect, of course, considering the U.S. never goes it alone, but rather is always joined by a *coalition*.

United Nations Charter

In no way applicable to indispensable nations.

Unpeople

Collateral damage in waiting.

U.S. Agency for International Development – USAID

Federal agency responsible for managing *Washington*'s *regime change* slush fund.[69]

U.S. Embassy

An overseas command and control center used by the U.S. to properly see to a local *change in the government*.[70]

---

[69] To take but one of the more recent cases of USAID meddling: From early 2010 to mid-2012, the U.S. State Department, through the USAID, created a social networking site in Cuba – a "Cuban Twitter" – with the intent of destabilizing the Castro government through the eventual mobilization of "smart mobs." Desmond Butler, Jack Gillum, and Alberto Arce. "US secretly created 'Cuban Twitter' to stir unrest." Associated Press. (3 April 2014).

[70] The old joke being: Do you know why there has never been a coup in the U.S.? Because there is no American Embassy in Washington D.C.

Victory

A *mistake* subjected to *positive thinking*.

Vietnam Syndrome

A troublesome aversion to *war* voiced by the *American people* after the U.S. *victory* in Vietnam. The Vietnam Syndrome was officially overcome in 1991, after the U.S. triumph in *Iraq*. As President George H.W. Bush elatedly declared: "By God, we've kicked the Vietnam Syndrome once and for all."[71]

Vietnam War

A *mistake*.

Violent Extremists

"[*Bad guy*] individuals who support or commit ideologically-motived violence to further [*bad guy*] political goals."[72]

Vital National Interests

The interests of *American small businesses*.

Volatile Region

A region in which *American* predominance of force is threatened by the existence of an *anti-access environment*.

War Crime

A serious violation of international humanitarian *law* committed by those defeated by *liberating American* forces. (For *American* violations of international humanitarian *law* during *war*, see *Isolated Incident*, Chapter 11.)

War Criminal

Any non-*American* who commits a *war crime*. There are, of course, no *American* war criminals, only *bad apples*.

---

[71] Quoted in: George C. Herring. "America and Vietnam: The Unending War." *Foreign Affairs*. (Winter 1991/92).
[72] A 2011 White House report on violent extremism defined "violent extremists" as "individuals who support or commit ideologically-motivated violence to further political goals." See "Empowering Local Partners to Prevent Violent Extremism in the United States." Whitehouse.gov. (August 2011): 1.

We Came. We Saw. He Died.

The triumphant 2011 words of Secretary of State Hillary Clinton upon receiving reports of the death of Libyan leader *Muammar Gaddafi*. Clinton's choice to channel Julius Cesar was meant as a confirmation that, yes, *America* is indeed an empire now and will create its own *reality*, thank you very much. And the new *reality* to be created in 2011 was one in which the Libyan *dictator* Gaddafi was to be lynched. It was all really quite simple: the lone indispensable nation had come to *Libya*, it had seen *Libya*, and the *Libya* it had seen had no room for a non-dead Gaddafi; thus, "he died."[73]

Weapons of Mass Destruction

The specter to be invoked whenever the *American people* express an initial skepticism toward a *preventive* or *preemptive war*.

White Man's Burden

See *Responsibility to Protect* and *Protecting Civilians*.

World's Policeman

A *state* acting within the international system as a cop would on his beat; that is, a *state* terrorizing and killing unarmed people of color with utter impunity.

Worth the Price

Sticking it to a *bad guy dictator* to the tune of a half-million dead children.[74]

---

[73] Corbett Daly. "Clinton on Qaddafi: 'We came, we saw, he died." CBS News. (20 Oct 2011).

[74] As former Secretary of State Madeleine Albright callously remarked when asked directly about the half million dead Iraqi children due to the U.S.-imposed sanctions regime against Iraq in the 1990s, "I think this is a very hard choice, but the price — we think the price is worth it." Channeling Albright, U.S. Senator Mark Kirk similarly voiced support for stiffer sanctions on Iran in 2011 by averring that, "It's okay to take the food out of the mouths of" innocent Iranians. Rahul Mahajan. "'We Think the Price Is Worth It': Media uncurious about Iraq policy's effects--there or here." *Extra!* (Nov 2001); Ali Gharib. "Sen. Mark Kirk: 'It's Okay To Take Food From The Mouths Of' Innocent Iranians." Think Progress. (12 Oct 2011).

10. The World

Then conquer we must, when our cause it is just.

-    *"The Star-Spangled Banner"*

Afghanistan

A *liberated*, yet frustratingly ungrateful nation.

Africa

An "under-polluted"[1] land containing a vast reservoir of *oil*. Yet, because of Chinese *meddling* across the continent,[2] African *oil* is not yet safely *American oil*. And thus, Africa "remains the Army's last frontier."[3]

America's Backyard

South and Central America; purview of the *U.S. military*'s SOUTHCOM.

Arab Street

Arab *public opinion*. Left unrestrained, the Arab Street would trigger nothing less than a *crisis in democracy* throughout the Arab world, and therefore must be placed under the paternal control of a local *strongman* or *liberating American* forces.

Arctic

A future *American* lake.[4]

---

[1] In 1991, while working as an economist at the World Bank, Larry Summers penned a memo in which he asserted: "I've always thought that under-populated countries in Africa are vastly UNDER-polluted." Summers' resume post memo: U.S. Treasury Secretary under Bill Clinton, president of Harvard University, and senior economic advisor to President Obama.

[2] As Secretary of State John Kerry remarked during his 2013 Senate confirmation hearing: "Now with respect to China and Africa, China is all over Africa — I mean, all over Africa. And they're buying up long-term contracts on minerals, on ... you name it. And there're some places where we're not in the game, folks. And I hate to say it. And we got to get in." "Kerry: Relations with China 'critical'." UPI. (24 Jan 2013).

[3] "3,000 soldiers to serve in Africa next year." *Army Times*. (8 June 2012).

[4] The Arctic is estimated to hold up to $1 trillion in hydrocarbons and rare earth minerals, which are likely to become extractable in the coming decades with growing

Asia-Pacific

A region portending impressive economic growth and dynamism, all of which is to be harnessed by the U.S. through the deployment of *American full spectrum dominance*. (See *America's Pacific Century* and *Pivot to Asia*, Chapter 9.)

Axis of Evil

The *states* (*Iran*, *North Korea*, and pre-2003 invasion *Iraq*) inexplicably uninterested in joining the *international community*.

Bahamas, the

A *NSA* listening post.[5]

Bahrain

Home of the U.S. Navy's 5th Fleet. Whatever else happens in Bahrain is irrelevant and ought to be ignored. *America*, after all, isn't a nation prone to *meddling*.[6]

Brazil

A valued ally (i.e., an intelligence *adversary*).[7]

---

ice melt attributable to climate change. Accordingly, the U.S. plans on being able to actively patrol the Arctic as early as 2020. Andrea Shalal. "U.S. Navy eyes greater presence in Arctic from 2025." Reuters. (28 Feb 2014).

[5] According to *The Intercept*, the NSA has clandestinely set-up backdoor access to the Bahamas' cellular telephone network, allowing the agency to "covertly record and store the 'full-take audio' of every mobile call made to, from and within the Bahamas – and to replay those calls for up to a month." Ryan Devereaux, Glenn Greenwald and Laura Poitras. "Data Pirates of the Caribbean: The NSA Is Recording Every Cell Phone Call in the Bahamas." *The Intercept*. (19 May 2014).

[6] As Bahrain unleashed a brutal crackdown on protesters in 2011, and as the U.S. readily condemned state "repression" in Libya, the U.S. stayed conspicuously silent on events in Bahrain. In fact, as State Department spokesperson Mark Toner commented in March 2011: "Our position towards Bahrain is crystal clear. We're going to continue to work with the Bahraini Government." Without question, the presence of the Navy's strategically important 5th Fleet factored heavily into Washington's indifference to the demands of Bahrainis on the streets. Marian Wang. "U.S. Stays Mum as Bahrain Unleashes Brutal Crackdown." ProPublica. (12 April 2011).

[7] As part of the Edward Snowden leaks, it was reported that the NSA spied on both Brazilian companies (including the state owned oil company Petrobras) and Brazilian citizens, including President Dilma Rousseff. The revelations led Rousseff to cancel

BRICS

The untrustworthy lot of emerging economies comprised of *Brazil, Russia,* India, *China,* and South Africa. The BRICS are to be dismissed for not knowing their proper place in *the world,* while any signs of their economic weakness is to be cheered as their rightful comeuppance.[8]

Canada

A semi-autonomous *American* province.

Castro, Fidel

The *CIA*'s white whale.[9]

Chad

Drone launching pad.[10]

Chavez, Hugo

The democratically elected *dictator/tyrant* of *Venezuela* from 1998 to 2013.

China

A large *anti-access environment* situated in the heart of Asia threatening to usurp *American* control of the *Asia-Pacific.*

Colombia

The *U.S. military*'s backyard staging hub.[11]

---

a 2013 state visit to Washington in protest. Jonathan Watts. "Brazilian president postpones Washington visit over NSA spying." *The Guardian.* (17 Sept 2013).

[8] As *Foreign Affairs,* the journal of the Council of Foreign Relations, cheered over the cooling economies of the BRICS in early 2014: "The BRICS are crumbling." Gildeon Rose and Jonathan Tepperman. "The Shape of Things to Come: Hot Markets to Watch." *Foreign Affairs* Vol. 93 No. 1 (Jan/Feb 2014): 2.

[9] The CIA concocted upwards of 600 assassination plots against Castro.

[10] The U.S. flies drones from a former French military base in Chad. See Craig Whitlock. "Pentagon set to open second drone base in Niger as it expands operations in Africa." *Washington Post.* (1 Sept 2014).

[11] In 2009, the U.S. signed a ten-year renewable basing agreement with Colombia, allowing the U.S. military access to seven bases within Colombia. As Benjamin Dangl reported, "a U.S. Air Force document states the deal offers a 'unique opportunity' for 'conducting full spectrum operations' in the region against various threats,

Cuba

A defiant upstart that is to be severely punished, lest the contagion of national *sovereignty* spread further into *America's backyard.*

Djibouti

Drone launching pad.[12]

East, the

The highly suspicious societies (*China, Russia,* and the various *Muslim* lands subjected to *American liberation*) that are to be both feared and hated.

Eastern Europe

A *NATO* growth area.

Egypt

A longtime purchaser of *American* military hardware, so let's just go ahead and call it a *democracy.*

Ethiopia

Drone launching pad.[13]

European Union – EU

An economic and political union of European states…"Fuck the EU."[14]

---

including 'anti-U.S. governments.'" Benjamin Dangl. "U.S. Bases in Colombia Rattle the Region." *The Progressive.* (March 2010).

[12] Until late 2013, the U.S. used its sprawling Camp Lemonnier base in Djibouti City to launch drones used for strikes in Somalia and Yemen. But after Djibouti raised concerns over the safety of American drones following a series of high profile crashes, the U.S. was forced to relocate its drone fleet to a remote airstrip outside the capital. Craig Whitlock and Greg Miller. "U.S. moves drone fleet from Camp Lemonnier to ease Djibouti's safety concerns." *Washington Post.* (24 Sept 2013).

[13] In 2011, the Air Force began flying drones out of an air base located in Arba Minch, Ethiopia. The drones are used for strikes within Somalia. "US launches drones from Ethiopia." Al Jazeera English. (29 Oct 2011).

[14] The quote is attributed to Victory Nuland, U.S. Assistant Secretary of State for European Affairs, and came as Nuland discussed with the U.S. Ambassador to Ukraine who the U.S. sought to have installed in the post-coup government in Kiev, as was all revealed in 2014 video posted to YouTube containing the audio of the call.

Free World

The societies of all *NATO* member countries and their dictatorial *client states*.

G-7

A generally productive international forum, where the serious issues facing *the world* are addressed by *the world*'s seven serious powers: the U.S. and its closest European hangers-on, plus *Japan*.

G-20

A less reliable, less productive international forum including agents of disorder like *China* and *Russia*.

Gaddafi, Muammar

The "mad dog of the *Middle East*"[15] and *dictator* of *Libya* from 1969 till the moment in 2011 when: *We came. We saw. He died.*

Gaza

A land habitually subjected to the *restraint* of the *lone democracy in the Middle East*.

Germany

A close ally and *forward operating base*, so clearly another intelligence *adversary*.[16]

Global South

An irrelevant patch of land home to an irrelevantly large group of people. As Secretary of State Henry Kissinger once remarked: "Nothing important can come from the South. History has never been produced in the South. The

---

Josh Rogin. "State Dept Official Caught on Tape: 'Fuck the EU.'" *The Daily Beast*. (6 Feb 2014).

[15] The words of President Ronald Reagan.

[16] According to documents made available by Edward Snowden, the NSA has tapped the personal cellphone of German Chancellor Angela Merkel for years, including prior to her even serving as chancellor. And then, during a German parliamentary investigation into U.S. spying coming as a result of such revelations, the U.S. was caught recruiting Germans to spy on the inquiry, leading Germany in July 2014 to expel America's top intelligence official working in the country. Greg Miller and Stephanie Kirchner. "Germany orders CIA station chief to leave over spying allegations." *Washington Post*. (10 July 2014).

axis of history starts in Moscow, goes to Bonn, crosses over to Washington and then goes to Tokyo. What happens in the South is of no importance."[17]

Great Britain

An *American* lapdog.

Guam

A Pacific *forward operating base*.[18]

Gulf Cooperation Council – GCC

An "Arab *NATO*" comprised of the *democracy* promoting Gulf monarchies.[19]

Haiti

What *Cuba* ought to look like. And what *Cuba* would look like if it weren't such a *rogue state*.

Homeland

A city on a hill.

Honduras

A shining *democracy* following the nation's 2009 U.S.-supported *change in the government*.

Hussein, Saddam

Iraqi *strongman*-cum-*the next Hitler* finally *deposed* by the U.S. in 2003. (See *Iraq War*, Chapter 9.)

International Criminal Court – ICC

International body responsible for holding (African) *war criminals*[20] to account for their crimes. And accordingly, a body in no way for the U.S. First,

---

[17] Quoted in: Stephen Kinzer. *Overthrow: America's Century of Regime Change From Hawaii to Iraq.* (New York: Times Books, 2006): 198.
[18] A U.S. territory, Guam hosts two U.S. naval bases and one U.S. air base.
[19] Vijay Prashad. *Arab Spring, Libyan Winter.* (Oakland: AK Press, 2012): 28.
[20] To date, all ICC prosecutions have targeted African leaders.

because the U.S. is not an African *state*. Second, because there are no *American war criminals*.[21]

Iran

An ancient land of rich *history*, which can be dated all the way back to 1979, when 52 *Americans* were for unexplainable reasons taken and held hostage for over one year.[22] Today, Iran consists of a large *anti-access environment* in the *Middle East*.

Iraq

From 2003 to 2011, a place of *stability*. Now, succumbing once again to *instability* as Baghdad becomes just a little too friendly with Tehran.

Israel

A democratic *state* for the Jewish people…which also just happens to have a large Arab population. Regardless, the *lone democracy in the Middle East*. Also, a recipient of generous *American* largesse[23] and a formidable storage hub for excess *U.S. military* equipment.[24]

Italy

A *forward operating base* for the looming *just war* with that irksome *revisionist power*.[25]

---

[21] The U.S. is not a party to the ICC.

[22] The U.S.-orchestrated 1952 coup, which imposed the Shah and his henchmen, has long since been sent down the vast American memory hole.

[23] U.S. aid to Israel can be measured in the billions, with the vast majority going to the Israel Defense Forces. In 2012, former IDF Chief of Staff Gabi Ashkenazi went so far as to claim that, "In the past three year…US taxpayers have contributed more to the Israeli defense budget than Israeli taxpayers." "Ashkenazi: Preserving US ties a security necessity." *Jerusalem Post.* (11 Sept 2012).

[24] The U.S. keeps $800 million in military gear and ordinances on Israeli soil. Under the terms of the storage agreement, Israeli forces are permitted to use the U.S. equipment and munitions in the case of an "emergency" (i.e., a bombing of Gaza, or what Israeli officials deem, "mowing the lawn"). Amos Harel. "U.S. to store $800m in military gear in Israel." *Haaretz.* (11 Jan 2010).

[25] In early 2015, the Pentagon announced plans to consolidate the 67,000 American troops stationed in Europe, with most troops to be sent to existing bases in either Italy or Germany. The move, the *New York Times* stated, comes as the U.S. seeks to "counter a more aggressive Russia." Helene Cooper. "U.S. Consolidates Forces in Europe to Save Money." *New York Times.* (8 Jan 2015).

Japan

A former U.S. nuclear testing site now functioning as a military depot holding the defense assets necessary for the *containment* of *China*.

King Abdullah bin Abdul Aziz al-Saud

A man of "remarkable character and courage" who served as the "revered leader" of *Saudi Arabia* from 2005 to 2015.[26]

Libya

Since *NATO*'s 2011 intervention, a place of *stability* where civilians are protected from all the perils of social tranquility.[27]

Mediterranean Sea

A *NATO* lake.[28]

---

[26] When the despotic King Abdullah died in January 2015, the U.S. political class rushed to heap praise on their favorite tyrant. The chairman of the Joint Chiefs of Staff, General Martin Dempsey, went so far as to announce an essay contest to "honor" the "remarkable character and courage" of the king. The submitted essays were not to be satirical. Meanwhile, U.S. Secretary of State John Kerry tweeted: "King Abdullah was a man of wisdom & vision. US has lost a friend & Kingdom of #SaudiArabia, Middle East, and world has lost a revered leader." See: Jim Garamone. "Dempsey Sponsors Essay Competition to Honor Saudi King." DoD News. (26 Jan 2015); John Kerry. Twitter.com. (22 Jan 2015). <https://twitter.com/JohnKerry/status/558465776370200576>

[27] NATO's 2011 "humanitarian intervention" in Libya was sold to Western public opinion as a mission to "protect civilians." As President Obama warned at the time, failing to intervene would "[stain] the conscience of the world." A year later, Ivo Daalder, then the U.S. permanent representative to NATO, went so far as to deem the toppling of Gaddafi and the destruction of Libya "a model intervention." And perhaps it was, just so long as one completely disregards the mission's purported pretext of protecting civilians. As Alan Kuperman notes in the establishment journal *Foreign Affairs*: "Before NATO's intervention, Libya's civil war was on the verge of ending, at the cost of barely 1,000 lives. Since then, however, Libya has suffered at least 10,000 additional deaths from conflict. In other words, NATO's intervention appears to have increased the violent death toll more than tenfold." Alan J. Kuperman. "Obama's Libya Debacle: How a Well-Meaning Intervention Ended in Failure." *Foreign Affairs* Vol. 94 No. 2 (March/April 2015): 66, 72.

[28] On NATO's Mediterranean encroachment, or "Mediterranean Dialogue," see: Nazemroaya. *The Globalization of NATO*, 134-152.

Mexico

Backyard play area for U.S. anti-narcotics agents.[29]

Middle East

A vast reservoir of *American oil*. (See *Carter Doctrine*, Chapter 9.)

Morales, Evo

An indigenous peasant absurdly fashioning himself to be the *president* of Bolivia. No chance is therefore to be missed to put Morales in his place.[30]

Mubarak, Hosni

Egypt's *strongman* and *our kind of guy* from 1981 to 2011.

Muslim World

A world to be comically misunderstood, irrationally feared, and hysterically hated – and then ultimately bombed.

New Europe

All the *resolute* European countries who joined the 2003 *coalition of the willing* against *Iraq*.

Nicaragua

A most unruly child.[31]

---

[29] According to a 2014 *Wall Street Journal* report, U.S. Justice Department personnel routinely partake in armed raids in Mexico dressed as Mexican Marines. As the paper reported, "about four times a year the U.S. Marshals Service sends a handful of specialists into Mexico who take up local uniforms and weapons to hide their role hunting suspects, including some who aren't on a U.S. wanted list." Devlin Barrett. "U.S. Raids Cartels as Mexican Marines." *Wall Street Journal*. (22/23 Nov 2014): A1.

[30] Morales's presidential jet was forced to land in Vienna, Austria in July 2013 on a return trip from Moscow, after having been denied entry into the airspace of several European Union countries on the suspicion that Edward Snowden might be aboard the plane. It is widely believed the EU nations were acting on behalf of the U.S.

[31] In 2006, an official with the International Republican Institute, a partner organization to the National Endowment for Democracy, "equated the relationship between Nicaragua and the United States to that of a son to a father. 'Children should not argue with their parents,' she said." Blum. *America's Deadliest Export*, 183.

Niger

Drone launching pad.[32]

Non-Aligned Movement

A totally irrelevant intergovernmental body comprised of over 100 *states* containing over half *the world*'s population. Ignore the Non-Aligned Movement.

Noriega, Manuel

A Panamanian *strongman* and *CIA asset* turned *dictator* and drug lord *deposed* by the U.S. in 1989. (See *Operation Just Cause*, Chapter 11.)

North Atlantic Treaty Organization – NATO

Washington's default *coalition*. More formally, a defensive military alliance of northern Atlantic *states*, which has long since broken free from the shackles of both defense and *geography*. Accordingly, the Alliance can now be found doing everything from imposing African *no-fly zones* to occupying *Afghanistan*.[33]

North Korea

A 1950s era U.S. bombing target. And now, the necessary *bad guy pretext* needed for the *marketing* of the *pivot to Asia* to the *American public*.

Old Europe

All the European countries too weak to join the 2003 *coalition of the willing* against *Iraq*.

---

[32] In early 2013, the U.S. announced it was setting up a Predator drone base in Niamey, Niger. And by September 2014, the U.S. had gained permission to fly drones from a second base, located in the city of Agadez. See: Eric Schmitt and Scott Sayare. "New Drone Base in Niger Builds U.S. Presence in Africa." *New York Times*. (22 Feb 2013); Whitlock. "Pentagon set to open second drone base in Niger as it expands operations in Africa."

[33] The 9/11 attacks accelerated the transformation of NATO into a truly global force. As Mahdi Darius Nazemroaya writes, "fighting terrorism became a central feature of the Atlantic Alliance's self-declared functions and responsibilities. These self-imposed responsibilities have allowed NATO to publicly transform; they have put the Atlantic Alliance on a permanent offensive footing, transforming it from a defensive military body." Nazemroaya. *The Globalization of NATO*, 131.

Organization of American States – OAS

At its best, a forum through which the U.S. is able to keep the upstarts in its backyard in line. At its worst, an irresponsible international body coddling the tyrants in Havana.

Organization of Oil Exporting Countries – OPEC

A most untrustworthy organization controlling far too much *American oil*.

Outer Space

America's sky.[34]

Pakistan

Drone firing range.[35]

Palestine

Israeli settlement.

Palestinians

The "invented people" who live in *Palestine*.[36]

Persian Gulf

Vital *American* waterway protected 24-7 by the U.S. Navy from any outside *meddling*. (See *Carter Doctrine*, Chapter 9.)

---

[34] The U.S. military's Space Command was created in 1985 with a mission to, "Provide Resilient and Affordable Space and Cyberspace Capabilities for the Joint Force and the Nation." The U.S. military's Joint Vision 2020, meanwhile, calls for full spectrum dominance across all domains, including space. See "Joint Vision 2020: America's Military: Preparing for Tomorrow." U.S. Department of Defense. (Washington DC: US Government Printing Office, June 2000): 6.

[35] According to the Bureau of Investigative Journalism, from 2004 to February 2015, there have been 413 U.S. drone strikes in Pakistan, killing 2,438-3,942 individuals, including 416-959 civilians.

[36] The words of former U.S. Speaker of the House Newt Gingrich. Associated Press. "Palestinians are an invented people, says Newt Gingrich." *The Guardian*. (9 Dec 2011).

Philippines, the

Drone launching pad.[37]

Qatar

Drone launching pad.[38]

Russia

A large *anti-access environment*, the epitome of evil, and a serial denier that *history is now over.* (See *Revisionist Power*, Chapter 9.)

Rwanda

The reason *we* must always militarily intervene to "protect civilians," lest *we* have another Rwanda – another *genocide* – on our hands.[39]

---

[37] As Micah Zenko and Emma Welch reported in *Foreign Policy*, "The Philippine government reportedly allows the United States to fly unmanned surveillance drones to monitor militants from the al Qaeda-linked group Abu Sayyaf on the island Mindanao. The most active site is in Zamboanga, one of the locations where the Joint Special Operations Task Force-Philippines is based. U.S. drones are said to have provided the location of prominent Abu Sayyaf militants that were subsequently killed in an air strike carried out by the Philippines Air Force in February 2012." Micah Zenko and Emma Welch. "Where the Drones Are: Mapping the launch pads for Obama's secret wars." *Foreign Policy*. (29 May 2012).

[38] The U.S. flies drones out of Al-Udeid Air Base in Qatar, where "Lawyers are stationed…24 hours a day to approve drone strikes carried about by the U.S. military." *Ibid.*

[39] On a recent example of Rwanda being used as a justification for U.S. military intervention, see: Anne-Marie Slaughter. "Obama should remember Rwanda as he weighs action in Syria." *Washington Post*. (26 April 2013).

    Commenting on the use of Rwanda as a justification for military intervention more broadly, Jean Bricmont writes: "The problem is that the mainstream discourse uses nonintervention in situations where it might have been justified (although it remains to be seen what would have been the nature and consequences of such an intervention) to prepare public opinion to accept other interventions that do in fact take place but in very different circumstances. The 'lessons of history' are always the same: denunciation of our supposed indifference to the suffering of others and encouragement of military intervention." Jean Bricmont, translated by Diana Johnstone. *Humanitarian Imperialism: Using Human Rights to Sell War.* (New York: Monthly Review Press, 2006): 51

Saudi Arabia

Guardians of *American oil* and loyal customers of *American* weapons manufacturers, whatever else the House of Saud does is of no importance.[40]

Serbia

Late 1990s U.S./*NATO* bombing target.

Seychelles

Drone launching pad.[41]

Somalia

Drone firing range.[42]

South China Sea

Given time, the South *American* Sea.

South Korea

What *North Korea* ought to be; you know, a *forward operating base*.[43]

---

[40] Substantial evidence exists linking members of the Saudi ruling family to the 9/11 hijackers. For instance, in 2014 testimony given from inside a U.S. supermaxim prison, former al-Qaeda operative Zacarias Moussaoui asserted that "he was directed in 1998 or 1999 by Qaeda leaders in Afghanistan to create a digital database of donors to the group. Among those he said he recalled listing in the database were Prince Turki al-Faisal, then the Saudi intelligence chief; Prince Bandar Bin Sultan, the longtime Saudi ambassador to the United States; Prince al-Waleed bin Talal, a prominent billionaire investor; and many of the country's leading clerics." Similar claims have been made by former U.S. Senator Bob Graham, who co-chaired the Congressional Joint Inquiry into 9/11. See: Scott Shane. "Moussaoui Calls Saudi Princes Patrons of Al Qaeda." *New York Times*. (3 Feb 2015); "Investigating the Saudi Government's 9/11 Connection and the Path to Disillusionment - Sen. Graham on Reality Asserts Itself pt 1." *The Real News Network*. (3 Oct 2014).

[41] The U.S. has been flying drones out of a base in the Seychelles since 2009. Craig Whitlock and Greg Miller. "U.S. assembling secret drone bases in Africa, Arabian Peninsula, officials say." *Washington Post*. (20 Sept 2011).

[42] According to the Bureau of Investigative Journalism, from 2007 to February 2015, there have been between 8-12 U.S. drone strikes in Somalia, killing between 23-102 individuals.

[43] The U.S. has just under 30,000 troops stationed in South Korea, with the Pentagon adding to that total as recently as 2014. Tony Capaccio and Nicole Gaouette. "U.S. Adding 800 Troops for South Korea Citing Rebalance." *Bloomberg*. (7 Jan 2014).

Syria

A means through which to weaken *Iran*, as the road to Tehran runs through Damascus.[44]

Third World

A *Cold War (old)* era U.S. bombing target and frequent location of *low intensity conflicts*.

Turkey

Drone launching pad.[45]

Ukraine

A means through which to weaken *Russia*.[46]

United Arab Emirates

Drone launching pad.[47]

United Nations

At its best, an international political body formed to lend legitimacy to U.S. *wars* and *no-fly zones*. At its worst, an anti-Semitic *mob* intent on delegitimizing the *lone democracy in the Middle East*.[48]

---

[44] Richard Haas, president of the influential Council on Foreign Relations, argued for U.S. airstrikes against Syria in August of 2013 "not simply to discourage them [the Syrian government] from using chemical weapons again, but to send a message to Iran." "U.S. Action on Syria Might Send Message to Other Nations, Reinforce Taboo." *PBS Newshour.* (26 Aug 2013). See also, Ben Schreiner "Targeting Iran on a Syrian Battlefield." *MRzine.* (9 Feb 2012).

[45] The U.S. flies drones out of the joint U.S.-Turkey airbase located in Incirlik, Turkey. Zenko and Welch. "Where the Drones Are."

[46] As former national security advisor to President Carter, Zbigniew Brzezinski, commented in his 1997 book, *The Grand Chessboard*, "Ukraine...is a geopolitical pivot because its very existence as an independent country helps to transform Russia. Without Ukraine, Russia ceases to be a Eurasian empire."

[47] The U.S. flies drones out of Al-Dhafra Air Base, United Arab Emirates. Zenko and Welch. "Where the Drones Are."

[48] The U.S. has used its position on the UN Security Council to veto measures condemning illegal Israeli behavior over 40 times.

United Nations Security Council

When granting authorization for *American wars*, a strong and powerful voice for the will of the *international community*. When failing to authorize such *wars*, a tragically "neutered" body.[49]

Venezuela

A sizable repository of *American oil* under the control of a rogue *regime* run by a bunch of uppity despots pandering to the dirty lower classes.[50]

West, the

The civilized *good guys* (i.e., the U.S., *Canada*, Europe, and *Japan*).

World, the

A battlefield.[51]

World Court

An utter non-entity ever since the day in 1986 when the Court had the temerity to actually issue a ruling against *the world*'s lone indispensable nation.[52]

---

[49] After both Russia and China vetoed a 2012 UN Security Council resolution calling for Syrian President Bashir al-Assad to step down, Secretary of State Hillary Clinton deem the resolution's failure a "travesty." She went on to deem the council "neutered." Arshad Mohammed. "Clinton calls U.N. vote a 'travesty.'" Reuters. (5 Feb 2012).

[50] As soon as Hugo Chavez came to power in 1998, the U.S. began a multifaceted campaign of destabilization against Venezuela (including the failed 2002 coup). And yet even after Chavez's passing in 2013, the U.S. campaign has continued apace. As Eva Golinger writes, the National Endowment for Democracy and USAID have "filtered more than $14 million to opposition groups in Venezuela between 2013 and 2014, including funding for their political campaigns in 2013 and for the current anti-government protests in 2014." Eva Golinger. "The Dirty Hand of the National Endowment for Democracy in Venezuela: Agents of Destabilization." *CounterPunch*. (25-27 April 2014).

[51] See Jeremy Scahill. *Dirty Wars: The World is a Battlefield*. (New York: Nation Books, 2013).

[52] The 1986 case, brought by Nicaragua, awarded reparations to Nicaragua for the U.S. role in supporting the Contra rebels. The Court's judgment was ultimately blocked by the U.S. in the United Nation's Security Council.

Yemen

Drone firing range.[53]

Yugoslavia

The birthplace of the *humanitarian intervention*.[54]

---

[53] According to the Bureau of Investigative Journalism, from 2002 to February 2015, there have been a confirmed 89-108 U.S. drone strikes in Yemen, killing 428-633 individuals, including 65-96 civilians.

[54] Sold as one of the first "humanitarian interventions," the U.S. and NATO bombardment of Yugoslavia was little more than a dressed up imperial endeavor. As Diana Johnstone explained in her book, *Fool's Crusade*: "In the 1990s, the US-led International Community was no longer interested in promoting state-building. Nation-state deconstruction was more compatible with economic globalization measures. Recalling the unswerving goal of U.S. policy is to keep Europe 'open to trade', Madeleine Albright has stressed that, with communism defeated, 'The struggle now is between democracy and extreme forms of nationalism'. The 'extreme' nationalism is likely to be the one thought to be least likely to fall in line with International Community economic dictates. Yugoslavia's traditional 'state-builders' drew less sympathy than the splitters. Held together, Yugoslavia might have been a potential source of independent foreign policy. Fragmented, it could easily be subdued or marginalized." Diana Johnstone. *Fool's Crusade: Yugoslavia, NATO and Western Delusions*. (New York: Monthly Review Press, 2002): 128-129.

11. A Global Force for Good

Poll: Public rejects 'Global force for good'

-   Navy Times, *2013*[1]

A Global Force for Good

The *U.S. military – isolated incidents* and all.

Abu Ghraib

Iraq prison at which *bad apples* within the *U.S. military* tortured, raped, sodomized, and killed prisoners from 2003 to 2004. In other words, an *isolated incident*.

AFRICOM

U.S. military's strategic *Africa* Command, located in Stuttgart, *Germany*. AFRICOM is responsible for *protecting civilians* in all the geopolitically important countries spanning the continent of *Africa*.

Air Force Global Strike Command

The military unit responsible for overseeing to the safety and security of the nation's nuclear weapons stockpile. And accordingly, a unit staffed by the very best of the best…or maybe not.[2] Well either way, it's only a bunch of nukes.

Air-Sea Battle

The *Pentagon*'s "preposterously expensive" model for a future *war* with *China*. Relying on the use of long-range bombers and stealth submarines to strike

---

[1] Sam Fellman. "Poll: Public rejects 'Global force for good.'" *Navy Times*. (5 Feb 2013).

[2] In 2013, the Global Strike Command was rocked by multiple scandals involving systemic cheating by nuclear launch officers on proficiency exams at Malmstrom Air Force Base in Montana and Minot Air Force Base in North Dakota. The same year, the Air Force sacked the head of the U.S. nuclear force, Major General Michael Carey. The cashiering of Carey followed an official visit to Moscow in which the two-star general engaged in heavy drinking and inappropriate fraternizing with "suspicious" foreign women. And then in 2014, the Air Force was again compelled to sack two more nuclear commanders. "US air force fires two more nuclear commanders amid leadership crisis." *The Guardian*. (3 Nov 2014).

anti-access environments deep inside *China* as part of an initial "blinding campaign," the battle concept promises to unleash "incalculable human and economic destruction." That said, Beijing still need not worry, for as the *unpeople* from Korea to Vietnam and *Afghanistan* to *Iraq* can personally attest, the *global force for good* only resorts to such wanton destruction as a very last resort.[3]

Al-Shifa

A menacing Sudanese civilian pharmaceutical factory bravely *taken out* by U.S. *cruise missiles* in 1998, because, well, *something had to be done* in the wake of the U.S. *embassy* bombings in East *Africa*.

All-Volunteer Force

A military force comprised of the conscripts of a shadow draft imposed on *American* youth of low socioeconomic status.

Annihilate

Kill.

Anti-Access Environments

The scarce places scattered about the globe still capable of repelling the tentacles of the U.S. *military*. The continued existence of such environments presents an ongoing threat to *vital national interests*.

Anti-Personnel Weapons

Military weapons specifically designed for the most *efficient* dismemberment and murder of various *unpeople*.

Apache

The native inhabitants of the Southwest U.S. who were subjected to *ethnic*

---

[3] The warnings of Air-Sea Battle being "preposterously expensive" and supremely destructive come from an internal Marine Corps assessment. In early 2015, the Pentagon rebranded Air-Sea Battle as the "Joint Concept for Access and Maneuver in the Global Commons," with an eye toward assuaging concerns from the Marine Corps and Army over the original Air-Sea Battle design's exclusion of land forces. See Greg Jaffe. "U.S. model for a future war fans tensions with China and inside Pentagon." *Washington Post*. (1 Aug 2012); Paul McLeary. "New US Concept Melds Air, Sea and Land." *Defense News*. (24 Jan 2015).

cleansing by the *American state* during the 1800s. The U.S. has since made amends with the Apache by naming a military attack helicopter – used in U.S. *campaigns* against various other native peoples in faraway lands – an Apache.[4]

Army of One

U.S. Army recruiting slogan acknowledging the future abandonment by the *American government* each enlisted soldier will ultimately face upon his or her discharge from the service.

Army Strong

U.S. Army recruiting slogan acknowledging the fact that it takes a special kind of strength to endure being an *Army of One*.

Asymmetrical Threats

Threats posed to the *Pentagon*'s various billion dollar weapons systems by the cheap, defensive weaponry fashioned by motivated *insurgents* fighting in *liberated* areas. Asymmetrical threats are to be combated by spending billions of more dollars on the creation of even more sophisticated weapons systems.

Asymmetrical Warfare

Detainee suicide.[5]

Bad Apple

A low level functionary responsible for the systemic crimes of the civilian military leadership. *Justice* prevails through the punishment of bad apples.

---

[4] Other examples of Native American names finding their way into the military lexicon include: the Black Hawk, Chinook, Comanche, Cheyenne, Kiowa, and Lakota helicopters. There is also the Tomahawk cruise missile. Meanwhile, the raid to kill Osama bin Laden was codenamed Geronimo.

[5] When three detainees suddenly died at the U.S. detention facility at Guantanamo Bay in 2006, the military quickly claimed the three had committed suicide, with base commander Admiral Harry Harris asserting, "I believe this was not an act of desperation, but an act of asymmetrical warfare waged against us." A later investigation by Scott Horton appearing in *Harper's* magazine showed the official claims that the detainees committed suicide to be simply beyond belief. Moreover, as an army whistleblower crucially revealed, the three deceased had been tortured at an off-the-books detention facility on the base the night of their deaths. See Scott Horton. "The Guantánamo 'Suicides': A Camp Delta sergeant blows the whistle." *Harper's.* (March 2010).

Battle Damage Repair

Blood *money*.[6]

Bay of Pigs Invasion

The failed 1961 invasion of *Cuba* by *CIA*-backed *rebels* occurring at the Bay of Pigs. The botched invasion was to provide all the proof necessary that President John F. Kennedy was a *weak leader*. So weak, in fact, that not till the sudden appearance of a magical bullet in Dallas, Texas on November 22, 1963 was the anxiety of every red-blooded anti-*communist* to finally subside.[7]

Be All That You Can Be

An old U.S. Army recruiting slogan. The catchphrase acknowledged that becoming cannon fodder for the U.S. *government* was all the Army thought potential recruits could ever really *hope* to be.

Black Hawk Down

A 1993 battle in Mogadishu, *Somalia* since lionized in *American culture*. The battle saw the downing of two U.S. Black Hawk helicopters and the death of 18 U.S. forces, along with more Somali *others*. The incident ultimately forced the U.S. to withdraw from *Somalia* and disengage from the country's hitherto *low intensity conflict*. With the introduction of the *drone*, however, the U.S. was able to once again reenter *Somalia* and resume its active involvement in the country's *low intensity conflict*.[8]

Blunt Momentum

Kill.

---

[6] According to a 2013 report in *The Nation* magazine, "the United States paid out more than $3.7 million in 'battle damage repair' [i.e., blood money] to Afghans in 2010. In 2011, that number jumped to nearly $12 million." Turse. "Blood Money."
[7] On the forces within the American government which conspired to assassinate Kennedy, see: James Douglass. *JFK and the Unspeakable: Why He Died and Why It Matters.* (New York: Simon and Schuster, 2008).
[8] In 2007, the U.S. resumed covert actions within Somalia. And according to the Bureau of Investigative Journalism, since then, there have been 8-12 U.S. drone strikes within the country and 8-11 additional covert operation, which have killed in total 63-243 Somalis. "US covert actions in Somalia" Bureau of Investigative Journalism.<http://www.thebureauinvestigates.com/category/projects/drones/drones-somalia/>

Body Counts

Something no *global force for good* can be troubled with.[9]

Building Partner Capacity

Training expendable foreigners to fight and die for *American* interests.

Bunker Buster

A diplomatic tool designed to *destroy* buried installations located deep within *anti-access environments*.

Campaign

A military operation undertaken as part of the *liberation* of a suppressed people, entailing the standard *liquating, neutralizing,* and otherwise *vaporizing* of all *liberty*-hating locals.

CENTCOM

U.S. military's strategic Central Command located in Tampa, Florida. CENTCOM is responsible for securing *America*'s *oil* throughout the *Middle East*.

Civilian Control of the Military

Doing whatever the *generals* say.

Cluster Bombs

An *anti-personnel weapon* posing a particular threat to civilians, especially children. And because of such concerns, a total of 84 nations have ratified an international treaty banning the use of cluster bombs. But not the *exceptional nation*. As the *U.S. State Department* explains, cluster bombs have "demonstrated military utility."[10]

---

[9] As U.S. Gen. Tommy Franks famously remarked in 2002, "we don't do body counts." (A brazen lie, incidentally, which was exposed by the cache of U.S. diplomatic cables published by WikiLeaks in 2010.) Similarly, in early 2015, Pentagon Press Secretary Rear Adm. John Kirby remarked, in regard to reports of civilian casualties in the U.S. bombing campaign against the Islamic State in Iraq and Syria: "We aren't getting into an issue of body counts." See John Broder. "A Nation at War: The Casualties; U.S. Military Has No Count Of Iraqi Dead In Fighting." *New York Times*. (2 April 2003); Julian E. Barnes. "U.S. Probes Civilian Casualties in Iraq, Syria." *Wall Street Journal.* (6 Jan 2015).

[10] U.S. Department of State. <http://www.state.gov/t/pm/wra/c25930.htm>

Counterinsurgency – COIN

A divide – kill – and rule anti-insurgency strategy deployed against the thanklessly *liberated*. (See *Fallujah*.)

Counterterrorism

The use of *violence* to weaken those who stoop to using *violence* against the M16-packing *good guys*.

Covert Actions

Never to be confused with missionary *work*, covert actions are clandestine military operations turned to as *war fatigue* grows; for the *vital national interests* must be protected, whether the *American people* are able to stomach it at any particular moment or not.[11]

Cruise Missile

The most favored instrument in the U.S. *diplomacy* toolkit.

Crush

Kill.

Cyberattack

Fingers crossed, *a new Pearl Harbor*.[12]

CYBERCOM

U.S. military's strategic Cyber Command located in Fort Meade, Maryland. CYBERCOM is responsible for ensuring no entity challenges the *NSA*'s ownership of the *Internet*.

---

[11] As Secretary of State Henry Kissinger once remarked, "covert action should not be confused with missionary work." Quoted in: Blum. *Killing Hope*, 244.

[12] In late 2012, then-Secretary of Defense Leon Panetta lobbied for greater spending on cyber warfare by warning of a "cyber-Pearl Harbor." And upon his nomination to become Secretary of Defense in December 2014, Ashton Carter referred to the leaks attributed to Edward Snowden as a "Pearl Harbor." As Carter remarked, "We had a cyber Pearl Harbor. His name was Edward Snowden." Elisabeth Bumiller and Thom Shanker. "Panetta Warns of Dire Threat of Cyberattack on U.S." *New York Times*. (11 Oct 2012); Craig Whitlock. "Ashton Carter, passed over before, gets picked by Obama to be defense secretary." *Washington Post*. (5 Dec 2014).

Cyber War

The certain future lifeblood of the digital economy

Death Squad

A *partner* nation *kill team* trained by the very best of the best in the killing business (i.e., the *global force for good*).[13] (See also, *School of the America's*.)

Defense Spending

The spending related to the offensive capabilities of the *U.S. military*. Increase defense spending, get more *wars*. And given that *war* is what sustains the *American* economy – the *American way of life* – no amount is ever too high when it comes to defense.[14]

Degrade and Destroy

Kill, for a sustained period of time.

Department of Defense

Department of *war*.

Department of Veteran Affairs

Federal department tasked with systematically underserving the needs of *veterans*.[15]

---

[13] The use of U.S. trained and equipped death squads was a hallmark of the U.S. dirty wars throughout Central America in the 1980s. The U.S. later exported the Central American model to post-invasion Iraq, with the training of Shiite death squads. Notably, the Iraq dirty war fell under the leadership of U.S. Ambassador John Negroponte, who served as Ambassador to Honduras from 1981 to 1985, and before that as an official at the U.S. Embassy in Saigon during the Vietnam War. Nicolas J.S. Davies. "U.S. Dirty Wars: Why Iraqis consider ISIS the lesser evil next to U.S.-backed death squads." *Z Magazine*. (Jan 2015): 39-43.

[14] Even accounting for the defense cuts proposed by Secretary of Defense Chuck Hagel in 2014, which would see a reduction in military personal not seen since prior to WWII, the U.S. still spends more on defense than Russia, China, and the United Kingdom combined.

[15] In mid-2014, the VA became embroiled in its latest scandal as it was revealed that numerous VA hospitals were denying lifesaving care to veterans and then covering up such actions through various bookkeeping schemes, including the use of secret waitlists and fraudulent appointment scheduling.

Depleted Uranium

A dangerously radioactive munition used by the *U.S. military* because its increased density and reduced diameter as compared to lead makes it a far more *efficient* killer.

Depose

Kill or topple a foreign head of *state*.

Desert Storm

The code name given to the first U.S. *war* with *Iraq* in 1990. *Desert Storm*, in addition to fulfilling the promise of the *Carter Doctrine*, vanquished the *Vietnam Syndrome* and served notice to *the world* that the *end of history* was to be ensured by U.S. *full spectrum dominance*.

Destroy

Kill.

Drones

Robotized killing machines offering a great advance forward in the conduct of warfare, guaranteeing any chosen conflict remains a *low intensity conflict*.

Eliminate

Kill.

Eradicate

Kill.

EUCOM

U.S. military's strategic European Command, located in Stuttgart, *Germany*. EUCOM is responsible for protecting the *free world* from *revisionist powers*.

Exterminate

Kill.

F-35 Joint Strike Fighter

A suspect jet flawlessly designed to funnel historic amounts of public cash into the private coffers of leading defense contractors.[16]

Fallujah

Iraqi city ravaged by high cancer rates and birth deformities. Unrelatedly, the same city falling under the siege of *depleted uranium*-discharging and *white phosphorous*-shelling U.S. forces in 2004.[17]

False Flag

An operation occurring solely in the minds of crazed conspiracy theorists. Involving the staging of an attack or incident in such a manner as to conceal the real perpetrator in order to later blame a foreign *state* or actor, a false flag operation aims to create the necessary *provocation* needed to launch a wider *war*. The U.S. would never consider conducting a *false flag* operation – ever. (See *Gulf of Tonkin Incident* and *Operation Northwoods*.)

Finish

Kill.

Forward Operating Base

A military base located near the location of the next *just war*. And hence the presence of U.S. forward operating bases on every continent.

Forward Positioned

The strategic positioning of troops and hardware for the next *war*.

---

[16] Lockheed Martin's F-35 Joint Strike Fighter, which was originally projected to cost $81 million per plane, is now estimated to cost $219 million or more per copy. And yet, the jet remains largely inoperable. As Avery Kleinman of the Project on Government Oversight explains: "As of now, the planes can't drop bombs and have only 2% of the necessary coding to be used in combat. During testing, pilots have ended up abandoning their futuristic helmets mid-flight due to the confusion they cause. The planes also can't fly in inclement weather, something a $60,000 Cessna can do." Avery Kleinman. "The Over Budget and Behind Schedule F-35." POGO. (17 Sept 2013).
[17] One study found that in the years since the 2004 U.S. siege of the city, birth malformations in Fallujah rose to "11 times higher than normal rates." Martin Chulov. "Research links rise in Falluja birth defects and cancers to US assault." *The Guardian*. (30 Dec 2010).

Free-Fire Zone

A *collateral damage* zone.

Friendly Fire

An attack against one's own forces occurring by *mistake* when trying to attack enemy forces. If such an attack were to, say, kill a prominent former football player turned soldier, spare no expense in covering up such an embarrassing revelation.[18]

Full Spectrum Dominance

The *Pentagon*'s stated quest for unrivaled military supremacy across all terrains and platforms: air, land, sea, *space*, cyber, and information. In other words, the *Pentagon*'s yearning for world domination.[19]

General

A future board member of a prominent defense contractor.[20]

Giving Aid and Comfort to the Enemy

Protesting against a *just war* in the streets.

Good War, the (i.e., WWII)

The U.S. firebombing of Dresden and Tokyo, nuking of *Hiroshima* and *Nagasaki*, and domestic interning of *Americans* of Japanese heritage.

Gulf of Tonkin Incident

A staged 1964 "attack" by North Vietnamese vessels on the USS *Maddox* occurring in international waters off the coast of North Vietnam. The

---

[18] The exampled alluded to being the military cover-up of the friendly fire death in 2004 of U.S. Army Ranger and former NFL player Pat Tillman.

[19] In the Pentagon's stated strategic vision for the year 2020, full spectrum dominance – described by the Pentagon as "the ability of US forces...to defeat any adversary and control any situation across the full range of military operations" – is declared to be the "overarching focus." "Joint Vision 2020," 6, 3.

[20] A 2012 report from the Citizens for Responsibility and Ethics in Washington "found 70 percent (or 76) of the 108 three-and-four star generals and admirals who retired between 2009 and 2011 took jobs with defense contractors or consultants." "Strategic Maneuvers: The Revolving Door from the Pentagon to the Private Sector." CREW. (2012).

"attack" served as the impetus needed for the U.S. bombing of North Vietnam and the escalation of the *Vietnam War*. (See *False Flag*.)

Haditha

Iraqi city in which 24 civilians were murders by U.S. Marines in November 2005. Another strikingly *isolated incident*.

Hamdania Incident

The 2006 murder of a detained Iraqi man in the village of Al Hamdania and the subsequent cover-up by U.S. Marines. Once more, an *isolated incident*.

Hellfire Missile

A $70,000 scalpel to be put to use in *surgical strikes*.

Highway of Death

The highway on which *American* forces gallantly massacred retreating Iraqi soldiers fleeing from Kuwait at the close of the *Gulf War*.[21]

Hiroshima

A message delivered to Moscow on August 6, 1945. The missive was intended to relay the fact that the U.S. was a truly exceptional *superpower* that was not going to be *soft on communism*. Coming attached to the message was well over 100,000 dead Japanese in *collateral damage*.

Ice Cream

The latest *consumer* comforts of the *homeland* (fast food, electronics, etc.) brought to the furthest imperial outposts.[22]

---

[21] In late February 1991, Iraq's Republican Guard began to withdraw from Kuwait back into Iraq along Highway 80. In a clear violation of international law, American pilots then proceeded to mow down the retreating Iraqis. As one American pilot recalled, "It was like shooting fish in a barrel." Mickey Z. "Highway of Death: 22 Years Later (What We're Up Against)." InformationClearingHouse.info. (20 Feb 2013).

[22] Attending a military contractor convention, David Vine writes of the use of "ice cream" to describe the perks found on U.S. military bases overseas: "[U.S. Marine Corps Major Patrick] Reynolds explained to the group how bases tend to expand exponentially over time. 'You start out small' with an outpost, he said, 'thinking you'll only be there for a week…. And then it's two weeks. And then it's a month. And then it's two months.' In the process, bases add facilities, food, and recreational

Iran Air Flight 655

An Iranian civilian passenger jet shot down in the *Persian Gulf* by the "exceptionally meritorious" *American* sailors of the USS *Vincennes* on July 3, 1988, killing all 290 people on board.[23]

Isolated Incident

The systemic crimes of *American* troops and policymakers committed during *criminal wars* of *aggression*.

Joint Special Operations Command – JSOC

An executive branch hit squad.[24]

Kill Team

Those *winning hearts and minds*.[25]

Kinetic Action

Any use of bombs and bullets with the intent of killing and maiming.

Lily Pad

A small, strategically located, and low-profile foreign military base. Lily pads

---

amenities, like steak and lobster, flat screen TVs, and Internet connections. The major said he and others in the military refer to these comforts collectively as 'ice cream.'" David Vine. "'We're Profiteers': How Military Contractors Reap Billions from U.S. Military Bases Overseas." *Monthly Review* Vol. 66 No. 3 (July/Aug 2014): 95.

[23] The commanding officer of the *Vincennes* at the time of the downing of Iran Air Flight 655, Captain William Rogers, was later awarded the Navy's Legion of Merit for his "exceptionally meritorious conduct."
<http://en.wikipedia.org/wiki/Iran_Air_Flight_655>

[24] JSOC is comprised of the U.S. military's most highly trained special operations commandos, including the Navy Seals. Journalist Seymour Hersh described the command's structure as follows: "It's an executive assassination ring essentially…the Joint Special Operations Command—JSOC it's called. They don't report to anybody, except in the Bush-Cheney days, they reported directly to Cheney." Eric Black. "Investigative reporter Seymour Hersh describes 'executive assassination ring.'" *MinnPost*. (11 March 2009).

[25] "Kill team" being the name conferred on members of the U.S. Stryker Brigade from Joint Base Lewis-McCord in Washington State who killed Afghans as sport. See "Winning Hearts and Minds" below and the accompanying footnote.

allow U.S. forces to easily traverse *the world*, jumping from base to base, *low intensity conflict* to *low intensity conflict*.[26]

Liquidate

Kill.

Mahmudiyah Killings

The 2006 gang rape and murder of 14-year-old Iraqi girl Abeer Qassim Hamza al-Janabi by five U.S. soldiers near Al-Mahmudiyah, *Iraq*. One more *isolated incident*.

Massive Ordinance Penetrator – MOP

A $16 million, 30,000-pound *bunker buster* designed to "get at any enemy, anywhere."[27]

Mercenary

Soldier for hire. Also, the best employment opportunity for those formerly an *Army of One*.

Message Force Multiplier

A media *military analyst*.[28]

---

[26] "Like real lily pads," David Vine writes, "bases have a way of growing and reproducing uncontrollably. Indeed, bases tend to beget bases, creating 'base races' with other nations, heightening military tensions, and discouraging diplomatic solutions to conflicts." David Vine. "The Lily-Pad Strategy: How the Pentagon Is Quietly Transforming Its Overseas Base Empire and Creating a Dangerous New Way of War." TomDispatch.com (15 July 2012).

[27] As Defense Secretary Leon Panetta remarked in 2012 on the MOP: "It's not just aimed at Iran. Frankly, it's aimed at any enemy that decides to locate in some kind of impenetrable location. The goal here is to be able to get at any enemy, anywhere." Adam Entous and Julian E. Barnes. "Pentagon Seeks Mightier Bomb vs. Iran." *Wall Street Journal*. (28 Jan 2012).

[28] A 2008 *New York Times* investigation cited internal Pentagon documents as repeatedly referring to media military analysts "as 'message force multipliers' or 'surrogates' who could be counted on to deliver administration 'themes and messages' to millions of Americans 'in the form of their own opinions.'" Barstow. "Behind TV Analysts, Pentagon's Hidden Hand."

Military Advisors

Combat troops fighting either a *war* officials have claimed to be winding down, or a *war* officials have yet to formally acknowledge.

Missile Defense

An offensive weapons system designed to intercept and destroy incoming missiles, thus permitting military commanders and policymakers the *freedom* to launch offensive attacks without having to *fear* the repercussions of a retaliatory strike.

Mutual Security

Pacts struck between the *U.S. military* and a foreign *state*, in which U.S. bases are permitted in return for U.S. promises to assure the continued security of the hosting *government* against possible threats, whether they be foreign or domestic (i.e., an excess in *democracy*). (See *Bahrain*, Chapter 10.)

Mutually Assured Destruction – MAD

A *Cold War (old)* era military doctrine holding that two rational acting *states* with nuclear weapons would not resort to using such weapons in *war*, for *fear* that doing so would assure the total destruction of both nations. In the modern age of *full spectrum dominance*, MAD is simply capitulation.

My Lai Massacre

The lone case of *criminal* behavior by U.S. forces in Vietnam to be found. A remarkably *isolated incident*.

Nagasaki

A second message delivered to Moscow on August 9, 1945. The missive was intended to reiterate the fact that the U.S. was a truly exceptional *superpower* that was not going to be *soft on communism*. The message again came with over 100,000 dead Japanese in *collateral damage*.

Navy SEALS

An *American death squad*.

Neutralize

Kill.

NORTHCOM

U.S. *military*'s strategic Northern Command located in Colorado Springs, Colorado. NORTHCOM is responsible for securing the *homeland* by putting the final nail in the coffin of *Posse Comitatus*.[29]

Obliterate

Kill.

Off

Kill.

Operation Falcon Freedom (i.e., the 2011 bombing of Libya)

An unequivocal message sent to *the world* by the U.S. and its *NATO* allies that all *states* abandoning their nuclear weapons programs in exchange for better relations with the *West* naively expose themselves to *regime change*.[30] Also, more generally, a much needed re-legitimizing of the *humanitarian intervention* in the post-*Iraq war* era.[31]

Operation Just Cause (i.e., the 1989 invasion of Panama)

A live-fire U.S. *war game* conducted in Panama in order to prep the *U.S. military* for Operation *Desert Storm*, which was to follow one year later. The *war game* also *liberated* the Panamanian people from a *strongman* turned *dictator*

---

[29] According to NORTHCOM's website, the command's mission "includes counter-drug operations and managing the consequences of a terrorist event employing a weapon of mass destruction," in addition to providing local authorities "civil support." <http://www.northcom.mil/AboutUSNORTHCOM.aspx>

[30] In 2003, out of a desire not to become the next Iraq, Libya renounced its WMD program in return for greater relations with the West. As even Richard Haass, the president of the quasi-official Council on Foreign Relations, has since been left to remark: "the entire exercise [the U.S./NATO intervention] – coming as it did a few years after Qaddafi had been induced to give up his unconventional weapons programs – probably increased the perceived value of nuclear weapons and reduced the likelihood of getting other states to follow Qaddafi's example." Richard Haass. "The Unraveling: How to Respond to a Disordered World." *Foreign Affairs* Vol. 93 No. 6 (Nov/Dec 2014): 74.

[31] As Vijay Prashad remarked on the significance of the Libyan war, "Interventionism is back, thanks to NATO's Libyan adventure." Prashad. *Arab Spring, Libyan Winter*, 234.

(*Manuel Noriega*) at the price of only over 1,000 Panamanians in *collateral damage*.[32]

Operation Northwoods

A 1962 proposal originating within the *Department of Defense*, which called for a series of *terrorist* attacks against targets within the United States to be carried out by *CIA* operatives. The proposal went on to suggest that these attacks would then be linked to the Cuban *regime* of *Fidel Castro*, as a means of ginning up popular support for a U.S. invasion of the island. (See *False Flag*.)

Operation Urgent Fury (i.e., the 1983 invasion of Grenada)

An attempt to kick the *Vietnam Syndrome* by chalking up a nice, quick *victory*. Unfortunately, the *Vietnam Syndrome* would persist for another eight long years, before finally meeting its end during *Desert Storm*.

Pacification

Terrorizing the ungrateful locals into a more respectful state of submission.

PACOM

U.S. military's strategic Pacific Command, located in Halawa Heights, Hawaii. PACOM is responsible for the *containment* of *China*.

Panjwayi Massacre

The March 2012 murder of 16 Afghan civilians by U.S. Army Staff Sargent Robert Bales in the Panjwayi District of Kandahar Province. Again, an *isolated incident*.

Pentagon

The largest office building in *the world*, the Pentagon is the place of employment for the nation's legions of future defense industry *consultants* and *lobbyists*.

Phase Zero

The first phase in the *U.S. military*'s six phased combat spectrum. Phase Zero is marked by an intolerable absence of conflict (what some may erroneously

---

[32] On Operation Just Cause as a prelude to the Gulf War, see: *The Panama Deception*. Dir. Barbara Trent. (1992).

deem to be a state of *peace*), which is to be passed doing everything possible
to ensure Phase Zero is short-lived.[33]

Phase 1

Leveling threats of *aggression* backed up by *coercive diplomacy*.

Phase 2

Unleashing *shock and awe*.

Phase 3

Boots on the ground, drones in the air.

Phase 4

Counterinsurgency.

Phase 5

Nation building while *Washington* rallies the *international community* anew against
the next *next Hitler*.

Post-Traumatic Stress Disorder – PTSD

The personal burden to long be endured by the *heroes* ever so prudently
shipped off to be "greeted as liberators."[34]

Precision Guided Munitions

See *Smart Bombs*.

---

[33] As Rosa Brooks explains: Following Phase Zero is Phase 1, "which is characterized
'by preparatory actions that indicate the intent to execute subsequent phases of
operation.' If deterrence [Phase 1] fails, Phase 2, 'seizing the initiative,' begins,
leading...to Phase 3, 'dominance' or 'sustained combat operations.' If successful, this
is followed by Phase 4, 'stabilization,' in which military forces restore basic security
and services. In Phase 5, the military works to restore civil authority. These tasks
completed, we once again circle back to Phase Zero." Rosa Brooks. "Portrait of the
Army as a Work in Progress." *Foreign Policy*. (May/June 2014): 46.
[34] As Vice President Dick Cheney asserted prior to the 2003 U.S. invasion of Iraq:
"I think things have gotten so bad inside Iraq, from the standpoint of the Iraqi
people, my belief is we will, in fact, be greeted as liberators." "Transcript: Interview
with Vice-President Dick Cheney." *Meet the Press*. (16 March 2003).

Preparing the Environment

A covert military incursion into a nation quickly moving up on *Washington*'s list of "to be liberated."

Private Contractor

See *Mercenary*.

Regional Security

The enforcement of *stability* by the *Pentagon*'s regional combatant commands.

Regionally Aligned Forces

The forces the Army plans to assign to specific regions around *the world* and train in region-specific linguistics and culture, because (1) *the world* is a battlefield, and (2) *American diplomacy* is run out of the *Pentagon*, not Foggy Bottom.[35]

Remove From the Battlefield

Kill.

Rogue Elements

Colluding *bad apples*.

School of the Americas

The former name of the *U.S. military training* school located as Fort Benning, Georgia; since 2001, known as the Western Hemisphere Institute for Security Cooperation. The school trains officers primarily from militaries in *America's backyard* in the ways of *counterinsurgency* and *enhanced interrogation techniques*.[36] (See *Death Squads*.)

---

[35] As Rosa Brooks, a supporter of Regionally Aligned Forces, admits: "Even if it doesn't reflect hegemonic U.S. ambitions, the RAF concept, taken to its logical extreme, does suggest that senior Army officials view the entire globe as a potential battlefield." Brooks. "Portrait of the Army as a Work in Progress," 46.

[36] Some of the more notorious School of the Americas graduates include: Panamanian dictator Manuel Noriega and Argentinian junta leaders Emilio Massera, Jorge Rafael Videla Redondo, and Leopoldo Galtieri.

Sexual Assault

A most serious offense threatening to negatively impugn the solid reputation of the armed forces. Sexual assaults are best left investigated by those with intimate knowledge of the issue; you know, those sexually assaulting their peers.[37]

Shake 'n' Bake

The combined use of high explosives and *white phosphorus* to "shake" and then "bake" the *collateral damage*. (See *Fallujah*.)

Shock and Awe

Good guy blitzkrieg.

Smart Bombs

Bombs equipped with precision guiding *technology*, assuring they always strike their dubiously selected target.

SOUTHCOM

U.S. military's Southern strategic command, located in Doral, Florida. SOUTHCOM is responsible for landscaping *America's backyard*.

Special Forces

Highly trained forces specializing in the execution of *collateral damage* the old fashioned way – on the ground and in person.

Status of Forces Agreement

An agreement signed by the *U.S. military* and any foreign *state* hosting *U.S. military* personnel. Such agreements ensure all U.S. soldiers caught raping or

---

[37] In 2013, "the chief of the Air Force's sexual-assault prevention program was charged with assaulting a woman outside a bar in Crystal City, Va., and grabbing her buttocks." The officer, Lt. Col. Jeffrey Krusinski, was later acquitted. But then in early 2014, it was revealed that the Army's top sex-crimes prosecutor, Lt. Col. Joseph Morse, was under investigation following "allegations that he groped a female lawyer at a sexual-assault conference in 2011." Craig Whitlock. "Army's top sex-crimes prosecutor faces groping allegation." *Washington Post*. (6 March 2014).

murdering locals come to safely passage out of country in order to face *justice* in the U.S.[38]

Stomp Out

Kill.

Stop

Kill.[39]

Stop-Loss

The military's once a soldier, always a soldier contract clause.[40]

Strategic Communications

Good guy propaganda.

Tactical Nuclear Weapons

Just another one of the options to always be left *on the table.*

Take Out

Kill.

Target-Rich Environment

Any *dispensable nation.*

---

[38] For instance, in 2014, the U.S. Embassy in Manila announced that it was going to retain custody of U.S. Pfc. Joseph Scott Pemberton under provisions of the visiting forces agreement, a document similar in intent to a status of forces agreement. Pemberton is accused of murdering a transgender Filipina woman. Similarly, as the *Marine Corps Times* reported, "In 2005, Lance Cpl. Daniel Smith was found guilty of raping a woman and was kept at the embassy [in Manila] until his conviction was overturned by appeal even though a judge ordered him released to local authorities." "U.S. will keep custody of Marine accused of murder in the Philippines." *Marine Corps Times.* (18 Dec 2014).

[39] Pentagon spokesperson Rear Admiral John Kirby: "When you drop a bomb from the air, something blows up, somebody, you know, gets stopped, and you have a tactical effect." "Department of Defense Press Briefing by Rear Admiral Kirby in the Pentagon Briefing Room." Department of Defense. (8 Oct 2014).

[40] Stop-loss allows the military to unilaterally extend a member's service beyond the timeframe agreed upon in one's enlistment contract.

Theatre (of Conflict)

The geographical area in which *American* forces are actively engaged in imposing *freedom* on an appreciative people.

Unmanned Aerial Vehicle

See *Drones*.

U.S. Military Training

Equipping *the world*'s next crop of *war criminals* with the all the necessary skills needed for their future success.

Vaporize

Kill.

War Games

Game planning world domination.[41]

Waste

Kill.

White Phosphorous

A civilized *chemical weapon* used by *good guys* against *bad guys*.[42]

---

[41] A 2012 *New York Times* report on a series of U.S. war games shed a little light on the truly global extent of the imperial designs held by Pentagon planners. As the *Times* reported: "Three times so far this year, the Joint Chiefs of Staff and the regional war-fighting commanders have assembled at a military base south of the capital, where a giant map of the world, larger than a basketball court, was laid out on the ground, giving the sessions an appearance of a lethally earnest game of Risk.

"The generals and admirals walked the world and worked their way through a series of potential national security crises, locked in debate over what kind of military — its size, its capability — the nation will require in the next five years." Thom Shanker. "Mapping Military Needs, Aided by a Big Projection." *New York Times*. (11 Sept 2012).

[42] The U.S. most famously deployed white phosphorous during its 2004 siege of Fallujah, Iraq. White phosphorus is a particularly insidious weapon, due to its ability to stick to human skin as it literally burns through one's flesh.

Winning Hearts and Minds

Carefully removing and collecting the locals' skulls, fingers, and teeth – and then urinating on the mutilated corpses.[43]

Wipe Out

Kill.

---

[43] In 2010, six U.S. Stryker Brigade soldiers from Joint Base Lewis-McCord in Washington State were charged with keeping body parts of Afghan fighters and civilians as trophies. Staging numerous attacks in order to create a pretext to attack civilians, members of the Stryker Brigade removed skull fragments, fingers, and teeth from their victims. In 2012, video emerged of U.S. Marines from the 3rd Battalion, 2nd Marines urinating on the corpses of what the Pentagon claimed were Taliban fighters in Afghanistan. Mark Boal. "The Kill Team: How U.S. Soldiers in Afghanistan Murdered Innocent Civilians." *Rolling Stone*. (27 March 2011); Matthew Green. "US and Kabul condemn troop abuse video." *Financial Times*. (12 Jan 2012).

12.   The War on Terror

That metadata doesn't look all that scary this morning.

- *Former director of the NSA Michael Hayden, the morning after the January 2015 terrorist attack on the French satirical magazine* Charlie Hebdo.[1]

9/11

A new Pearl Harbor.

Adversary

The *NSA* term for those – friends, allies, *rogues states*, you, and everybody else – the agency snoops on.[2]

Al-Qaeda

The justification for the *war on terror* ("We must take the fight to al-Qaeda, lest they take it to us.") and a most useful tool in the pursuit of *vital national interests* ("We must intervene here, there, and everywhere, lest al-Qaeda gain a *safe haven*."). (See also, *Khorasan Group.*)

Answering in the Least Untruthful Manner

The means through which one may lie through one's teeth during congressional testimony and not be charged with perjury.[3]

---

[1] Andrew Desiderio. "Hayden Defends NSA Metadata After Paris: 'Doesn't Look All That Scary' Anymore." Mediaite. (8 Jan 2015).

[2] During a tape recorded July 2013 NSA recruiting seminar at the University of Wisconsin-Madison, two NSA recruiters repeatedly referred to those the agency targets for surveillance (i.e., everyone) as "adversaries," while those within the government requesting intelligence from the agency were referred to as "clients." When graduate students asked the recruiters to define "adversary," the two officials were at a lost. This, despite the fact that the officials purported to be language specialists. See Madiha R. Tahir. "The NSA Comes Recruiting." The Mob and the Multitude. (2 July 2013). <http://mobandmultitude.com/2013/07/02/the-nsa-comes-recruiting/>

[3] During a March 2013 Senate committee hearing, Director of National Intelligence James Clapper was asked whether the National Security Agency was collecting "any type of data at all on millions or hundreds of millions of Americans." Clapper responded, "No," before going on to clarify, "Not wittingly." A short three months later, however, Clapper's lie was exposed: the NSA, as the Edward Snowden leaks

Associated Forces

Groups the U.S. *government* claims are linked to *al-Qaeda* and thus legitimate targets in the *war on terror*. That said, don't spend too much time trying to find out who such groups actually are, because it's classified, you know, to protect *national security*.[4]

Authorization for Use of Military Force (2001)

The gift that keeps on giving.

Automatic License Plate Readers – ALPRs

Surveillance devises used to scan and read car license plates in conjunction with date, time, and location. ALPRs are an integral part of the frenzied effort of *law* enforcement agencies the nation over to increase their haul of "little goodies" amassed via *asset forfeitures*.[5]

Balancing Liberty and Security

Evoking security to *destroy liberty*.

---

confirmed, does indeed wittingly collect data on hundreds of millions of Americans. But when asked later to explain his apparent perjury, Clapper asserted that he had merely "responded in what I thought was the most truthful or least untruthful manner." And with that, official Washington swiftly moved on from the entire affair, as if Clapper's illegal lie had simply never occurred. Marcy Wheeler. "Clapper Couldn't Even Do Better Than 'Least Untruthful' with a Day's Notice." Empty Wheel. (11 June 2013).

[4] U.S. officials often speak of targeting al-Qaeda and its "associated forces," but when ProPublica tried in 2013 to determine who exactly the U.S. government deems to be an "associated force," a Pentagon spokesperson told the news organization "revealing such a list could cause 'serious damage to national security.'" Cora Currier. "Who Are We at War With? That's Classified." ProPublica. (26 July 2013).

[5] According to a 2015 report in the *Wall Street Journal*, the Justice Department is using ALPRs strategically placed on major highways, in combination with those routinely used by state and local law enforcement agencies, to maintain a national database to "track in real time the movement of vehicles around the U.S." Many of the devices used to feed the database, the paper notes, "also record visual images of drivers and passengers, which are sometimes clear enough for investigators to confirm identities." A DEA email on the program viewed by the *Journal* describes the "primary purpose" of the program to enhance asset forfeiture. (See "Asset Forfeiture," Chapter 5.) Devlin Barrett. "U.S. Spies on Millions of Cars." *Wall Street Journal*. (27 Jan 2015): A1, A2.

Big Data/Metadata

The means through which the *government* and *corporations* learn more revealing, intimate details about your life than your friends or family will ever know.[6]

Black Sites

Where *ghost detainees* and *isolated incidents* unite.

Bulk Collection

The collection of every *American*'s "private" communications undertaken in order to form a haystack from which a needle may be extracted.[7]

Camp Bondsteel (Kosovo)

Gitmo east.[8]

---

[6] The use of big data to intrude on the privacy of individuals is by no means limited to the state. The private sector, too, has become quite adept at exploiting personal data in order to enhance consumer marketing. The retail giant Target, for instance, is able to use data collected from customers to determine when a woman is pregnant, often even before her own family becomes aware. "In one famous case," Alice Marwick writes, "the father of a teenage girl called Target to complain that it was encouraging teen pregnancy by mailing her coupons for car seats and diapers. A week later, he called back and apologized; she hadn't told her father yet that she was pregnant." (See Alice Marwick. "How Your Data Are Being Deeply Mined." *New York Review of Books* Vol. LXI No. 1 (9 Jan 2014): 22-24.)

And yet, as advanced as the data collection of corporate America has become, it may just be surpassed by the data analysis strategies of political campaigns, as evidenced in President Obama's 2012 reelection campaign. As John Nichols and Robert McChesney report, the Obama campaign was able to use its vast collection of voters' personal data to "determine which person should contact another person to get that person to vote for Obama and precisely what type of message would be most effective." Nichols and McChesney go on to quote Obama campaign manager Jim Messina remarking that, "Corporate America, Silicon Valley were knocking down the door trying to hire these guys [the Obama campaign data analysts]." See Nichols and McChesney. *Dollarocracy*. 238, 240.

[7] As General Keith Alexander, former head of the NSA, once averred on his surveillance philosophy: "You need a haystack to find a needle." David Sanger and Eric Schmitt. "N.S.A. Imposes Rules to Protect Secret Data Stored on Its Networks." *New York Times*. (18 July 2013).

[8] As William Blum writes, "In November 2005, following a visit [to Camp Bondsteel], Alvaro Gil-Robles, the human rights envoy of the Council of Europe, described the camp as a 'smaller version of Guantánamo.'" Blum. *America's Deadliest Export*, 160.

Categorical Watchlisting

Racial profiling for a post-racial *society*.[9]

Civil Liberties

The *freedoms* granted in order to protect the rights of minority groups against the will of the majority; unless, of course, such rights in any way hinder the *war on terror*.

Classified Information

Any information implicating particularly embarrassing or even *criminal* activity on the part of *government* officials.

COINTELPRO

A far-reaching *Cold War (old)* era domestic spying program levied against the *American public*, which will surely never be replicated by a now clearly contrite and restrained *American* military-intelligence apparatus.

Collect It All

The internal motto of the *NSA*, meant to capture the very essence of the agency's oh-so "limited"[10] surveillance *work*.[11]

---

[9] The use of "categorical watchlisting" in the compiling of U.S. terror watchlists was revealed in a 2014 exposé by Jeremy Scahill and Ryan Devereaux. As the two explain: "While the nomination process [for terror watchlists] appears methodical on paper, in practice there is a shortcut around the entire system. Known as a 'threat-based expedited upgrade,' it gives a single White House official the unilateral authority to elevate entire 'categories of people' whose names appear in the larger databases onto the no fly or selectee lists. This can occur, the guidelines state, when there is a 'particular threat stream' indicating that a certain type of individual may commit a terrorist act.

"This extraordinary power for 'categorical watchlisting' – otherwise known as profiling – is vested in the assistant to the president for homeland security and counterterrorism, a position formerly held by CIA Director John Brennan that does not require Senate confirmation." Jeremy Scahill and Ryan Devereaux. "Blacklisted: The Secret Government Rulebook For Labeling You a Terrorist." *The Intercept*. (23 July 2014).

[10] "Limited" being the buzzword all officials cling to once their not-so-limited illegal spying is revealed to the public. As President Bush insisted once his own NSA spying program was exposed by the *New York Times* in late 2005: "This is a limited program designed to prevent attacks on the United States of America – and I repeat: limited." "Bush defends NSA spying program." CNN. (1 Jan 2006).

[11] "Far from being a frivolous quip," Glenn Greenwald writes, "'collect it all' defines the NSA's aspiration, and it is a goal the NSA is increasingly closer to reaching. The

Computer Search

An illegal *CIA* hack.[12]

Dark Side

A place completely shaded from *freedom* jeopardizing things like the *Constitution*, the *Bill of Rights*, *Habeas Corpus*, etc.[13]

Department of Homeland Security

Department tasked with brining the *war on terror* into the *homeland*.

Detainee Suicide

A *good guy* murder of a *bad guy* nobody needs to know about. (See *Asymmetrical Warfare*, Chapter 11.)

Dirtbox

A simulated cell tower used as a surveillance device capable of collecting all identifying information off one's cellular phone. As part of the ongoing national effort to collect ever larger quantities of hay in search of a needle, the U.S. Marshals Service regularly loads dirtboxes onto planes for reconnaissance flights across the U.S.[14]

---

quantity of telephone calls, emails, online chats, online activities, and telephonic metadata collected by the agency is staggering. Indeed, the NSA frequently, as one 2012 document put it, 'collects far more content than is routinely useful to analysts.' As of mid-2012, the agency was processing more than twenty billion communications events (both Internet and telephone) from around the world *each day*." Greenwald. *No Place to Hide*, 98.

[12] A December 2014 *New York Times* article on the illegal CIA hacking of computers used by Senate staffers working on the Senate Intelligence Committee's report on the agency's torture program ran with the headline: "Investigators Said to Seek No Penalty for C.I.A.'s Computer Search." (*NYT*, 19 Dec 2014.)

[13] As Vice President Dick Cheney remarked five days after 9/11, while speaking on *Meet the Press*: We "have to work, though, sort of the dark side, if you will...We've got to spend time in the shadows in the intelligence world. A lot of what needs to be done here will have to be done quietly, without any discussion, using sources and methods that are available to our intelligence agencies, if we're going to be successful."

[14] According to the *Wall Street Journal*, "The U.S. Marshals Service [dirtbox] program, which became fully functional around 2007, operates Cessna aircraft from at least five metropolitan-area airports, with a flying range covering most of the U.S. population." The "dirtboxes" on board such surveillance aircraft work by mimicking

Disposition Matrix

A *government* created spreadsheet containing the names of those the U.S. has marked for assassination, along with the resources to be expended on their murder. Such a kill matrix is seen as key to institutionalizing *kill lists* to the point where future *administrations* will come to see no reason not to continue with *state* assassinations – no reason not to *look forward, not backward*.[15]

Double Tap

A two-phased *drone* strike, a "double tap" involves an initial strike, followed soon after by a second strike targeting those on the ground responding to the victims of the first. Although perhaps appearing unseemly, the second "tap" is quite justified, given that only *terrorists* would come to the aid of targeted *terrorists*. And it is assured that the targets of the first "tap" are indeed *terrorists*, given that they have been subjected to a *drone* strike in the first place.[16]

Enhanced Interrogation Techniques

Truth serum; or, *good guy torture*.[17]

Espionage

The unauthorized leaking of information to the media.

Espionage Act of 1917

Law passed as the U.S. entered "the *war* to end all *wars*" by a remarkably

---

"cell towers of large telecommunications firms and trick cellphones into reporting their unique registration information." This allows "investigators to scoop data from tens of thousands of cellphones in a single flight, collecting their identifying information and general location." Devlin Barrett. "Americans' Cellphones Targeted in Secret U.S. Spy Program." *Wall Street Journal.* (13 Nov 2014).

[15] As the *Washington Post* reported in late 2012, Obama administration officials "seem confident that they have devised [with the Disposition Matrix] an approach that is so bureaucratically, legally and morally sound that future administrations will follow suit." Greg Miller. "Plan for hunting terrorists signals U.S. intends to keep adding names to kill lists." *Washington Post.* (23 Oct 2012).

[16] As the *New York Times* reported, the U.S. "counts all military age males in a strike zone as combatants…unless there is explicit intelligence posthumously proving them innocent." Becker and Shane. "Secret 'Kill List.'" *New York Times.*

[17] The architects and defenders of the CIA's torture program repeat ad nauseam that accurate intelligence was gleaned from the agency's program. A 2014 Senate report on the program, however, found no such intelligence successes linked to the torture of detainees.

prescient *Congress* able to anticipate the grave threat to come, nearly a century later, by *government whistleblowers*.[18]

Extraordinary Rendition

The *CIA* chaperoning of *ghost detainees* on one-way trips to *black sites*.

Five Eyes

The post-*Good War* spying alliance formed between the U.S., Australia, *Canada*, New Zealand, and *Great Britain*. The alliance allows each member country to share intelligence gathered on each other's citizens, thus allowing each nation's intelligence service to skirt any imprudent domestic *laws* prohibiting the practice of blanket domestic surveillance.

Foiled Terror Plot

The grand public disclosure of the latest *FBI entrapment* scheme.

Foreign Intelligence Surveillance Court – FISC

The secret court tasked with promptly rubber stamping all requests made by the *FBI* and *NSA* to snoop on *American citizens*.[19]

Fourth Amendment

The constitutional protection against unreasonable searches and seizures; that is, all searches and seizers occurring absent a warrant issued with probable cause. As was intended when enacted in the early days of the *American* Republic, the Fourth Amendment in no way applies to any form of electronic communication, or anything else potentially related to the *war on terror*.

Freedom of Speech

The absolute right of *corporations* to market their products, along with the restricted right of *American citizens* to speak, so long their speech doesn't come to impinge on the *profitability* of *corporations*, damage the *war on terror*, or both.

---

[18] The Obama administration has brought seven cases under the Espionage Act involving leaks by government officials. Only three such cases had been brought previously.

[19] Of the more than 33,900 government surveillance requests made in the first 33 years of its existence, the FISC declined a mere 11. Evan Perez. "Secret Court's Oversight Gets Scrutiny." *Wall Street Journal.* (9 June 2013).

Ghost Detainee

A disappeared *unperson*.

Gitmo

America's "battle lab."[20]

Habeas Corpus

The right enshrined in the *Constitution* entitling every citizen under arrest to be brought before a judge or court to face his or her charges. Obviously, a rather negotiable right in the context of the *war on terror*.[21]

Hacker

Whistleblower.[22]

Homegrown Terrorism

The design, manufacture, and eventual export of *American*-made bombs, missiles, *drones*, guns, bullets, tanks, jets, etc.

Homeland Security

That which requires the endless bombing of faraway lands (when in doubt,

---

[20] "Battle lab" being the term used by Gitmo's first intelligence commander, Major General Michael Dunlavey, and his successor, Major General Geoffrey Miller. As a 2015 Seton Hall Law Center for Policy and Research report explained, "Every lab must have its test subjects and GTMO was no different; its rats were human beings, detainees." By subjecting detainees, or "rats," to torture, the report continues, "The government sought information on the most effective ways to torture a human physically, information on the most damaging ways to break a man psychologically, and insight as to just how far the human body could be pushed in pain and terror before organ failure or death. Upon arrival, detainees were routinely given psychosis-inducing drugs and were held in isolation for up to 30 days without access to human contact, including the International Committee of the Red Cross." Mark P. Denbeaux, Jonathan Hafetz, Joshua Denbeaux. "Guantanamo: America's Battle Lab." Seton Hall Law Center for Policy and Research. (Jan 2015).
[21] In 2002, American citizen Jose Padilla was arrested for allegedly plotting a "dirty bomb" attack within the U.S. Classified as an "enemy combatant," Padilla was held in solitary confinement for 3½ years before charges were even brought against him.
[22] In June 2013, President Obama dismissively referred to NSA whistleblower Edward Snowden as a "29-year-old hacker." Julian Pecquet. "US 'won't scramble jets' to capture 'hacker' Snowden, says Obama." *The Hill*. (27 June 2013).

hit *Iraq*), in addition to the snatching up of every *American*'s personal communications.

Imminent Threat

A threat which may or may not materialize in the immediate future, but nonetheless justifies the urgent *targeted killing* of an *American terrorist*.[23]

Incidental Collection

The illegal collection of every *American*'s personal electronic data by the *NSA* made legal because – whoops! – they only collected it incidentally.

Intelligence Target

One of the select few subjected to *NSA* surveillance. Namely, only those who speak on phones or browse the *Internet*...along with all those who happen to be *Muslim*. (See also, *Adversary*.)

Internet, the

NSA surveillance device.

ISIS/ISIL/The Islamic State

Just the latest reason *something must be done* "before we all get killed here at home."[24]

---

[23] In a leaked 2011 Justice Department memo outlining the legal rationale for the killing of American citizens by drone, government lawyers argue that such a killing would be legal as long as (1) the target is a ranking al-Qaeda figure; (2) he or she poses an "imminent threat of violent attack"; and (3) that capture is not "feasible." The definition of what constitutes an "imminent threat," however, is constructed in such a way as to make any threat materializing at any future date to be "imminent." As the Justice Department memo states: "the condition that an operational leader present an 'imminent' threat of violent attack against the United States does not require the United States to have clear evidence that a specific attack on U.S. persons will take place in the immediate future."
See:<http://msnbcmedia.msn.com/i/msnbc/sections/news/020413_DOJ_White_Paper.pdf>

[24] In September 2014, Sen. Lindsey Graham criticized President Obama's airstrikes against the Islamic State in both Iraq and Syria as being too weak. As Graham shrieked, "This president needs to rise to the occasion before we all get killed back here at home." Evan McMurry. "Sen. Graham: Obama Must Stop ISIS 'Before We All Get Killed Here at Home.'" Mediaite. (14 Sept 2014).

Khorasan Group

An illusory group terrorizing the dreams of those consulting with *official sources*.[25]

Kill List

The list compiled by the U.S. *government* containing the names of all the *terrorists* to be *taken out*.

Lone Wolf Attack

A small-scale attack perpetrated by an assailant working alone, which nonetheless requires that (a) *civil liberties* be suspended at home,[26] and (b) bombs dropped abroad.

Military Tribunal

A military "court" designed to convict – and only convict – *unlawful enemy combatants*.[27]

---

[25] The "Khorasan Group" made its first appearance in the U.S. media in late 2014, as the U.S. began bombing targets in both Iraq and Syria as part of its war against the Islamic State or ISIS. Although seemingly springing from little more than the imaginations of "official sources," the Khorasan Group was quickly presented as a threat far surpassing that of even ISIS itself. As Glenn Greenwald and Murtaza Hussain wrote at the time, the rapid concoction of the Khorasan Group served to both sustain public support for American bombing and provide a veneer of legality to the campaign. And thus, as Greenwald and Murtaza noted, "After spending weeks depicting ISIS as an unprecedented threat – too radical even for Al Qaeda! – administration officials suddenly began spoon-feeding their favorite media organizations and national security journalists tales of a secret group that was even scarier and more threatening than ISIS, one that posed a direct and immediate threat to the American Homeland. Seemingly out of nowhere, a new terror group was created in media lore." Glenn Greenwald and Murtaza Hussain. "The Fake Terror Threat Used To Justify Bombing Syria." *The Intercept*. (28 Sept 2014).

[26] The 2013 bombing of the Boston Marathon being a case in point. Recall that in launching a city-wide manhunt for a 19-year-old suspect, officials ordered the residents of one of America's largest cities to "shelter in place," as their city was laid siege by National Guard troops and militarized police forces conducting house to house searches in clear violation of the Fourth Amendment.

[27] In April 2014, the *New York Times* reported that the FBI had approached a member of the defense team for one of the men accused by the government of plotting the 9/11 attacks. The FBI reportedly asked the individual working on the detainee's military tribunal questions on the case, even having him sign an agreement not to divulge their conversation. This last step went so far as to turn a member of the

Muslim

A modern-day *communist*. That is, an untrustworthy person to be kept under the strictest of surveillance.[28]

National Security Agency – NSA

Proud owner of the global *Internet*.

National Security Letter

A subpoena issued by the *FBI* during an investigation related to *national security*, which bars recipients from even acknowledging that they have received such a letter. Obviously necessary because the *war on terror* supersedes the right to *freedom of speech*. And in the end, the *war on terror* is really a *war* fought to protect *American freedoms*. So, it certainly reasons that such *freedoms* can't be allowed to get in the way of those trying to protect them.

No-Fly List

A list of purported *terrorists* and recalcitrant snitches banned from flying within the U.S.[29]

---

defense team into an FBI informant. The case was just the latest evidence of government meddling in the military tribunal process. It had been previously disclosed that the government had eavesdropped on confidential conversations between defendants and their lawyers. Furthermore, the Pentagon was forced at one point to acknowledge that it had "inadvertently" searched and copied defense lawyers' emails, although it claimed nobody read them. As Christopher Jencks, a Southern Methodist University law professor and a former military prosecutor, remarked on the military tribunal process to the *Times*: "If this were any other country's system…'The reaction would be, 'Oh my gosh. What a kangaroo process.''" Matt Apuzzo. "Covert Inquiry by F.B.I. Rattles 9/11 Tribunals." *New York Times*. (18 April 2014).

[28] Five of the more prominent American Muslims to fall under the NSA's dragnet, as *The Intercept* reported in mid-2014, include: Faisal Gill, Asim Ghafoor, Hooshang Amirahmadi, Agha Saeed, and Nihad Awad. Respectfully that's a Republican Party operative and former Department of Homeland Security official; a defense attorney representing clients charged with terrorism; a Rutgers University professor of international relations; a former professor of political science at California State University; and the executive director of the Council on American-Islamic Relations. Glenn Greenwald and Murtaza Hussain. "Meet the Muslim-American Leaders the FBI and NSA Have Been Spying On." *The Intercept*. (9 July 2014).

[29] In 2014, four American Muslims filed suit against the FBI, accusing the agency of placing them on the no-fly list as a means to either intimate them into becoming FBI

Nobody is Listening to Your Calls or Reading Your Email

The *NSA* is monitoring your calls and storing your emails.[30]

Patriot Act

2001 *law* lifting legal constraints on the *government*'s ability to snoop on the private affairs of *American citizens*. In particular, the *law* permits the *government* to access *American*'s records regarding their banking, business, education, travel, and library history. Quaint stuff, really, in the age of *Prism* and *XKeyscore*.[31]

Police State

A *state* in which individual civil, economic, and political rights are curtailed by the surveillance of ever-present *police* and intelligence services. The snooping on every *American* undertaken by the *National Security Agency* does not make the U.S. a police state, given that domestic spying in *America* is undertaken not as a means to curtail individual *freedom*, but strictly as a means to secure it.

Potential Terrorist Threat

An anti-*war* rally.[32]

---

informants or punishing them for refusing to become snitches. Spencer Ackerman. "No-fly list used by FBI to coerce Muslims into informing, lawsuit claims." *The Guardian*. (22 April 2014).

[30] In the wake of the NSA domestic spying revelations made possible by Edward Snowden, President Obama was quick to assure the American public that, "Nobody is listening to your telephone calls." Of course, as dubious a claim as that is, there's really no need to listen to the content of one's calls when you're collecting metadata, as the NSA most assuredly is. Indeed, as Stewart Baker, the former general counsel of the NSA, commented on metadata: "Metadata absolutely tells you everything about somebody's life. If you have enough metadata you don't really need content.... [It's] sort of embarrassing how predictable we are as human beings." Quoted in: Alan Rusbridger. "The Snowden Leaks and the Public." *New York Review of Books*. (21 Nov 2013).

[31] Remarkably, Wisconsin Rep. James Sensenbrenner, co-author of the Patriot Act, has deemed NSA spying to be "excessive and un-American." Ryan J. Reilly. "Jim Sensenbrenner, Patriot Act Author, Slams 'Un-American' NSA Verizon Phone Records Grab." *Huffington Post*. (6 June 2013).

[32] In 2007, the ACLU obtained Pentagon documents related to the department's Threat and Local Observation Notices program. As the ACLU noted: "Protests against the war in Iraq were a common trigger for TALON reporting. For example,

PRISM

A tightly controlled and rather limited *NSA*-run anti-*terrorism* program, collecting and storing the communications of only those who use the *Internet*.[33]

Privacy

The right of *super donors* to have their political contributions remain anonymous. Every other aspect of one's "private" life is not to be subject to such confidentiality, given that the protection of fundamental liberties, such as the right to privacy, requires the evisceration of said liberties, per that whole *balancing liberty and security* thing.

Range-R Radar

An advanced radar device used by *law* enforcement agencies to peer through house walls in order to determine whether anyone is inside. Because those not actively searching the *Internet* or talking on the phone must be watched too.[34]

---

a protest entitled 'Stop the War NOW!' was reported as a potential terrorist threat in a March 2005 TALON. The TALON describes the protest, aimed at a military recruiting station and federal building in Akron, Ohio, as including a rally, march, and 'Reading of Names of War Dead.'" "No Real Threat: The Pentagon's Secret Database on Peaceful Protest." ACLU. (17 Jan 2007). <https://www.aclu.org/national-security/no-real-threat-pentagons-secret-database-peaceful-protest>

[33] As *The Guardian* reported in 2013, PRISM allows the NSA to tap directly into the systems of the largest service providers and collect: "email, video and voice chat, videos, photos, voice-over-IP (Skype, for example) chats, file transfers, social networking details, and more." Glenn Greenwald and Ewen MacAskill. "NSA Prism program taps in to user data of Apple, Google and others." *The Guardian.* (6 June 2013).

[34] As a 2015 report by *USA Today* found, "at least 50 U.S. law enforcement agencies have secretly equipped their officers with" Range-R radar devices. According to the paper, law enforcement agencies "began deploying the radar systems more than two years ago with little notice to the courts and no public disclosure of when or how they would be used." Using radio waves, the radars are able "to zero in on movements as slight as human breathing from a distance of more than 50 feet. They can detect whether anyone is inside of a house, where they are and whether they are moving." Brad Heath. "New police radars can 'see' inside homes." *USA Today.* (20 Jan 2015).

Rectal Hydration

An *enhanced interrogation technique* in which a detainee's food is pureed and then inserted rectally for feeding, because, well, why not?[35]

Responsible Father

A father not subjecting his son to a *state* assassination by happening to appear on a U.S. *kill list*.[36]

Salt Pit (or COLBALT)

A *CIA*-run "dungeon" north of Kabul, *Afghanistan*.[37]

---

[35] At least 5 detainees put through the CIA's "enhanced interrogation" program were subjected to "rectal hydration." This, despite the lack of any "documented medical necessity." According to a CIA official quoted in the Senate Select Committee on Intelligence's 2014 report on the agency's torture program, "rectal hydration" was instead administered in an effort to gain "total control over the detainee." Senate Select Committee on Intelligence. "Committee Study of the Central Intelligence Agency's Detention and Interrogation Program: Executive Summary." (3 Dec 2014): 82.

[36] In 2012, former White House Press Secretary Robert Gibbs was asked what legal grounds the U.S. government had for its October 2011 killing in Yemen by drone of 16-year-old American citizen Abjulrahman al-Awlaki. The sage advice of Gibbs? Get a better father. As Gibbs advised the deceased al-Awlaki, "I would suggest that you should have a far more responsible father." Of course, Abdulrahman's aforementioned irresponsible father, the American citizen Anwar al-Awlaki, was subjected himself to a targeted killing in September 2011 – a decision President Obama deemed "an easy one." See Just Foreign Policy. "Robert Gibbs Blames Al Awlaki 16 Year Old Son's Death By Drone On His Having A Terrorist Father." YouTube. (26 Oct 2012). <http://www.youtube.com/watch?v=_pOUFHTN1G4>

[37] "Dungeon" being the word the prison's chief of interrogations used to describe the facility. As the Senate's 2014 report on CIA activities at the Salt Pit, or COBALT, adds: "CIA detainees at the COBALT detention facility were kept in complete darkness and constantly shackled in isolated cells with loud noise or music and only a bucket to use for human waste. Lack of heat at the facility likely contributed to the death of a detainee [Gul Rahman]…At times, the detainees at COBALT were walked around naked or were shackled with their hands above their heads for extended periods of time. Other times, the detainees at COBALT were subjected to what was described as a 'rough takedown,' in which approximately five CIA officers would scream at a detainee, drag him outside of his cell, cut his clothes off, and secure him with Mylar tape. The detainee would then be hooded and dragged up and down a long corridor while being slapped and punched." Senate Select Committee on Intelligence. "Committee Study of the Central Intelligence Agency's Detention and Interrogation Program: Executive Summary," 4.

Signature Strike

A U.S. *drone* strike targeting unknown individuals exhibiting the behavior common to *terrorists* (e.g., living beneath a prowling *drone*). Everyone killed by a *drone*, though, is a *terrorist* – proven by the mere fact that he or she was killed by a *drone*. Unless, of course, evidence is to arise after one has already been dismembered by a *Hellfire missile* indicating that one wasn't in fact a *terrorist*.[38] But in that case, they were still just an *unperson* turned *collateral damage*, so who really cares?

Soft on Terror

Exhibiting a fleeting moment of hesitation just prior to ordering the next *drone* strike.

Spy

Whistleblower.[39]

State Secrets Privilege

A special privilege the U.S. *government* may claim during a legal proceeding in order to avoid having to reveal evidence it claims will threaten *national security*. Such a "trust us, we're honest, good people" privilege is vital to responsibly safeguarding *classified information* otherwise imperiled by a volatile legal proceeding.[40]

---

[38] According to the U.S., all military age males in a drone strike zone are considered to be terrorists, unless proven not to be terrorists after their death. Becker and Shane. "Secret 'Kill List.'" *New York Times*.

[39] In a January 2014 appearance on *Meet the Press*, the chair of the House Intelligence Committee, Rep. Mike Rogers, charged, without providing any evidence, that Edward Snowden was working as an agent of the Russian government. As Rogers speculated: "Let me just say this. I believe there's a reason he ended up in the hands, the loving arms, of an FSB agent in Moscow. I don't think that's a coincidence." On the same program, the chair of the Senate Intelligence Committee, Sen. Diane Feinstein, commented, when asked if she agreed that Snowden received aid from Russia in order to leak NSA documents: "He may well have. We don't know at this stage. But I think to glorify this act is to set a new level of dishonor." Dominic Rushe. "Intelligence chair: NSA leaker Edward Snowden may have had Russian help." *The Guardian*. (19 Jan 2014).

[40] On the first use of the State Secrets Privilege by the Bush administration, see: Sibel Edmonds. *Classified Woman: The Sibel Edmonds Story*. (Alexandria: Sibel Edmonds, 2012).

Stingray

A ground-based *dirtbox* used by *police* departments to track one's location and scoop up all the text messages, emails, and photos off one's phone perhaps missed by the U.S. Marshals jettisoning about in their spy planes overhead.

Suspected Terrorist

A *dangerous radical.*

Targeted Killing

The precision killing of a suspected *terrorist*, along with all the women and children attending the same wedding party.[41]

Terror Plot

The careful planning by *FBI* agents to deploy *mosque crawlers* in an attempt to recruit disenchanted *Muslim* men to sign onto fictitious attacks against *American civilians.*

Terror Tuesdays

Tuesdays at the White House, where the *president* and his national security team convene to pour over the "macabre 'baseball cards'" comprising the U.S. *kill list* and solemnly deliberate on who will be marked next for a *targeted killing.*[42]

Terrorism

The use of *violence* – or the threat of *violence* – in an attempt to instill widespread *fear* to attain goals that are political, economic, religious, or ideological in nature. Oh wait, that can't be, because that would mean...

---

[41] In December 2013, a U.S. drone strike in Yemen's al-Baitha province struck a wedding convoy, killing 14 and injuring 22 others. Such crimes, however, are commonplace to the U.S. drone campaign. As a 2014 analysis of U.S. drone strikes by the human-rights group Reprieve found, "Attempts to kill 41 men resulted in the deaths of an estimated 1,147 people, as of 24 November" 2014. See: Hakim Almasmari. "Yemen says U.S. drone struck a wedding convoy, killing 14." CNN. (13 Dec 2013); Spencer Ackerman. "41 men targeted but 1,147 people killed: US drone strikes – the facts on the ground." *The Guardian.* (24 Nov 2014).

[42] Becker and Shane. "Secret 'Kill List.'" *New York Times.*

Terrorist

All those killed, unless proven innocent in their death, by the U.S. *government*. Well that, and *animal rights activists* and *environmentalists*.[43]

Terrorist Organization

A politically inconvenient organization – whether it be domestic, foreign, violent, nonviolent, whatever.

Terrorist Training Camp

A training ground and *safe haven* for *terrorists*. For example, south Florida.[44]

Torture

Bad guy enhanced interrogation techniques.

Traitor

Whistleblower.[45]

Transportation Security Administration – TSA

Federal agency tasked with ensuring all the nation's flyers are properly groped, prodded, and strip-searched prior to travel.

Treason

The betrayal of the *American government* by an *American citizen*...or an Australian one.[46]

---

[43] See "Animal Rights Activist" and "Environmentalist," Chapter 1.

[44] As William Blum remarks on south Florida: "It should be noted that for nearly half a century much of southern Florida has been one big training camp for anti-Castro terrorists. None of their groups – which have carried out many hundreds of serious terrorist acts in the US as well as abroad, including bombing a passenger airplane in flight – is on the State Department [terrorist] list." Blum. *America's Deadliest Export*, 42.

[45] House Speaker John Boehner and former Vice President Dick Cheney are among those who have deemed Edward Snowden a traitor. Former U.S. Ambassador to the UN John Bolton, meanwhile, went so far as to state that Snowden "ought to swing from a tall oak tree." Josh Feldman. "John Bolton: Snowden 'Ought to Swing from a Tall Oak Tree.'" Mediaite. (16 Dec 2013).

[46] In 2010, when asked his thoughts on the U.S. Justice Department not yet charging Australian – yes, Australian – Citizen Julian Assange with treason, Senator Joseph

Truth

That which must be destroyed.[47]

Unlawful Enemy Combatant

A "battle lab" rat. (See *Gitmo.*)

Useful Intelligence

The false and fabricated claims extracted from tortured detainees coming in handy whenever endeavoring to sell a *war* to the *American public.* [48]

Lieberman mused, "I don't understand why that hasn't happened yet." See Zaid Jilani. "Lieberman: 'I Don't Understand' Why The Department Of Justice Hasn't Charged Australian Assange With Treason." Think Progress. (7 Dec 2010).

[47] As James Risen observes: "Of all the abuses America has suffered at the hands of the government in its endless war on terror, possibly the worst has been the war on truth. On the one hand, the executive branch has vastly expanded what it wants to know: something of a vast gathering of previously private truths. On the other hand, it has ruined lives to stop the public from gaining any insight into its dark arts, waging a war on truth." James Risen. *Pay Any Price: Greed, Power, and Endless War.* (New York: Houghton Mifflin Harcourt, 2014): 230.

[48] The CIA torture apologists are oft to crow about all the useful intelligence gleaned from the agency's program. But what, exactly, was this useful intelligence? And was it even accurate? The answer to the latter, as multiple Senate reports have concluded, is no. As for the former, a 2009 report by Jonathan Landay in *McClatchy* helps explain the utility of the false intelligence. As Landay wrote: "A former senior U.S. intelligence official familiar with the interrogation issue said that Cheney and former Defense Secretary Donald H. Rumsfeld demanded that the interrogators find evidence of al Qaida-Iraq collaboration.

'There were two reasons why these interrogations were so persistent, and why extreme methods were used,' the former senior intelligence official said on condition of anonymity because of the issue's sensitivity.

'The main one is that everyone was worried about some kind of follow-up attack (after 9/11). But for most of 2002 and into 2003, Cheney and Rumsfeld, especially, were also demanding proof of the links between al Qaida and Iraq that (former Iraqi exile leader Ahmed) Chalabi and others had told them were there.'

It was during this period that CIA interrogators waterboarded two alleged top al Qaida detainees repeatedly — Abu Zubaydah at least 83 times in August 2002 and Khalid Sheik Muhammed 183 times in March 2003 — according to a newly released Justice Department document."

In other words, knowing that faced with torture, one will admit to anything, the point of the CIA torture program in 2002 and 2003 seems to have been to fortify the phantom link between al-Qaeda and Iraq, so to then better sell the Iraq war to the American public. This being the very essence of useful "intelligence." Jonathan

War on Terror

An indefinitely profitable global *war* <u>of</u> terror.

Watchlist

A tightly controlled *government* maintained list comprised of *terrorists, suspected terrorists,* and those suspected of being a *suspected terrorist,* along with all those in any way associating with any of the above.[49]

Waterboarding

An *enhanced interrogation technique* in which a detainee is put through the paces of an aggressive hydration program in order to extract *useful intelligence.*[50]

Whistleblower

A traitorous and loathsome *spy* usurping the democratic process by exposing the workings of the people's *government* directly to the people themselves.

XKeyscore

NSA computer system pivotal in the agency's continued ownership of the global *Internet.* XKeyscore allows *NSA* analysts to identify and track an individual's digital fingerprint by reading an *adversary*'s emails, browsing

---

Landay. "Report: Abusive tactics used to seek Iraq-al Qaida link." *McClatchy.* (21 April 2009).

[49] As Scahill and Deveraux explain: "Because the government tracks 'suspected terrorists' as well as 'known terrorists,' individuals can be watchlisted if they are suspected of being a suspected terrorist, or if they are suspected of associating with people who are suspected of terrorism activity." Scahill and Devereaux. "Blacklisted." *The Intercept.*

[50] A Senate report on the CIA's torture program found that contrary to the repeated claims of Bush administration and CIA officials, no actionable intelligence was obtained through waterboarding or other torture techniques. Yet, as the Senate report found, the CIA manipulated intelligence reports to create the impression that valuable information was obtained via the waterboarding of detainees. As one U.S. official commented to the *Washington Post* on the Senate's report: "The CIA described [its program] repeatedly both to the Department of Justice and eventually to Congress as getting unique, otherwise unobtainable intelligence that helped disrupt terrorist plots and save thousands of lives. Was that actually true? The answer is no." Greg Miller, Adam Goldman and Ellen Nakashima. "CIA misled on interrogation program, Senate report says." *Washington Post.* (31 March 2014).

history, and protected passwords.[51] Of course, despite the capacity to read one's emails, the agency would never actually do such a thing. (See *Nobody is Listening to Your Calls or Reading Your Email*.)

---

[51] As a NSA presentation slide on XKeyscore leaked by Edward Snowden read: "the program covers 'nearly everything a typical user does on the internet', including the content of emails, websites visited and searches, as well as their metadata." As *The Guardian* noted further, "Analysts can also use XKeyscore and other NSA systems to obtain ongoing 'real-time' interception of an individual's internet activity." Glenn Greenwald. "XKeyscore: NSA tool collects 'nearly everything a user does on the internet'." *The Guardian.* (31 July 2013).

Index

Ben Schreiner writes on U.S. politics and foreign policy. His work has appeared in *Common Dreams*, *CounterPunch*, *Dissident Voice*, *Global Research*, *Z Magazine*, and many others. His media appearances include RT and Press TV. He earned a degree in politics from Willamette University in Salem, Oregon. His work can be viewed at www.workingleft.blogspot.com.